Fabric furnishings

Fabric furnishings

Margaret G Butler and Beryl S Greves

B T BATSFORD LIMITED   LONDON

© Margaret G Butler and Beryl S Greves
First published 1972

ISBN 0 7134 2754 X

Designed by Charlotte Baron
Filmset in Monophoto Baskerville 11 on 12 point by
Filmtype Services Limited, Scarborough, Yorkshire
Printed in Great Britain by The Anchor Press, Tiptree, Essex
and bound by William Brendon, Tiptree, Essex
for the publishers
B T Batsford Limited
4 Fitzhardinge Street, Portman Square, London W 1

Contents

Our purpose in preparing this book is to present the results of our research into soft furnishings to those who are interested in making personal contributions to the décor of their homes. We hope, also, that the information will be useful to teachers and students who are planning work in this aspect of home-making, and to those studying this topic for Advanced Level examinations.

In the first section we have attempted to give some guidance in the basic principles of interior décor, but also to encourage individuality. The interior of the home should reflect the personalities of the occupants, and offer congenial surroundings for both their leisure and their activities.

We hope the sketches in section two will suggest some ideas, and help people to create an individual treatment of room décor.

In this present age of mass production, individuality is tending to be destroyed. Craftsman-designed articles can now only be bought for very high prices and more women are expressing their individuality by making things for themselves. We have concentrated, therefore, on the articles we felt most people would be tempted to make. We hope to encourage those who feel hesitant, as we have tried to show how to think about soft furnishings for the home as a preliminary step, and to give clear directions for measuring, shopping, preparing and making.

In many cases it is impossible to buy the exact requirements of colour, pattern and texture. We hope to encourage women to make the article instead of buying unsatisfactorily.

The problem of measurement has been dealt with in as straightforward a way as possible, and a comparable Imperial measurement is given in brackets beside each metric measurement. There is no attempt to make these metric and Imperial measurements directly equivalent: this would often give a sizing which would be unrealistic in use. To clarify this situation we have included a table at the end of the book to show the comparable measurements we have used up to 254 mm (10 in.). Measurements above this can be found by adding from within the table. However, in some cases, we found that the actual metric conversion gave greater accuracy in a calculation. An example of this occurs in the café curtain section.

We presume that people will be aware both of the necessity of using fitting lines to give accuracy in the finished size of articles, and also have a knowledge of basic sewing stitches.

In order to give clarity in diagrams, some tacking stitches have been omitted. In all cases, the placing of tacking is advised in the text, and it is wise to follow this advice. Goods results are obtained only if adequate preparation is made, and most fabrics, especially those available for soft furnishing, need holding firmly in position for final stitching. Once the final stitching has been completed, and usually before pressing, tacking stitches should always be removed and machine thread ends fastened off securely. As this occurs so frequently, we have omitted saying it in the text.

Wherever possible cross references have been given to avoid unnecessary repetition and to offer full directions for the stages of work for each article included in the book.

Clacton-on-Sea   *MGB and BSG*

Note

'See *figure 00*' is a direction to the reader to study the figure and caption before proceeding to the next step, whereas '*figure 00*' illustrates the previous point.

Introduction

The extensive selection of soft furnishing fabrics available in the shops today, allows everyone the freedom to express their individuality in their own home or room. Never before has there been so much scope for the homemaker, as wide ranges of colour, texture and design are to be found in all furnishing shops and stores. This choice has made people view the planning of interior décor with increasing interest and pleasure.

Interior décor covers the treatment of all that makes the appearance of a room: the decoration of walls and ceiling, the floor covering, furniture and soft furnishing. It is the setting of the day to day living of the family or occupant; it declares the function of each room and the discernment of the woman responsible for its choice.

The purpose of this book is to deal with one aspect of interior décor, namely soft furnishings; to examine the items included under this heading, and to select those which most girls and women can make for themselves. The information in the following pages is intended to help and encourage them to be adventurous and successful in their efforts, so that they can make a personal contribution to the beauty, comfort and economy of their room or home furnishings.

Soft furnishings include the following items:
carpets and rugs
curtains
loose covers
bed coverings
cushions
lampshades

Carpets will obviously have to be bought and probably rugs too, although some people enjoy making rugs as a hobby.

Large, heavy curtains, especially if lined or interlined, may have to be made to order on account of their size, weight and bulk. Lighter curtains can be handled more easily, and by careful following of instructions may be undertaken by anyone. If inexperienced, begin by making the kitchen and bathroom curtains and, as confidence develops, proceed to the bigger, more expensive ones.

Loose covers require an accurate pattern for each chair. These patterns must be hand made and a certain knowledge of shaping, cutting and fitting is essential for good results. The study of loose cover construction is best made after some experience has been gained with simpler articles which are lighter and easier to handle. Fewer homes, nowadays, have furniture which demands this type of cover. They can always be made to measure, by order, if the family budget allows. Failing this, the manufacture of stretch covers is developing in a very interesting way. A wide range is already available which may appeal to many people, and it will be worth noticing the increase in the ranges of fabric, colour and design as they appear in the shops.

The increasing use of electric blankets, combined with central heating has brought about a drastic change in bed fashions. The traditional bedspread and eiderdown, though still available, are declining in popularity.

Many people prefer to conceal an eiderdown during the daytime by using a cover chosen to blend with the room décor. This cover may be a simple throw-over type, or fitted, according to the use of the room or individual taste. The simple covers are frequently bought, but can be made at home very easily if this solves problems of matching fabric. Fitted covers are available in a limited range, therefore people may find it desirable to make their own.

Cushions are expensive to buy, with the exception of simple types of scatter cushion. It is convenient to make cushions as they are small, easy to handle and prove economic as they often utilise oddments of fabric. When patterns are required, they are comparatively easy to make. Some practice in the making of box cushions is excellent as a background to the later making of loose covers and fitted bed-covers.

Lampshades are costly, and it is often diffi-cult to find the size, shape, colour and fabric desired. Simple ones, which can be most attractive if suitably chosen, are very easy to make. With experience, interesting styles of greater difficulty can be designed and made at home. The making of lampshades is one of the most economic fields of soft furnishing.

1 Planning décor

Colour, pattern and texture are the three essential things to consider when planning the décor of a room. Not, however, as isolated factors, but in close relationship, so that the whole effect is pleasing and harmonious. As these factors are of such importance to the whole, consider each one separately and then decide how to relate them into one scheme.

COLOUR

Colour cannot be seen unless there is light, and the degree of light will effect the intensity of the colour. White light is made up of all the hues of the spectrum, that is purple, blue, green, yellow, orange and red. The colours are so balanced and blended, that the effect is colourless. The six hues can be distinguished if white light is passed through a prism, and the true colour of an object is only seen in white light. However, the source of light is not colourless. The colour of daylight varies according to the presence or the absence of the sun and the light from open fires, candles and incandescent light bulbs is yellowish. Some fluorescent lights have a strong red content. Depending on the surface texture of the object, the light shining on it may be reflected or absorbed. Therefore these factors control the colours that are seen.

Confidence is needed to use colour successfully. Many people are inclined to play for safety and use dullish colour combinations. Alternatively, a person without any colour sense is likely to make glaring errors. We are all aware of colour, and on entering a room we react, consciously or unconsciously, to the use of colour in that room.

Before colour can be used with safety and success, it is necessary to have an understanding of its composition. There is much confusion about the language of colour, and to clarify this problem the following breakdown may be helpful.

Colour can be divided into three groups:

a Primary colours Red, blue, yellow
These are colours which cannot be made by mixing other colours.

b Secondary colours These are made by the combination of two primary colours.
Red and blue give purple
Blue and yellow give green
Yellow and red give orange

c Tertiary colours These are obtained by mixing two secondary colours.
Examples of tertiary colours are:
a Purple and orange give russet.
b Orange and green give citron.
c Green and purple give olive.

Hues

A hue is any primary, secondary or tertiary colour without either black or white added.

In addition to hues, there are the neutrals which are black and white, and the tones between black and white which are the greys.

Tone, shades and tints

Tone is the degree of lightness or darkness, irrespective of colour.

Shades are made by adding black or grey to any hue.

Tints are made by adding white to any hue.

Therefore, colour can be modified in three ways:
a By mixing two hues together
b By the addition of black or grey
c By the addition of white.

The effect of black and white

Whereas white reflects light, black absorbs it. Therefore a hue with white added will give apparently more light than the same hue with black added. White will absorb colour around it and give a general softening effect. Black, on the other hand, intensifies adjacent colours or those seen against it.

Similarly light greys will have the same effect as white, and dark greys as black, although to a lesser degree.

Complementary colours

Each primary colour has a contrasting colour which is the secondary colour made by the two remaining members of the primary group. Therefore the *complementary colour* of:
RED is GREEN (mixture of blue and yellow)
BLUE is ORANGE (mixture of yellow and red)
YELLOW is PURPLE (mixture of red and blue)

Thus we prove that the complementary colour of a primary colour is a secondary colour and vice versa.

The influence of colour

When two colours are adjacent, each will appear to partake of the complementary of the other, eg when blue is adjacent to red, the blue appears to have a content of green, and the red of orange.

When a colour and its complement are adjacent, each one will increase in intensity. There is a similar result with tone: a dark tone and a light tone are both intensified when seen beside or against each other.

Harmony of colour

This is most easily obtained by selecting one colour as the basic colour of the scheme and supporting it with colours which include the same basic colour in their composition, eg blue as a basic colour can be teamed with hues of purple and turquoise. In addition a colour harmonises with its own tints and shades, and also with black, white or grey.

Contrast of colour

This can be achieved in one of two ways:
a By colour contrast, eg red with its complementary which is green, or a hue of each of these colours.
b By tone contrast, eg a dark hue with a light hue of the same colour, eg dark blue and light blue.

Effects of colour

Drab colours are depressing; bright primary colours are stimulating. Colour used in discord is restless and tiring. Alternatively, carefully selected colours give a feeling of peace and well being. Colour can also be used to give a feeling of warmth or coolness.

Using colour to create an illusion

A room with difficult proportions can be made more pleasing in appearance by a skilful use of colour. Dark tones and strong colours will help to make too long a room appear shorter, too wide a room appear narrower and too high a ceiling appear lower. Alternatively, the opposite effect can be achieved by using light tones and tints.

PATTERN

Pattern is formed by the planned repetition of a design, but a design can be used singly to decorate a surface or form. In order to achieve success, the pattern or design should be related to the form, object or area to which it is applied. Scale is of equal importance. A design, whether used singly, or in repetition to form a pattern, should always be in proportion to the object or area to be covered, eg a picture window can take a large repeating design, whereas a small upholstered chair requires a smaller unit of design in the pattern.

The repeating units of design create a rhythm which balances the content of the pattern. Over a large area it is the rhythm which gives as much pleasure as the design, and this must be remembered when cutting lengths and joining widths for curtains, and when hanging wallpaper.

Pattern is of two main types:

a Geometric or abstract, eg stripes, circles, squares and variations of these.

b Organic or natural, eg plant or other forms taken from nature.

Plant and animal forms are often stylised by designers, giving a certain geometric quality.

Pattern in a room can relieve flat areas of colour and add focal points of interest. The areas in a house which may take pattern are:

    walls and curtains
    ceiling
    upholstery
    floor
    bed furnishings

In addition to these, pictures and ornaments may also be used to add interest to plain areas. Consider the following points when choosing a colour scheme:

1   Never use too many patterns in the same scheme. Although each pattern may be pleasing on its own, it will lose much of its interest when used with several others and the whole effect will become disturbing and restless.

2   Usually two patterns can be used successfully in a scheme if linked with the colour and texture of the other surfaces, and will give a pleasing whole.

3   Pattern is best displayed if surrounded by a plain or complementary theme.

4   Geometric patterns, on the whole, are more easily used together than floral ones. Often two geometric patterns can be used in the same scheme successfully, whereas it is best to keep to one floral one, and use it with a geometric design if more than one pattern is desired.

5   It should be remembered that patterns are essentially decorative. As one tires more easily of patterned areas than plain ones, they must be chosen with care so that they give a lasting pleasure.

6   Patterns are affected by fashion trends, but a design of quality will continue to give pleasure even after a fashion has changed. This can be seen by the range of traditional and classical designs in textiles available today.

7   The pattern on a curtain fabric is seen on a draped area. Therefore the pattern should not be distorted or lost when the curtains are open.

8   Patterns are useful in that they are more practical, showing up dirt and stains less quickly, and also in wear and tear.

TEXTURE

The word texture is derived from the Latin *texere*, meaning to weave. It is not now solely confined to the surface appearance of fabric, but is used in relation to any surface.

Unlike colour and pattern, texture can be appreciated by touch as well as by sight. It is an important factor in adding interest to a scheme. It is found on all surfaces in the home, and ranges from very smooth, shiny surfaces such as french polished wood, mirrors, gloss paint and stainless steel etc to rough, dull ones such as pile rugs, tweed furnishing fabrics, and rush matting, with degrees of smoothness and roughness in between.

It can be used to replace pattern and to supply decoration; creating space where too much pattern would give enclosure. Texture gives atmosphere and depth to a scheme, so should be varied. Contrast in texture is as important as contrast in colour, or contrast of pattern with plain. When used in conjunction with colour, it can affect the tone value of the colour, eg the same hue used for gloss paintwork and a shaggy rug will appear different, as the painted wood will reflect light and the pile of the rug will absorb it, hence giving an apparent difference in tone.

Texture can affect colour in a similar way to

the use of black and white, giving light and shade. Rough surfaces will suggest warmth, whereas smooth ones will give a colder appearance.

Texture should be related to purpose. A smooth surface is best used where easy cleaning is required, such as in the kitchen. Rough surfaces naturally trap more dust and, therefore, should be used with discrimination. For example, a floor surface is fairly easily cleaned and can be treated with a rough texture, ie a carpet. A wall surface presents more problems and rough textures should only be used in a limited area. Rough textures are perhaps best restricted to the soft furnishing items in the scheme.

THE OCCASIONS WHEN DECOR IS CONSIDERED

The need for a new décor scheme could arise in the following circumstances: planning one's own bedroom, establishing oneself in a bed-sitting-room, setting up a new home on marriage, moving into a new house or refurbishing an existing one. Sometimes, therefore, interior décor is planned from the beginning, whereas at other times it must be planned round some existing furniture and furnishings.

Theoretically the bare shell is the easiest starting point. One can begin by considering the architectural weaknesses of the room and the arrangement of the electrical installations, so that any major constructional alterations can be made before the final décor is planned. Once these alterations have been carried out, the rooms are ready for furnishing. Each one now must be considered for its individual characteristics and use. When planning, consider the size and shape of the room and its aspect, as these points guide in the initial choice of colour, pattern and texture.

As the floor covering, if to be carpet, and the furniture are the most expensive items to be bought, these should be chosen first. Then the wall and ceiling finish decided, followed by the soft furnishing items.

In the other circumstances mentioned, there will be a nucleus of furniture and probably furnishings which will continue in use. So the plan, in fact, will have to stem from these, and they must be considered along with the size, shape, aspect and purpose of the room. Should new pieces of furniture and/or carpeting be required, these must, of course, be chosen first on account of their cost.

2 Curtain styling

Curtains are an expensive and important item in an interior décor scheme. Therefore time and thought should be given to deciding on their style and colour, and the type and texture of fabric to be used. During the day windows provide the source of light in a room and they immediately attract attention. For this reason they are often made a special feature in the décor. This is particularly true when other architectural features, such as a fireplace, are missing. On certain occasions they need a subtle treatment so that they add to the scheme but do not predominate. For example, if the view outside the window is displeasing, the focal point of the scheme should be set to draw attention away from the window area. Alternatively, of course, if a bold window treatment is desired, subsidiary net curtains may be hung to mask the view. If the view is attractive, the curtains should frame the view and not predominate to the point of detracting from it. This is the case with picture windows overlooking an attractive garden. However, further problems arise here, as usually there is a large expanse of curtain when they are drawn together at night. In this case the choice of fabric should not be so subtle that the curtains completely blend into the background. A textured fabric, as opposed to a brightly coloured or patterned one, will usually overcome this problem, the texture providing adequate interest in artificial light, and not detracting from the view in daytime.

When choosing curtains it should be remembered that window treatment can set the mood of the scheme. Curtains may create a formal setting, be exciting and dramatic, or subtle and relaxing.

The size and proportion of the window in relation to the room is all important. Clever curtain styling can disguise poor proportions and help the room to take on a more pleasing appearance. A tall, narrow window can be made to seem wider and shorter by choosing sill length curtains, extending the fitment beyond the window frame, thus exposing the maximum amount of window, and by the addition of a valance or pelmet. The stress thus becomes horizontal rather than vertical. Horizontal stripes or patterns will give further emphasis. However, if the ceiling is rather low, care should be taken not to over-emphasise the horizontal theme. Conversely, a short, wide window can be made to look longer and narrower by choosing floor-length curtains with a tall heading and no pelmet. This effect can be further emphasised by keeping the fitment to the width of the window frame, thus concealing part of the window when the curtains are hung. Vertical stripes and patterns will also help to create the illusion, providing the ceiling is not too high. If a pelmet is desired it should be fitted slightly above the window frame, so that the length is not reduced.

Windows must be studied critically before the style of the curtain is finally chosen. Although two windows in a house may be the same shape and size, this does not necessarily mean that they require exactly the same treatment. For example, in a kitchen, sill length curtains at a horizontal window would be a practical choice, whereas the same shape of window in a lounge may look better with floor length curtains.

The style of curtain must be decided before the track or fabric can be bought. In some cases it may be necessary to use an already existing track, which to some extent will dictate the style of curtain. If the track really is unsuitable for the style of curtain best suited to the scheme, it is worth the extra expense of a new track to guarantee a satisfactory finish.

There are many types and shapes of window in existence, but it is possible to fit them into a few general categories. The following sketches show some basic window shapes, and ways of treating them to suit a particular scheme.

VERTICAL WINDOWS

These windows are easy to curtain providing the casement opens outwards. They may be hung with either draw or café curtains. Decide first whether the vertical plane is to be stressed, or whether the setting would be improved if a horizontal appearance were to be given to the window.

In period settings, with high ceilings, the vertical plane is best stressed. Floor length curtains accentuate the vertical plane and retain the slender proportions of the window. Swags, tails and elaborate pelmets may be used with this kind of treatment. In modern settings, with low ceilings, the window fits better into the scheme if the horizontal plane is stressed. This is achieved by extending the curtains beyond the window on either side. A pelmet helps to reduce height and is useful when treating a pair of windows on the same wall, as it can be used to combine the two and give a unified and horizontal appearance to the window area.

If the window opens inwards, it is necessary to extend the curtains beyond the frame to prevent their becoming entangled when the window or door is open.

1 (*above*) Vertical or tall, narrow window. These windows are usually single-hung or double-hung sash windows, or casement windows, although a single french door gives a similar shape

2 (*below*) A vertical window with floor length curtains, hung from an unobtrusive track, giving a focal point to a half-landing

19

3 *(above)* The furniture unit controls the length of the curtains. The horizontal theme is emphasised by an extended curtain track and the shallow pelmet.

4 *(opposite)* A pair of identical windows set in the same wall. The theme here is planned to stress the vertical plane and give slender proportions by treating the windows separately. It is important to unite them either with a small piece of furniture, a wall ornament or both, suitably chosen for a period setting, as this gives a more balanced appearance. To give a softer effect, subsidiary net curtains have been added

5 *(opposite below)* The same pair of windows treated to give a contemporary setting. The horizontal plane is being stressed by the addition of a third curtain over the wall space between the two windows. The pelmet, here, unites the pair of windows and gives the appearance of one large window

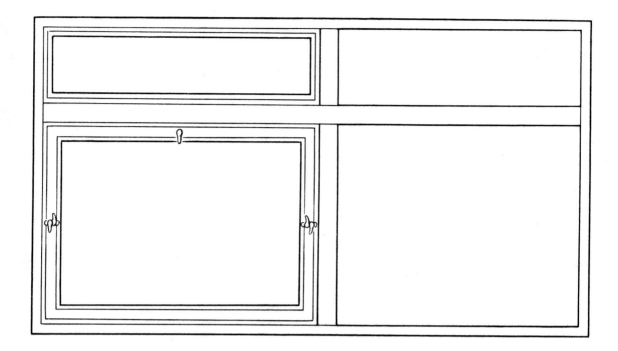

HORIZONTAL WINDOWS

This shape is found in the following types of window: casement, pivot, picture and glass wall. The horizontal plane is generally stressed when treating any of these, but the length of the curtains can be varied to suit the position of the window.

Shallow windows and those set high in the wall, are best treated with sill length curtains. This also applies if furniture is placed in front of the window, or if fitments or radiators are set below the window. Radiators present a special problem, and if there is not a wide sill to the window, it is wise to install a ledge above the radiator to protect the curtains from the heat. The sill or ledge will determine the length of the curtains. If these problems do not arise, floor length curtains may be used successfully. In some cases long curtains improve the proportions of the window and give a more pleasing appearance. Again the curtains should be set beyond the window frame if the window opens inwards within the curtained area.

6 *(above)* A horizontal window with opening section on pivots. This could also be a casement type window

7 *(opposite above)* An inset window which controls the length of the curtains. This shows a practical treatment for a kitchen

8 *(opposite below)* Sill length curtains with a decorative valance to suit a cottage setting

22

9 A more elegant treatment for a contemporary bedroom.
The curtain track has been extended a little way beyond the
window to balance window width with curtain length

The deeper window (*figure 10*) is the original ranch type; *figure 11* shows the shallower modern adaptation. These windows are usually set high in the wall.

A ranch window is usually treated with sill length curtains, although café curtains can be used to suggest more window area.

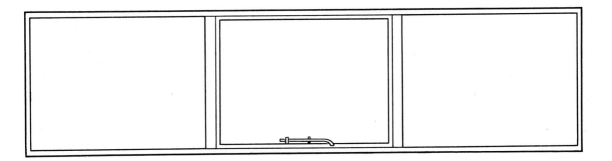

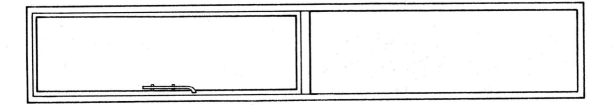

10 *(above)*   A ranch window

11 *(below)*   A shallow ranch window

12 *(above)* Sill length curtains kept to the window area. This would be an excellent opportunity to make use of a semi-sheer fabric

13 *(opposite above)* The proportion of this particular scheme has been improved by the use of café curtains hung from the base of the window, giving an apparently larger window area

14 *(opposite below)* An asymmetric treatment, with the built-in fitment controlling the curtain length. Although not generally used with ranch windows, the longer curtain suggested in this case connects the window with the fitment, giving a more pleasing appearance to this area of the room

PICTURE WINDOWS AND GLASS WALLS

Any picture window is best treated with simple, bold curtains, but care must be taken not to cover ventilation points.

A glass wall usually consists of basic window units, combined with each other to form a wall of glass. Sliding glass doors sometimes form part of the unit. It may be treated as one window, or the area may be broken with curtains hung at the division points as well as the sides. If there are sliding glass doors, the curtains must not interfere with this area.

15 *(above)* A picture window may be composed of one large, fixed pane, or be a combination of a fixed pane with other sections which will open

16 *(opposite above)* As there is no wall space on the left, an asymmetric treatment prevents coverage of the window area. If a pair of curtains are more satisfying, a semi-sheer fabric would prevent cutting out too much light

17 *(opposite below)* A simple, bold treatment for a glass wall. This styling could also be used for a picture window but, in this case, the track may need to be extended on one or both sides of the window, and the curtains hung from the ceiling

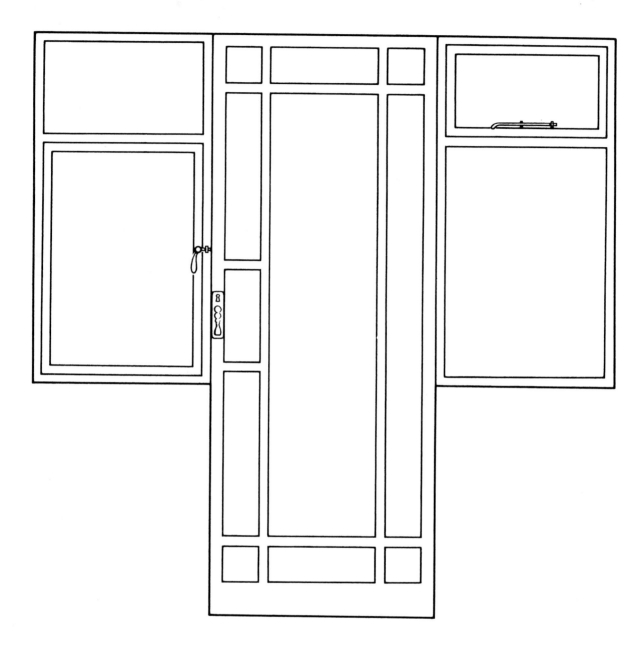

FRENCH DOORS

French doors vary in style and may have a
double or single door, sometimes flanked by
one or two small windows. In all cases floor
length curtains give the most suitable treatment. The most important factor, always, is to
allow the doors to open easily.

18   A single french door with small side windows

19 Floor length curtains used to enhance the vertical plane of
the door, thus giving a more pleasing whole to the single french
door with small side windows. In most cases the door and
window area is set in from the corners of the room. This
distance may not be the same on both sides of the window. It
is best to extend the track either side, equal in amount to the
shorter measurement, unless there is very little in the differing
measurements. In that case, set the track across the full width
of the wall to give a balanced effect

31

20 *(above)*   Single french door with one side window. The long curtains give a balanced effect. The use of a pelmet provides a horizontal line to suggest width

21 *(right)*   A double french door

22 *(above)* As the fitment takes the necessary wall space for a second curtain, an asymmetric treatment is necessary here to allow easy use of the doors. Alternatively, if the doors were wooden, sheer curtains could be attached to the framework, but these would give no coverage at night.

23 *(below)* The period setting requires a formal treatment, and gives scope for the use of a more luxurious fabric with day-time holdbacks

33

There are three main types of bay window, the angled bay, the square bay and the rounded bay or bow window.

There is no real difficulty in curtain styling for bay windows, but some styles will require a high meterage (yardage) of fabric. This type of window often forms a special feature in the room décor, and usually looks its most effective if the curtains are simply styled. A flexible track must be chosen so that it can be bent to follow the angle or curve of the bay. Floor length curtains for a bay window with a projecting sill, must be fitted with a suitable track with extension brackets, or if a wooden pelmet is used, the track must be set to the back of the pelmet. In either case the curtain must clear the sill to prevent distorting the drape of the fabric.

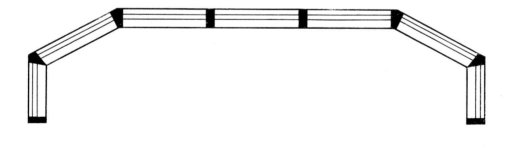

24   Plan of an angled bay window. This may contain 3 or 5 windows, or sometimes 7 as shown in this diagram

25   An angled bay with 5 windows, treated with floor length curtains. Two curtains are suggested to allow maximum light to the room. A wooden pelmet unites the curtains and emphasises the shape of the bay

26   Four apron length curtains have been used at this angled bay window as, being larger in size, it will provide adequate light. The bay has been turned into a special feature in the room by the addition of window seats which control the length of the curtains

27   Plan of a square bay window. This shape of bay may
contain an odd number of windows, or an even number as
shown here

28   The window-seat fitment in this square bay demands
either sill length curtains or, as shown here, floor length
curtains hung from the wall which completely screen off the
bay when closed. Many people use this screening off
treatment, even without a seat fitment, to prevent draughts

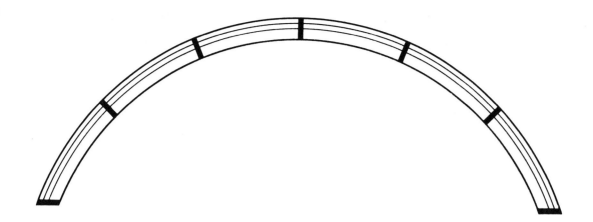

29   Plan of bow or circular bay window. These vary in size
and in the number of windows comprising the unit

30   A simple treatment of two floor length curtains which
give added elegance to the window shape, and suit the period
room furnishings. A similar treatment would be equally
attractive for a smaller bay window

DORMER WINDOWS

Dormer windows can be difficult to curtain. It is often better to consider the wall as a whole, rather than the individual window, and fill in the space below the window with a fitment or piece of furniture. Unless privacy is required, semi-sheer fabrics are a good choice, as dormer windows often restrict light.

31   Tiered, sill length café curtains give an attractive appearance to this difficult window

32   An ideal situation for the use of a semi-sheer fabric. A business-like treatment for an attic study

There is a wide range of curtain tracks available in the shops. Each one has a special feature, or is designed for a special purpose. Therefore it is important that thought should be given when buying, and the most suitable type and style chosen. Any track, regardless of style, should be strong enough to carry the weight of the curtains it will have to support, and it is an advantage if it is easily fitted. In use the track should give easy movement without putting undue strain on the curtains as they are closed and opened. A good track should be durable and, even with constant use, it should operate quietly without jamming or rusting.

There are many heading tapes available which give rigid headings. These are decorative in themselves and, therefore, require no pelmet. If these heading tapes are chosen, it is essential that the curtain track is unobtrusive when the curtains are open, unless a decorative fitting, such as a rod, is used to form a special feature of the window treatment.

Curtain tracks can be either face-fixed to the wall, or top-fixed to the ceiling. Some tracks can be used in one position only; others, of which Rufflette Trimtrack is an example, can be either face fixed or top fixed. *Figure 33 and 34* show this in section.

The following section illustrates and describes a selection of present day curtain tracks.

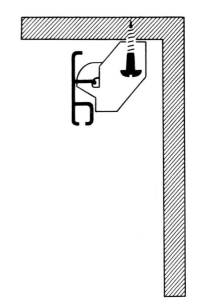

33 *Rufflette Trimtrack* face fixed to the wall

34   The same track top fixed to the ceiling

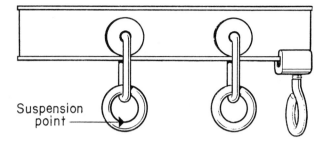

35   Front view of the track

Suspension
point

1   TRACKS TO USE WITH A VALANCE OR PELMET

a   *Rufflette Standard Track*

This metal track has been in use for many years, and remains popular as it is strong and durable. It will carry very heavy curtains if metal wheeled runners are used. The metal runners are not particularly quiet in use, but a slight touch of silicone wax will help to reduce the noise and give smoother running. Plastic gliders are quieter in use, but will support less weight of curtaining than the metal runners. The track requires regular cleaning and waxing to keep it in good condition.

R.S.

Lining

This track is available with overlap sets, valance rails and cording sets, for both straight runs and bay windows. Extension brackets can be bought to allow curtains to clean wide window sills without distorting the drape of the fabric. The track, which may be either top fixed or face fixed, is available in lengths from 91·4 cm (3 ft), complete with all necessary fitments.

36   Fixing a curtain to the runner rings

40

b Rufflette Keytrack

This track is made from strong plastic, and is available in plain white, or with a teak veneered finish. It will support an average curtain weight, but is not suitable for very heavy curtains. The nylon gliders render the track smooth running and quiet in use. It is easy to keep clean. Specially designed overlap and cording sets are available. The track may be bent to fit any shape of window, including strongly curved or angled bays, and may be top fixed or face fixed.

Keytrack is sold in ready-cut lengths from 122 cm (4 ft) to 304·8 cm (10 ft), in 152 mm (6 in.) stages. It is also available in 335·3 cm (11 ft), 365·8 cm (12 ft), 396·2 cm (13 ft), 426·7 cm (14 ft), and 500·4 cm (16 ft 5 in.) lengths. All necessary fitments are supplied with the track.

c Rufflette Cleartrack

This is made from translucent, non-corrosive plastic. It is sufficiently strong for the average weight of curtaining, but is not suitable for very heavy curtains. The plastic gliders help to make it smooth running and quiet. It is easily cleaned. A plastic cording set is available for straight runs. The track is flexible and can be bent to fit curved areas such as bay windows. It can be top fixed or face fixed. It is available in any length from 91·4 cm (3 ft), complete with all necessary fitments. There is a light, plastic valance rail available.

d Swish Nylonglyde

See section 2d
A valance rail is available for use with this track.

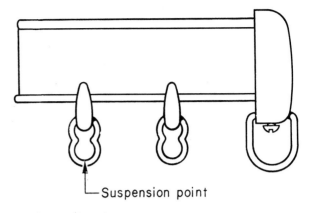

37 *Rufflette Keytrack*

e Harrison Style

This is a white plastic rail which is given added strength by means of a steel reinforcing strip which runs through the centre of the rail. Its special feature is the fixing brackets which are easy to fix, and also give easy removal of the rail for decorating and spring-cleaning purposes. The rail, which is bendable by hand for curved and angled windows, may be either top fixed or face fixed. It is buyable in lengths from 111·8 cm (3 ft 8 in) to 365·8 cm (12 ft).

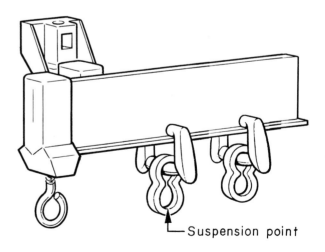

38 *Harrison Style*

f Harrison Glideway

This is a white PVC plastic rail with a steel reinforcement. The brackets, gliders and end stops are made from nylon. The rail is siliconised to ensure smooth, quiet running and is easily cleaned. Overlap and cording sets are available, and a matching valance rail is supplied. It is bendable by hand to any shape required, and may be either top fixed or face fixed. It is buyable in lengths from 91·4 cm (3 ft) to 426·7 cm (14 ft) in 305 mm (12 in.) stages. It is also supplied to retailers in coils, so that any required length can be bought.

2 TRACKS TO USE WITHOUT A VALANCE OR PELMET

a Rufflette Trimtrack

So that it will suit any décor, *Trimtrack* is made with the following variety of finishes:
i white plastic, which may be used as it is, or painted to blend with its surroundings
ii a light oak or teak veneered finish, on strong, light-weight plastic
iii non-corrodible aluminium with either a gilt or a silver milled finish.
 The unobtrusive, plain plastic, and the decorative gilt, silver and simulated wood styles, make these tracks most suitable for use without a pelmet.

Trimtrack runs smoothly and quietly, and is easily cleaned. A specially designed cording set is available for straight runs. The plastic styles may be bent round a gentle curve, but are not suitable for strong curves such as bay or corner windows. The aluminium styles are only suitable for straight runs.
 Any one of the *Trimtrack* range may be used with most curtain styles, but they are particularly suitable for use with tall heading tapes, as the glide fixtures, which hang below the rail, require a sufficiently deep heading to conceal the track when the curtains are hung. *Trimtrack* may be top fixed or face fixed.
 Trimtrack is available in ready-cut lengths from 91·4 cm (3 ft) to 274·3 cm (9 ft) in 152 mm (6 in.) stages. It is also available in 304·8 cm (10 ft), 365·8 cm (12 ft) and 426·7 cm (14 ft) lengths. All the necessary fitments are supplied with this track.

b Rufflette Keytrack

Refer to section 1b
When using *Keytrack* without a pelmet, a sufficiently deep heading is required to conceal the track when the curtains are hung, as the glide fixtures hang below the rail.

c Rufflette Cleartrack

Refer to section 1c

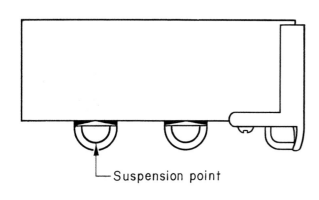
—Suspension point

39 *Rufflette Trimtrack*

40 *(left) Swish* curtain hook

41 *(right) Swish Dutch* hook

This track can be used successfully without a pelmet, as its transparency causes it to blend in with the background. As for *Keytrack*, a sufficiently deep heading is required.

Swish Tracks

These tracks are made from unplasticised polyvinyl chloride (UPVC) compound. They are non-inflammable and are resistant to abrasion, acids, alkalis, oils and grease. The tracks are easy to fix and run quietly and smoothly. They are easily cleaned with a soft cloth and a detergent solution. It is wise to give them an occasional rub with a silicone-based furniture polish to keep the gliders running smoothly on the track. Specially designed cording sets are available for straight runs with all *Swish* tracks.

Swish curtain hooks, *figure 40*, which are made to be used with *Swish* tracks, are available in clear or cream polystyrene, and also in nylon. They are similar in character to *Rufflette R4* and *R5* hooks. The nylon hooks are stronger. Both types of hook may be left in the curtains during laundering, as they cannot rust and will withstand normal washing temperature without damage.

The *Swish Dutch* hook, *figure 41*, is made to use with all standard tapes to give single pinch pleats. A universal bracket is supplied with *Swish Nylonglyde*, *De-Luxe* and *Sologlyde* (see section 3b) so that they can be used either for top fixing or face fixing. *Swish* tracks are available in lengths of 91·4 cm (3 ft) to 228·6 cm (7½ ft) in 152 mm (6 in.) stages.

d   Swish Nylonglyde

Nylonglyde is a fairly strong track, cream in colour. It is suitable for use with or without a valance or pelmet, as it is narrow and relatively unobtrusive. The track is given an antistatic treatment to reduce the collection of dust, so it is clean in use. It can be bent by hand to fit any curved area. All the fittings for this track are moulded in nylon. *Nylonglyde* is most useful as a subsidiary track when sheer curtains are to be used with the main ones. If used without a pelmet, a sufficiently deep heading is required to conceal all fitments.

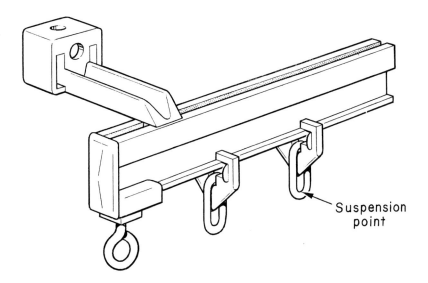

Suspension point

42   *Swish Nylonglyde*

43

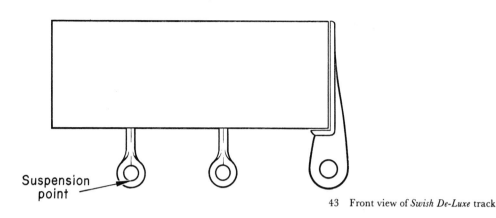

Suspension
point

43   Front view of *Swish De-Luxe* track

e   Swish De-Luxe

Swish De-Luxe track is made in cream, but it may be painted if this will make it blend better with the interior décor scheme. It is a strong track and will support most curtain weights. It is suitable for use without a pelmet because all fittings and moving parts are concealed. The rail can be bent by hand for most curved areas, but it is unwise to attempt to bend it for sharp curves. The fittings for this track are moulded in cream nylon, and the nylon gliders are siliconised to reduce friction and ensure smooth running. Metal extensions are available if the track is to be fitted away from the wall. These form a common support if two tracks are to be used, eg *Nylonglyde* for sheer curtains and *De-Luxe* for the main curtains. *Swish De-Luxe* track may be top fixed or face fixed. It is buyable in lengths from 91·4 cm (3 ft) to 213·4 cm (7 ft) in 152 mm (6 in.) stages.

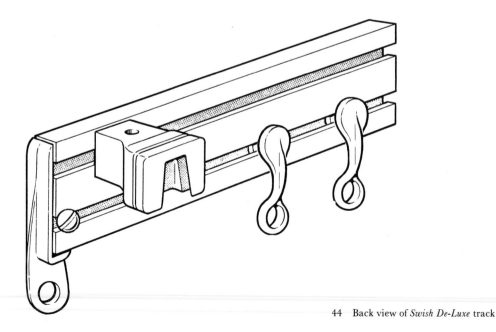

44   Back view of *Swish De-Luxe* track

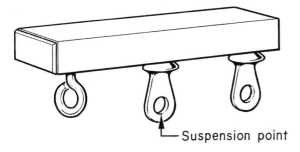

—Suspension point

45a Front view of *Swish Furni-Glyde* track

45b Side view of *Swish Furni-Glyde* track, showing rail with glider in position

f Swish Furni-Glyde

This is a simple track, essentially suitable for straight runs. It may be fixed inside the window area, either to the ceiling or to the wall, and takes up the minimum amount of space. It is ideal for kitchen and bathroom windows which require sill-length, inset curtains, see *figure 7*, page 23. There is a specially designed button-hook for use with this track, which hooks into the runners. A plain hem is made at the top of the curtain, instead of using tape, and the buttonholes are worked at intervals along this. The curtains are then buttoned onto the button-hooks. This is a useful arrangement for windows which require simple curtains for frequent, quick laundering, eg summer chalets and house-boats.

Furni-Glyde can also be used for hanging folding doors, room dividers, and as a wardrobe fitment for hanging clothes. A specially designed wardrobe hook is available. It is, in fact, a very adaptable track with many uses, some of which are not specifically related to Soft Furnishings.

Furni-Glyde is top fixed for use with curtain hooks, but is face fixed for use with button-hooks. It is sold in ready-cut lengths from 91·4 cm (3 ft) to 243·8 cm (8 ft), in 305 mm (12 in.) stages. All necessary fitments are supplied with the track.

Silent Gliss

Silent Gliss supply a variety of rails made from an aluminium alloy with an anodised satin-silver finish. They are strong but light in weight. The rails are siliconised to enable the nylon gliders to run smoothly and quietly along the track. The rails are supplied in lengths from 91·4 cm (3 ft) to 426·7 cm (14 ft). They may be cut by hand, but must be bent by the makers for fitting curved and angled windows. The *Silent Gliss* includes tracks suitable for deep and pencil pleated headings, as well as tracks with built-in draw cords for curtains meeting and overlapping in the centre. Rails for hand operated curtains are supplied complete with gliders, stops, screws and/or supports. Cord drawn rails are fully assembled ready for fixing.

45

The following three rails are suitable for hand operated curtains:

g Silent Gliss 1021

This rail should be face fixed to the bottom edge of the batten.

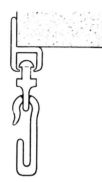

46 Cross-section, showing track in position

h Silent Gliss 1025

A similar rail to 1021, but suitable for top-fixing to wood.

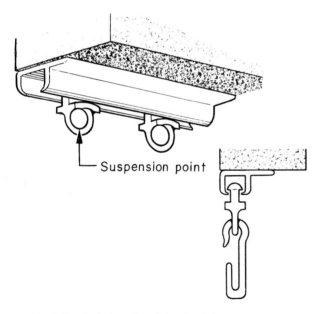

47a *(left)* Back view of track showing it fixed in position

47b *(right)* Cross-section of track

i Silent Gliss 1080

This rail may be either top fixed or face fixed to most surfaces, and is designed to be used with a deep or pencil pleated heading.

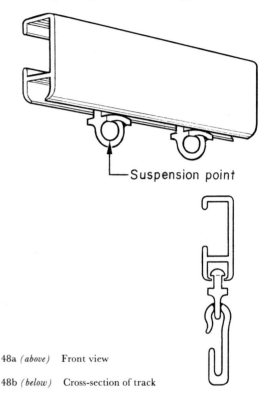

48a *(above)* Front view

48b *(below)* Cross-section of track

j Harrison Style

Refer to section 1e

When using this track without a pelmet, a sufficiently deep heading is required to conceal the track when the curtains are hung, as the gliders hang below the rail.

k Harrison Glydeway

Refer to section 1f, and the heading information given for *Harrison Style*.

Harrison Neta Rails

A series of three rails made from silver anodised aluminium. The rails are siliconised to give smooth, quiet running and, in each style, the nylon glider rings are slotted into a channel.

46

These are not suitable tracks for very heavy curtains.

l Neta 958

This track is suitable for top fixing, but if face fixing is desired, a conversion bracket is available.

m Neta 959

This track has to be face fixed.

Both *Neta 958* and *Neta 959* are light in weight, and relatively strong. They are available in lengths from 91·4 cm (3 ft) to 500·4 cm (16 ft 5 in.). They are similar in character to *Silent Gliss 1021*.

n Neta 960

This is a four-channel section, corded rail, and is suitable for top fixing straight runs up to 426·7 cm (14 ft).

o Harrison Extenda Corded Rail

This rail is suitable for straight runs, and is assembled for operation from the left hand side. However, it can be adjusted easily for right hand operation if desired. It is packed in two standard sizes, 139·7 cm (4 ft 7 in.) and 238·8 cm (7 ft 10 in.), but, as the name implies, it can be extended to fit most windows. *Extenda Corded Rail* is suitable for face fixing.

p Rolls Superglide

This rail is made from ivory plastic or an aluminium alloy with an anodised satin-silver or gold finish. The front, with its non-tarnishable, reeded surface, is designed to be used without a pelmet. The glider channel and bracket fixing rib are concealed. Brackets and pulleys are made from nylon, and the gliders and master slides from *Delrin*. It is a corded rail which may be bent for curved areas such as bay windows. Extension brackets are available to give window sill clearance. For straight runs of 304·8 cm (10 ft) or more, and for bay windows, special cording sets are made. The track may be top fixed or face fixed.

Superglide rails are sold in stock lengths from 122 cm (4 ft) to 243·8 cm (8 ft), in 152 mm (6 in.) stages, and from 274·3 cm (9 ft) to 457·2 cm (15 ft), in 305 mm (12 in.) stages.

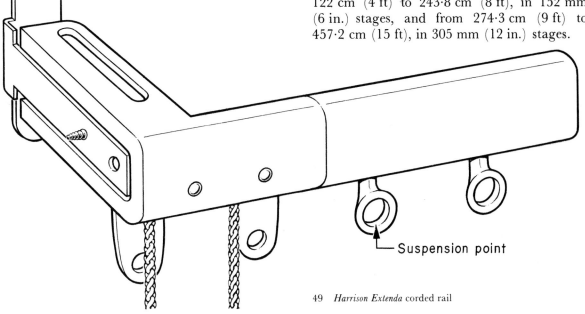

Suspension point

49 *Harrison Extenda* corded rail

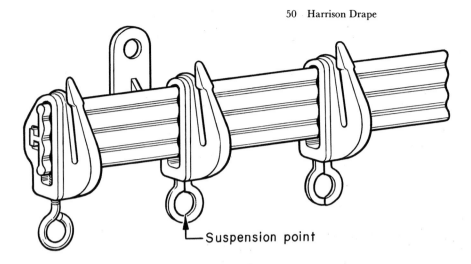

—Suspension point

3 TRACKS COMBINED WITH GLIDER HOOK UNITS

a *Harrison Drape*

This rail is made from anodised aluminium with a gold or silver finish, and has a fluted surface. It is siliconised to reduce noise and is bent easily to fit most window shapes. The special, and at one time unique, feature of this rail is the combined glide hook. The hook, which is made from nylon, can be snapped onto the rail after being inserted into the curtain tape, if the position of the fitment allows. Otherwise the hooks are left in position permanently and the curtain tape pockets slipped over them. When convenient, the hooks can be left in the curtain for laundering. The glide hook has a ring at the base to accommodate the special hooks required for *Hi-Style*, *Deep* and *Easy* pleat tapes.

A specially designed cording set is available, but only for straight runs. The rail is supplied in standard lengths from 91·4 cm (3 ft) to 426·7 cm (14 ft) complete with brackets, glide hooks and fixing screws.

The rail may be either top fixed or face fixed. A joining bridge is available for runs longer than 426·7 cm (14 ft), and should be fitted at the centre of the window, where the two curtains meet.

b *Swish Sologlyde*

Refer to section 2, *Swish* tracks, page 43, for general information. The *Sologlyde* track is less expensive than the *De-Luxe* track. The glider and hook are in one unit and clip into position over the top of the track. It can be bent by hand to suit any curve.

c *Decorail*

This rail is made by the Mono Curtain Rail Company Limited. It is designed to be used without a pelmet, and is available in white, white with either a silver or a gold band, and white with Fleur de Lys motifs on a gold band.

Decorail is strong and yet sufficiently flexible to be bent by hand to fit most windows. The combined hook and glider clips over the rail in a similar way to *Harrison Drape*. The rail may be either top fixed or face fixed, and is buyable in any required length.

SOLARBO PELMETS

These are available in various styles, from a simple painted, or veneered wood finish, to a more elaborate, sculptured pelmet. All the pelmets have a built-in, twin-grooved track, and the curtains are hung by means of specially

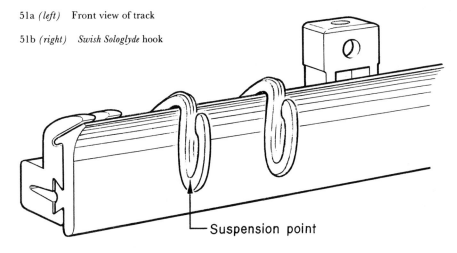

51a *(left)* Front view of track

51b *(right)* *Swish Sologlyde* hook

Suspension point

designed runner-hooks which slip into the grooves of the track. This system is unique to *Solarbo*.

Solarbo Unidrape tape, which has buttonholes along its length, is used in conjunction with the *Solarbo* runner-hooks. A plain hem is made along the top of the curtain, the point of the curled hook pierces the fabric, and the runner-hooks are twisted through the hem. The *Unidrape* tape is then 'buttoned' over the wooden balls of alternate runner-hooks. This automatically pleats up the curtain and provides two rows of runner-hooks, one row attached to the tape and one row free. The taped runner-hooks slot into the back groove of the pelmet, and the untaped runner-hooks slot into the front groove.

The conventional draw-cord tape and hook

52 *(left)* The *Solarbo* runner-hook, which is a wooden ball fitted with a sharply pointed, curled hook

53 *(right)* The *Solarbo* runner, which has a wooden ball fitted with a ring to take an ordinary curtain hook

method of hanging the curtains can be used, but *Solarbo* runners are required for slotting into the pelmet and holding the curtain hooks.

Solarbo products are not available on the ordinary retail market, but must be ordered by post from Solarbo Limited, of Lancing, Sussex, who will supply a catalogue on request. The products can also be seen in the London showrooms.

Bay window fitments have to be made by the makers to the size and shape required.

CURTAIN POLES AND RODS

Curtain poles and rods are once more becoming fashionable, and a reasonable range is available on the market. They are usually fitted with large rings, each having a smaller ring at the base to take the curtain hook. Alternatively, the rings can be stitched to the curtain tape. They are designed to be used without a pelmet, and are intended to form a decorative feature at the top of the window. They are best used in conjunction with deep or pencil pleated headings.

Kirsch produce a variety of rods, including a rectangular one called *Atavio*. This rectangular rod is available in three different styles, with a finish of either satin black or antique bronze.

49

The first is adjustable for windows between 76·2 cm (30 in.) to 127 cm (4 ft 2 in.), and 381 cm (12 ft 6 in.) to 685·8 cm (22 ft 6 in.). The second style can be cut to any desired length, and the third is designed to be used with café curtains. There is a choice of finish to suit personal taste. The rings for these rods are rectangular.

Kirsch circular rods are available in various styles and finishes, including white, walnut, black and plain wood. This latter one can be painted to suit a particular décor scheme. Rods are also available in anodised aluminium with bronze, antique brass, antique white and gold, and with *Alumigold* finishes.

Solarbo make an extendable brass or plain white rod in four lengths, which will fit any window between 76·2 cm (30 in.) and 609·6 cm (20 ft). For example, a 76·2 cm (30 in.) rod will extend to 122 cm (48 in.), and a 365·8 cm (12 ft) rod will extend to 609·6 cm (20 ft).

W. A. Hudson Limited produce a cornice pole with pineapple-shaped finials, covered in glossy white plastic. This is easily cleaned. It is available in three basic lengths, but extension units can be bought which adapt for windows up to 365·8 cm (12 ft).

4 Fabrics

FIBRES

The basic unit of any fabric is a fibre. A fibre is thin and hair-like, varying in length from 6 mm ($\frac{1}{4}$ in.) upwards. Fibres chosen to form the basic units of textile fabrics must contain sufficient strength, flexibility, length and fineness to be spun into yarn. There are two kinds of textile fibre used for this purpose:

a Filament

This is a continuous length of very fine fibre. Silk is a natural fibre in filament form. The filaments of man-made textiles are made by a machine spinning process.

b Staple

This is the name given to fibres which are short in length, and have to be twisted together to spin a yarn which can be used as a very long length to compare with filaments. Cotton and wool are natural fibres of staple length. Man-made fibre filament can be cut into staple form.

YARN

Yarns are the threads prepared for weaving. They are made either of staple fibres which have been spun (ie twisted) together, or of a group of lightly twisted filaments. In this case the twisting merely holds the filaments together. It is not required for the production of yarn length as in staple.

As staple and filaments are both variable according to their source, so yarns made from them will vary in appearance, quality and texture. However, it is true to say that filament yarns are usually smoother, thinner and more lustrous than staple yarns.

Obviously the colour, pattern and finish of fabrics play large parts in giving variety to the final product, but it is the initial preparation of the yarn which offers the greatest scope to the fabric manufacturers. Fancy yarns can be prepared in special ways to produce slub, loop, gimp or other effects which give interesting texture and colour to the finished cloth.

Yarns can be highly twisted in spinning so that they are hard and strong, or conversely, they can be more loosely twisted to form softer, more pliable threads.

WEAVING

The appearance, durability and texture of a fabric depend on the way in which it is made, as well as on the yarn. One of the most usual ways of making cloth is by weaving on a loom. Commercially, fabric is woven in set lengths called pieces, which vary in length according to the width and weight of the cloth. The width of the cloth varies, too, according to type.

Cloth is woven by the right-angled interlacing of threads. This can be done in a variety of ways, but all weaving is done on one foundation method. Parallel warp threads are set up first in the loom, and form the threads which run up and down the length of the cloth. The loom holds these warp threads tautly in place, while weft threads are woven through them by means of a shuttle. The weft threads pass over and under the warp threads, to and fro across the width of the cloth, setting at right angles to the warp.

Warp threads are subjected to strain during the weaving process. Therefore it is necessary for them to be made from strongly spun yarn. Weft threads, which journey across and in and out of the warp during weaving, usually need to be softer and more pliable.

At each edge of the warp the threads are packed a little more closely together. As the weft thread turns round the end warp thread to retrace its journey across the cloth, a firm, close edge is made. This is the selvedge.

It is easy to see the arrangement of warp and weft threads, and the formation of the selvedge, if a piece of coarse cloth is examined closely, or through a magnifying glass.

GRAIN

The warp and weft threads, which compose the weave of the cloth, provide the fabric with two grains, the warp grain and the weft grain. These two grains give balance to the cloth when it is in use. The warp grain will be stronger than the weft grain as explained in the previous section. It is important to place these grains accurately when cutting and sewing cloth.

EXAMPLE 1   A square cushion should have all four edges cut straight with the grains, ie two edges cut with the warp and two cut with the weft.

EXAMPLE 2   Curtains must be cut with their side edges and length seams straight with the warp. The top and bottom edges must be straight with the weft. In this way the curtains are balanced with the grains and will hang evenly and straight.

Net is not woven on a loom and, therefore, does not have warp and weft grains. It is made on special machines which either twist or loop the yarn. On close examination, it will be seen that lines of small holes run along the length and across the width of the net, thus providing two obvious directions. These are called the mesh of the net. It is necessary to balance net with the mesh in the same way that woven fabric must be balanced with the grain.

FABRIC FINISHES

Fabrics are usually given some type or types of finish during manufacture to render them more attractive and/or more convenient in use. The finishes in most general use are:

1   *Mercerisation.*

This finish is only applied to cotton. It is useful as it provides extra lustre, absorbancy, dye affinity and strength, and also helps to render the fabric crease resistant.

2   *Shrink resistance*

Fortunately most fabrics can be treated with this finish and, providing other factors are suitable, curtains and covers can often be washed at home, thus saving the expense of dry-cleaning.

3   *Dyeing*

The quality of dye-stuffs used varies according to the type and use of the fabric for which it is intended. Therefore the dye-stuffs can affect the price of the fabric. The tenacity of a dye is one of its most important qualities, and one which is related to the fabric being dyed, as some fabrics hold dye more readily than others. The word 'fast' as applied to dyes, refers to this tenacity. No dye can be guaranteed 100% 'fast' in all circumstances. Dyed fabrics are usually resistant to some or all of the following conditions: light, sun, water, suitably chosen washing powders or liquids and friction.

4   *Printing*

A coloured pattern can be applied fairly cheaply to one side of fabric by various methods of printing. The better the quality of the print, the more clearly visible it is on the reverse side of the fabric. With the *Duplex* system, a pattern can be printed on both sides of fabric in exact position.

Other finishes useful for soft furnishing fabrics are moth-proofing, crease-resisting, stain-repelling and soil-retarding. Fabrics with these finishes should be labelled accordingly.

To keep reasonable prices, the finishes imposed are restricted according to the use of the fabric, eg curtain fabric should resist sunlight, but need not be water-repellent.

SOILING OF FABRIC

A prime cause of this is dust which persistently attacks everything. Another cause is pollution by the atmosphere which brings dirt in several ways:

a from smoky fires
b from internal combustion engines
c from the incomplete combustion of oil in heaters.

The introduction of smoke abatement regulations have brought relief to housewives, but until this is general, soot will be a menace in the atmosphere. (If a fire is over-stoked it smokes freely, producing tarry secretions. As these burn, soot is given off by the flames.)

Sulphur dioxide is produced by the burning of coal and oil. This gas will dissolve in water vapour, and so droplets of acid are introduced into the atmosphere. All these unpleasant components of the atmosphere damage fabrics.

LOSS OF COLOUR

Loss of colour through fading is a common problem with soft furnishing fabrics. There are several causes of fading. The most common are water and the ultra-violet rays in natural light. It is advisable to test the washing reaction on a scrap of fabric if there is any doubt. First well soak the piece, and then wash it in hot water with detergent. If, when dried, there is no loss of colour apparent, the fabric can be pre-sumed fast for washing, but if loss of colour does result, it will be best to dry-clean.

FABRIC CHARACTERISTICS

When buying soft furnishing fabrics it is essential to make the best selection for the purpose. The advantages and disadvantages of the fibres must be considered in relation to the use of the fabric in the home. It is not possible to find a perfect fibre which will suit any situation, but most fibres have special characteristics which make them suitable for particular purposes.

When choosing curtains the drape of the fabric is important, and the fabric should be held up in the shop to test its hanging appearance. Soft, pliable fibres give good drapability to fabrics.

Upholstery and loose covers need fabric with body which offers a firm, solid feel when handled. This is given to the fabric by the weight and stiffness of the fibres and yarns.

Carpets and blankets require fibres which have a good loft quality, ie they must be resilient and springy, so that they do not remain compressed after use, but spring back to their original state.

Lustre gives beauty to fabric, but should not be confused with shine. Lustrous fabrics respond to light with a subdued richness, whereas shiny surfaces tend to dazzle in light.

Colour is also a contributory factor to the beauty of a fabric, and fibres which absorb dye readily, produce cloth which has a pleasing depth of colour.

The following tables indicate the tendencies of the fabric fibres in general use for modern soft furnishing fabrics:

FIBRE AND FIBRE FORM	STRENGTH AND DURABILITY	RESILIENCE AND ELASTICITY	ABSORBENCY	INFLAMMA-BILITY
COTTON Staple	Strong and hard-wearing Weakened by strong sunlight	Fair creases readily Tears fairly easily	Very good	Burns readily, especially if napped
LINEN Staple	Very strong and hard-wearing; stronger when wet Weakened by long exposure to sunlight	Poor—creases very readily in its pure form, but is usually blended or mixed with other fibres to overcome this deficiency	Very good	Burns readily, but more slowly than cotton
WOOL Staple	Moderately strong, weaker when wet	Very good	Good	Burns slowly—smoulders
SILK Filament in natural form Made into staple form if required	Strong Weakened by strong sunlight Reduced in strength by weighting	Very good sheds creases readily in its pure form, but this quality deteriorates with weighting	Very good	Burns slowly—smoulders
VISCOSE RAYON Filament, or staple if required	Fairly strong weaker when wet Weakened by prolonged exposure to sunlight	Fair	Very good	Burns readily

CHEMICAL PROPERTIES	FINISHES	USES	CARE	PRICE RANGE
Will withstand: alkalis cold dilute acids weak chlorine, and other weak bleaches if rinsed out thoroughly	Dyeing: good affinity Can be: mercerised glazed Can be rendered: shrink resistant crease resistant flame resistant water repellent stain repellent drip-dry minimum-iron	Used in most fields of soft furnishing and household textiles	Soils readily, but washes easily	Inexpensive to moderately expensive
As for cotton	Dyeing: fairly good affinity; however, with selected dyestuffs the colours are fast to light and washing Can be mercerised, can be rendered crease resistant	Used for curtains, loose covers and household linen in 100% form, and also mixed or blended with other fibres	Washes easily	Expensive
Will not withstand: concentrated acids concentrated alkalis Dilute acids may be used safely Dilute alkalis should be used with care	Dyeing: very good affinity Can be rendered: shrink resistant water repellent stain repellent moth-proof	Mainly carpets and upholstery Often blended for carpets	Fairly easy	Moderately expensive to expensive
Will not withstand: concentrated acids concentrated alkalis Always rinse thoroughly after using weak solutions of these	Dyeing: very good affinity Weighting often added	Used very little today, but sometimes for more luxurious accessories	Dry-cleaning recommended	Very expensive
Will not withstand: concentrated alkalis cold concentrated or hot dilute acids	Dyeing: good affinity Can be embossed, Can be rendered: crease resistant flame resistant water repellent stain repellent	Used extensively in all fields of soft furnishing	Fairly easy	Inexpensive

FIBRE AND FIBRE FORM	STRENGTH AND DURABILITY	RESILIENCE AND ELASTICITY	ABSORBENCY	INFLAMMA-BILITY
MODIFIED RAYONS 1 *Sarille* Staple only	Fairly strong	Fairly good	Very good	Burns readily
2 *Durafil*	Strong and hard-wearing	Good	Good	Burns readily
3 *Vincel*	Strong and hard-wearing	Fair	Good	Burns readily
4 *Evlan* and *Evlan M*	Strong	Good	Good	Burns slowly —smoulders
ACETATE Filament or staple as required *Dicel*, filament form *Celafibre*, staple form	Fairly weak weaker when wet weakened by prolonged exposure to sunlight	Fairly good	Fair	Burns and melts
TRIACETATE *Tricel* filament or staple as required	Moderately strong	Good	Moderately poor	Burns and melts, but less readily than *Acetate*
POLYAMIDES Nylon *Bri-nylon* *Blue C nylon* *Celon* *Banlon* *Enkalon* Filament or staple as required	Very strong Weakened by prolonged exposure to sunlight	Very good	Poor	Melts and tends to drop away

CHEMICAL PROPERTIES	FINISHES	USES	CARE	PRICE RANGE
As for *Viscose rayon*	Dyeing: good affinity	Blankets and candlewick bed-covers	Fairly easy	Inexpensive
As for *Viscose rayon*	Dyeing: good affinity	Blended with other man-made or natural fibres for upholstery fabrics	Fairly easy	Inexpensive
As for *Viscose rayon*	Dyeing: good affinity	On its own or in blended form for household textiles	Fairly easy	Inexpensive
As for *Viscose rayon*	Dyeing: good affinity	Carpets, upholstery, curtains and loose covers	Fairly easy	Moderately expensive
Will not withstand: concentrated acids, concentrated alkalis Dissolves in acetone	Dyeing: good affinity, with good fastness to light now suitable dyes and dyeing methods have been developed	Used in a limited way for curtains and upholstery fabrics *Celafibre* also used in blended form for carpets	Requires careful attention	Moderately inexpensive
As *Acetate*	Dyeing: good affinity Can be heat-set	For candlewick bed-covers and as washable fillings	Easy	Moderately inexpensive
Will withstand alkalis weakened by acids	Dyeing: good affinity, now suitable dyes and dyeing methods have been developed Can be: heat set embossed nylonised (to increase absorbency) Can be rendered: stain repellent further water repellent	Used in most fields of soft furnishing and household textiles, either on their own, or in blended form	Easy	Moderately expensive

FIBRE AND FIBRE FORM	STRENGTH AND DURABILITY	RESILIENCE AND ELASTICITY	ABSORBENCY	INFLAMMA-BILITY
POLYESTERS *Terylene* *Dacron* *Tergal* Filament or staple as required	Very strong, with a good resistance to light	Very good	Poor	Retracts and melts, with a tendency to drop away
ACRYLICS *Orlon* *Acrilan* *Courtelle* *Dralon* Usually staple	Fairly strong	Good	Poor	Does not burn readily
MOD-ACRYLICS *Teklan* *Dylan* Filament or staple as required	Fairly strong Good resistance to sunlight	Good	Poor	Flame resistant
GLASS Filament or staple if required	Extremely strong, but weakened by abrasion	Poor	Poor	Non-inflammable

CHEMICAL PROPERTIES	FINISHES	USES	CARE	PRICE RANGE
Generally resistant to acids and alkalis	Dyeing: good affinity, now suitable dyes and dyeing methods have been developed Can be heat-set Fine net can be given an anti-flare finish	As *Polyamides*	Easy	Moderately expensive
Will withstand: dilute acids dilute alkalis	Dyeing: good affinity, now suitable dyes and dyeing methods have been developed. Can be heat-set Can be rendered: stain repellent water repellent	Curtains Blankets Carpets on their own or in blended form Upholstery	Easy	Moderately inexpensive
Will withstand: dilute acids dilute alkalis	Dyeing: good affinity, now suitable dyes and dyeing methods have been developed	Curtains Carpets Rugs	Easy	Moderately expensive
Will withstand: acids alkalis Will not withstand: chlorinated dry cleaning solution	Dyeing: good affinity Coronizing, which can incorporate: cleaning, heat-setting, relaxing (to improve handle and drapability) and dyeing, in one continuous process can be delustered can be rendered water repellent	Mainly for curtains	Requires careful attention	Moderately expensive

The bast fibres

Jute
relatively strong and readily available
generally used in its natural colour
good affinity for dyes
Uses for starched and glued buckram for
pelmets, wall coverings, upholstery, bedding
foundations and carpet backings
Inexpensive

Ramie
white, lustrous and durable, but coarse, stiff
and lacking in elasticity
good affinity for dyes
sometimes blended with cotton, mohair, vis-
cose and nylon
Uses in a limited way for inferior upholstery
and furnishing fabrics
Inexpensive

The leaf fibre

Sisal
strong and hard-wearing with a naturally good
colour and lustre
good affinity for dyes
Uses for matting, some carpets and in upholstery, also for table mats
Inexpensive

The seed fibres

Coir
a coarse, brown fibre obtained from coconut
husks
Uses for door-mats and for stuffing upholstered furniture.
Moderately expensive

Kapok
light in weight
Soft when new, but loses its buoyancy after
some use
Uses for padding and stuffing.
Moderately expensive

Care labels are attached to almost all ready-made soft furnishing goods. Fabric bought by the yard should be classified in the shop so that the nature of the fibre content is known. It is also wise to enquire whether it has been given any special finish. The correct care for the fabric can then be found by studying the carefully devised eight washing codes of the Home Laundering Consultative Council.

The range of fibres used in modern fabric manufacture, while giving a wide and attractive selection of materials, has added to the complexities of washing and cleaning. The eight wash codes, if carefully followed, overcome this problem and guide the housewife into the best washing and drying treatments for the fabric in her home.

The standard iron settings now shown on modern electric irons, give guidance in the finishing of articles after washing.

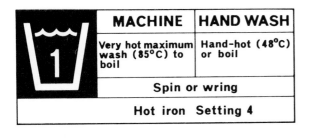

	MACHINE	HAND WASH
1	Very hot maximum wash (85°C) to boil	Hand-hot (48°C) or boil
	Spin or wring	
	Hot iron Setting 4	

54 A typical care label as found on white cotton or linen articles without special finishes

STANDARD WASHING TEMPERATURES
WITH EXPLANATION OF TEMPERATURE

Warm wash 40°C Pleasantly warm to the hand
Hand-hot wash 48°C As hot as the hand can bear
Hot wash 60°C Hotter than the hand can bear, the temperature of water coming from many domestic hot taps
Very hot 85°C Water heated to near boiling temperature
Boil 100°C

STANDARD IRON SETTINGS

Setting 1   Cool   Courtelle Acrilan Orlon
Setting 2   Warm Acetate   nylon   *Terylene Terylene* mixtures *Tricel* wool
Setting 3   Medium hot Rayon   or   modified rayons, eg *Vincel* or *Sarille.*
Setting 4   Hot   Cotton or linen.

The following table combines the wash code and iron settings to guide the care of soft furnishing fabrics in use in the home.

FIBRE	WASH CODE	MACHINE WASH	HAND WASH	FINISHING
White cotton and linen articles without special finishes	**1**	Very hot maximum wash (85°C) to boil	Hand hot (48°C) or boil	Hot Setting 4
		Spin or wring		
Cotton, linen or rayon articles without special finishes— colours fast at 60°C	**2**	Hot maximum wash (60°C)	Hand hot (48°C)	Medium hot Setting 4 or 3
		Spin or wring		
White nylon	**3**	Hot medium wash (60°C)	Hand hot (48°C)	Warm iron (if necessary) Setting 2
		Cold rinse, short spin or drip dry		
Coloured nylon, *Polyester*, cotton and rayon articles with special finishes, acrylic/cotton mixtures	**4**	Hand hot medium wash (48°C)	Hand hot (48°C)	Warm iron (if necessary) Setting 2
		Cold rinse, short spin or drip dry		

FIBRE	WASH CODE	MACHINE WASH	HAND WASH	FINISHING
Cotton, linen or rayon articles—colours fast at 40°C, but not at 60°C	**5**	Warm medium wash (40°C)	Warm (40°C)	Medium hot Setting 3
		Spin or wring		
Acrylics, acetate and triacetate, including wool mixtures, *Polyester*/wool blends	**6**	Warm minimum wash (40°C)	Warm (40°C)	Cool iron Setting 1
		Cold rinse, short spin. Do not wring		
Wool, including blankets and wool mixtures with cotton or rayon Silk	**7**	Warm minimum wash (40°C)	Warm, do not rub (40°C)	Warm iron (if necessary) Setting 2
		Spin. Do not hand wring		
Washable, pleated articles containing acrylic, nylon, *Polyester* or triacetate fibres Glass fibre fabric	**8**	HAND WASH ONLY		Ironing unnecessary Detrimental to glass fibre fabric
		Warm rinse, hand hot final rinse, drip dry		

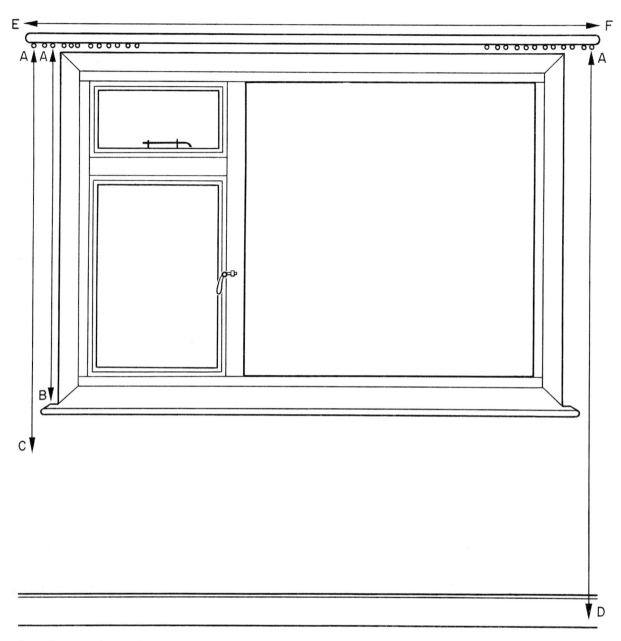

A   Suspension point
AB Sill length   EF Length of track to calculate
AC Apron length   width of curtaining required
AD Floor length

55   Taking measurements for curtains

5 Preparing for curtain making

MEASURING FOR CURTAINS

A new fitment may be necessary to replace an old one or to provide for a different style of curtain. If this is required, it must be attended to before beginning to measure, as the track has to be used when taking both length and width measurements.

When choosing the style, a decision must also be made about the curtain length, ie sill, apron or floor length.

Sill length (*a*) for inset windows the curtains just skim the sill (*b*) for normal windows the curtains just cover the sill board

Apron length The curtains hang 100 mm to 230 mm (4 in. to 9 in.) below the sill

Floor length The curtains clear the floor by 25 mm (1 in.)

Measuring the length

Measure from the suspension point to the desired length, using preferably a pocket steel rule. (A tape measure is not recommended because of lack of stiffness, but can, of course, be used if a steel rule is not available.) This measurement gives the initial length required. Certain other measurements have to be added to this before the fabric length can be ascertained with accuracy.

a Heading allowance. This varies according to the tape selected. (See heading tape section on page 92.)

b Hem usually 75 mm (3 in.).

c Shrinkage. If the fabric chosen is not guaranteed shrink resist, allow 30 mm per metre. (1 in. per yard.)

Calculating the width

This depends on the weight of the fabric and the weight of the heading. Light fabric and

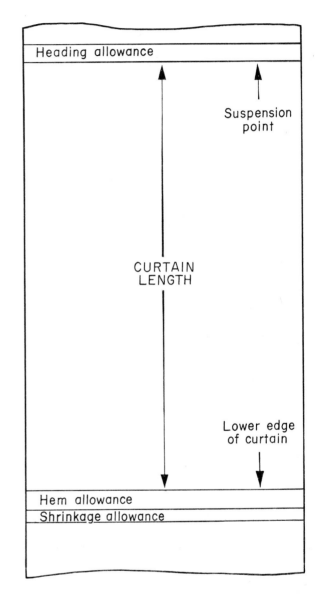

56 Measuring the length

sheers are usually made up with more fullness than heavy fabric, but certain heading styles, eg deep pleat using commercial tape, require careful calculation to allow for the regularity of the pleating. An adequately full curtain will always hang and look better than one which is skimped in fullness. Sometimes it is wiser to buy a slightly less expensive fabric in order to have the more desirable fullness.

The width is always based on the fitment, as in many cases this extends beyond the window frame. Therefore, measure the full width of the track. Thin fabric needs twice (minimum fullness) to three times (maximum fullness) the track measurement, divided between the number of curtains to be used at the window. Heavier fabric needs 1·3 ($1\frac{1}{3}$) (minimum fullness), to twice (maximum fullness) the track measurement, divided between the number of curtains.

Before the final width can be calculated accurately, it is essential to consider the following three points carefully if a minimum fullness has been allowed. The maximum fullness usually supplies sufficient fabric to provide for them.

a seam allowance if curtain widths need to be joined

b side hems on unlined curtains: side turnings on lined curtains

c the central overlap of the curtains when drawn, if this is provided by the fitment

The following examples give guidance in calculating the length of curtain fabric to buy:

Window A 167·5 cm wide × 218·5 cm long (66 in. wide × 86 in. long)
Minimum fullness—1·3 ($1\frac{1}{3}$) × track length
Plain fabric

Calculation of curtain width
Fullness is 1·3 ($1\frac{1}{3}$) × width
In this case 1·3 × 167·5 cm = 223·3 cm ($1\frac{1}{3}$ × 66 in. = 88 in.)
Divide this answer by the fabric width, ie 122 cm (48 in.)

$$\frac{2233}{1220} = 1 \cdot 830 \left(\frac{88}{48} = 1\tfrac{5}{6} \right)$$

Two full widths, therefore, give a surplus of fabric, which will allow for side finishes and overlaps, without reducing the fullness.

Calculation of curtain length
218·5 cm + 75 mm heading + 75 mm hem + 60 mm shrinkage = 239·5 cm
(86 in. + 3 in. heading + 3 in. hem + $2\frac{1}{2}$ in. shrinkage = $94\frac{1}{2}$ in.)

To find quantity to buy
Multiply the total length by the number of widths required,
ie 239·5 cm × 2 = 479 cm ($94\frac{1}{2}$ in. × 2 = 189 in.)
ie 4·79 metres (5 yd 9 in.)
Quantity to be bought is, therefore, 4·8 metres ($5\frac{1}{4}$ yds)

Window B 228·5 cm wide × 101·5 cm long (90 in. wide × 40 in. long)
Average fullness—1·5 ($1\frac{1}{2}$) × track length
Plain fabric

Calculation of curtain width
Fullness is 1·5 ($1\frac{1}{2}$) × width
In this case 1·5 × 228·5 cm = 342·8 cm ($1\frac{1}{2}$ × 90 in. = 135 in.)
Divide this answer by the fabric width, ie 122 cm (48 in.)

$$\frac{3428}{1220} = 2 \cdot 809 \left(\frac{135}{48} = 2\tfrac{39}{48} \right)$$

This shows that 3 widths are required, necessitating 1·5 ($1\frac{1}{2}$) widths per curtain.

The calculation of curtain length is worked out by the method already shown for *Window A*. To find the quantity to buy, multiply the total length by the number of widths required, in this case 3. This will necessitate splitting one width of fabric and joining each half to a full width, thus making each curtain 1·5 ($1\frac{1}{2}$) widths wide. The half widths must be joined so that they hang at the outer edges of the window.

Window C 244 cm wide × 175·5 cm long (96 wide × 69 in. long)
Maximum fullness—2 × track length
Plain fabric

Calculation of curtain width
Fullness is 2 × width
In this case 2 × 244 cm = 488 cm (2 × 96 in. = 192 in.)
Divide this answer by the fabric width, ie 122 cm (48 in.)

$$\frac{488}{122} = 4 \left(\frac{192}{48} = 4 \right)$$

This shows that 4 widths of fabric are required, necessitating 2 widths per curtain.

The calculation of curtain length is worked out by the method already shown for *Window A*. To find the quantity to buy, multiply the total length by the number of widths required, in this case 4.

Buying wide width fabric

Wide width fabric is 183 cm (72 in.) wide, and is available in a limited range. Therefore it is not wise to calculate on this measurement in the first instance. The calculation can be adjusted when shopping, as this measurement replaces a width and a half exactly, thus eliminating seaming. If in the original calculation 2 widths of 122 cm (48 in.) were required, it raises problems that have to be solved by deciding whether the fullness can be reduced or increased. In many cases it will probably be better to buy 122 cm (48 in.) width.

Buying patterned fabric

Patterned fabric requires special thought in planning to give a uniform and pleasing appearance to the curtains when they are hanging at the window. Each unit of design must come in the same position on each curtain, so that they will balance across the window. Also a whole design should be visible at the lower end of each curtain after the hem has been turned. As the heading is usually ruched in some way, a broken design is less conspicuous here. To ensure that the pattern is arranged to give these balanced results, it is often necessary to waste small amounts of fabric in between each length when cutting out the curtains (*see figure 57 overleaf*).

It is important to take to the shop the measurements and calculations worked out for plain fabric. When patterned fabric is chosen and the length of the design forming the pattern repeat can be measured, it will be possible to work out the extra amount of fabric required, with the help of the salesman if necessary. This extra fabric can be used for pelmets or accessories in the scheme if adequate.

Curtain lining

Unlined curtains, although more economical, do not always provide as satisfactory a finish as lined curtains, although they are more practical for bathroom, kitchen and some bedroom curtains. They can also give a very attractive appearance if modern, openweave fabric suits the décor of the room.

The choice of curtain fabric will often determine whether a lining is required. Lining fabric is available in a limited range, and only in cotton, although it may be given a finish, selling under the trade name of *Milium*. A lining will give additional weight, therefore improving the drapability of the fabric. Fibres damaged by strong light will be protected by a lining. It will also act as a draught barrier when the curtains are closed. The insulation quality is increased by the use of *Milium* for the lining fabric. Lined curtains eliminate the need for identical curtain fabric in every room in order to achieve uniformity from the outside of the house. The lining gives the uniformity desired, and allows a free choice of curtaining for each décor.

Linings can be made in one of two ways, ie either attached to the curtain or made detachable and suspended from the heading tape. This latter method is useful for lining curtain fabric which requires different washing treatment from cotton. This problem does not arise if the curtains are dry-cleaned. The amount of

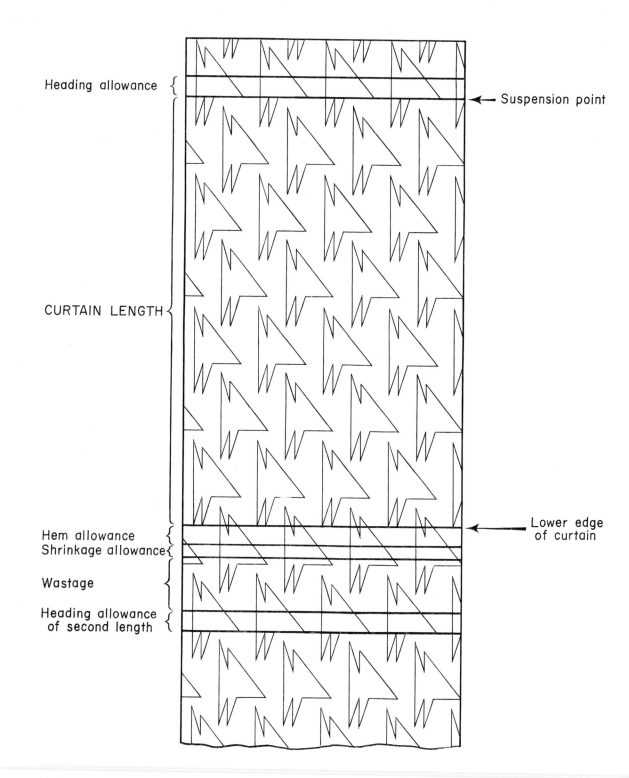

Heading allowance

Suspension point

CURTAIN LENGTH

Lower edge
of curtain

Hem allowance
Shrinkage allowance

Wastage

Heading allowance
of second length

57   Measuring patterned fabric

lining fabric required varies according to the method chosen.

To calculate the amount of fabric to buy for an attached lining, refer to the original calculation for the curtain fabric. The lining requires 50 mm (2 in.) less per curtain length, as the lining is set above the hem line of the curtain.

The length calculation for detachable linings varies according to the heading tape in use, and is, therefore, dealt with in the section on heading tapes, (page 92).

Buying soft furnishing fabrics

This is an important piece of shopping and adequate preparation should be made for it. The following general points should be considered carefully:

1 Buy according to the purpose of the room, choosing from a sensible price range and trying to obtain value for the money spent.
2 Check whether the fabric has been treated for shrinkage, and consider whether the shrinkage allowance in the estimated length is adequate.
3 Cheap fabric is sometimes dressed to improve its body, but this will be removed in the first wash. To check for this, examine the fabric closely and note the looseness of the weave compared with the apparent firmness of the fabric. If in doubt, rub a corner to see if the finish is permanent.
4 Remember to ascertain the fibre content and any special finishes given to the fabric, so that the correct method of cleaning may be selected.
5 Examine the fabric carefully for flaws. These should be marked on the selvedge by the manufacturer.
6 With printed patterns check that the dye has penetrated the yarn. If it is only on the surface of the fabric, it will tend to rub off if subjected to abrasion.
7 When buying patterned fabric, look closely to detect the grain. Then examine the design and check that it has been printed accurately in line with the grain. This is most important. If the pattern is inaccurately printed, the cutting of the fabric presents a great problem. If cut with the grain, the pattern comes out of alignment; if cut with the pattern, the cloth will be off grain and will not set evenly.
8 Always go shopping with the exact measurements required so that adequate fabric is bought, as it may be difficult to match it at a later date. If too long a length is bought, unnecessary expense is incurred. The wasted money could have been used towards buying better quality fabric, or for some other purpose.

When buying fabric for curtains, it is necessary to know which type of heading is needed for use with the curtain fitment, and to have considered the colour, pattern or texture of fabric which will suit the room. Along with the general points already listed, the following additional points apply specifically to the buying of curtain fabrics:

1 Buy furnishing fabric and not dress-weight fabric as a general rule, unless, for example, check gingham suits a kitchen or bathroom scheme.
2 View the curtain fabric draped, and hanging with the daylight behind it, this will often suggest whether the fabric needs to be lined. Also a pattern looks quite different when draped, than when seen on a flat surface. Check the effect of artificial light on the fabric as colours may appear to alter.
3 As curtains are subjected to strong light, colour fastness is an important consideration. Some manufacturers guarantee their fabric fadeless.

Most of the equipment required is simple and can usually be supplied by the contents of the home work box as shown by the following list:

Cutting-out shears   General purpose scissors
A tape-measure   Pins   Needles   Thimble
Tailor's chalk

A sewing machine, however, is an essential item for parts, if not all, of curtain making. It is necessary to use the correct size machine needle for the type of curtain fabric. The machine needles should be chosen according to the following guide:

Fabric	Machine Needle	
Heavy	Singer	size 16
	Continental size 100	
Medium to Light	Singer	size 14
	Continental size 90	
Light	Singer	size 14 or 11
	Continental size 90 or 80	

Thread. This should blend with the fabric in weight, fibre content and colour as nearly as possible. Cotton, mercerised cotton, silk and synthetic threads are available and it is worth while taking trouble to buy the correct thread, as it will give the most satisfactory result, both in construction and wear.

CUTTING OUT

Adequate space is required on account of the length of the fabric involved. In most homes, cutting out has to be done on the floor.

Preparation of the fabric

Straighten one weft edge, either by pulling a thread as a guide for cutting, or by fraying, until one thread runs across the complete width.

Marking the fabric for cutting

Work with the fabric open to its full width, so that the marking and cutting are done on single cloth. Add together the curtain length plus the heading, hem and shrinkage allowances and, beginning at the prepared weft edge, measure this length along the selvedge, marking it with a pin. Repeat the measuring the required number of times. Check that the planned lengths are accurate and then withdraw a thread across the width to guide the cutting. If the weave is clearly defined, it is possible to cut alongside a weft thread without withdrawing one.

Most curtain fabrics have a textured surface of some type which will respond to light, and it is necessary to ensure a uniformity of light and shade when the curtains are hanging at the window. After preparing the weft edge ready for measuring and cutting the curtains, study the fabric and decide whether the first curtain length will look best hanging with the prepared weft edge at the heading or the hem end of the curtain. Having decided, pin a paper label at the edge to state which end of the curtain it is to be. When marking the remaining curtain lengths, label each one to correspond.

Patterned fabric is sometimes found to have its design printed off grain as mentioned previously. If you are faced with this difficult problem, it is best to cut with the design to appease the eye, and hope that the off grain cut will not lead to too much difficulty in use; as when the fabric is washed, the grain will try to re-establish its correct position, and may cause the weft edges to slant. It will, of course, be necessary to choose the direction of the design and then mark the heading and hem positions as for plain fabric.

THE ORDER OF CONSTRUCTION FOR CURTAINS

All curtains are made in a similar order of construction whether they are large, small, lined or unlined. Unless this method is followed, the finished result will lack accuracy and a smart appearance. (*See the table on the following page.*)

GENERAL POINTS ABOUT CURTAIN MAKING

Selvedge edges If poor, these should be trimmed off, but good ones may be used in seams and side hems. If the selvedge is used, it should be snipped diagonally at 25 mm (1 in.) intervals to relax its tightness and to prevent puckered seams and edges, (*figure 58*).

Joining half-widths Half-widths, when necessary, should be seamed to the full widths, so that when the curtains are hanging, the half-widths come to the outer edges of the window frame.

Matching stripes and patterns at seams When making the seams, stripes and patterns must be matched at the stitching line. To do this, set the

UNLINED CURTAINS	CURTAINS WITH LINING SET BY HAND	CURTAINS WITH LINING SET MAINLY BY MACHINE
Seaming the widths	Seaming the widths	Seaming the widths
	If more than one width is to be used in a curtain	
Side hems	Side turnings	Seaming lining to curtain
Heading	Locking	Locking
Hem	Attaching lining to side turnings	
	Heading	Heading
	Hems on curtain and lining sections	Hems on curtain and lining sections

seam from the right side, using slip-tacking along the stitching line of the seam, (*figure 59*).

Turn back the upper layer of fabric, and the seam is ready for machining on the wrong side along the seam line. A second line of tacking, worked along the seam line on the wrong side, may be necessary before machining on slippery fabric.

In some cases this matching of the pattern may give unequal width turnings. On lined curtains, this may necessitate trimming away a little of the fabric on one or both turnings after joining. On unlined curtains the trimming of the turnings is dealt with during the construction of the seam.

Heading In each case it will be necessary to set the heading before the hem is made, as indicated in the construction table. As there is a range of headings available, and they are chosen according to style, it is not possible to outline setting of a specific heading for each type of curtain. For this reason the setting of

each heading tape is dealt with in a separate section. Reference must be made to this section for the particular tape in use when this stage of the construction is reached.

Hems Hems are usually made with a 12 mm ($\frac{1}{2}$ in.) first turning, but a turning up to the full width of the hem may be made to accommodate the extra material allowed for shrinkage. The finished width of a curtain hem is usually 65 mm ($2\frac{1}{2}$ in.). It is wise to hang curtains for several days, if possible, before making the lower hems, as the weight of the fabric often causes the curtains to drop. The surplus length gained may have to be trimmed off, unless it can be incorporated in the first turning of the hem, or a deeper hem made.

When handling semi-sheer fabrics, study the special guiding points on page 136.

Throughout the remainder of this section, instructions are given for making curtains of various types.

72

58 A selvedge edge with diagonal snipping

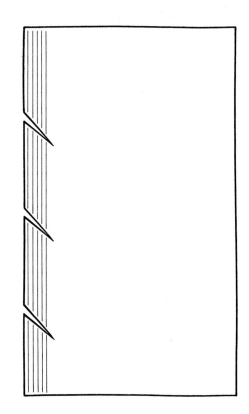

59 Fold back one edge to the wrong side along the fitting line and place it along the corresponding pattern line of the other edge of the seam. Pin and slip-tack along the fold

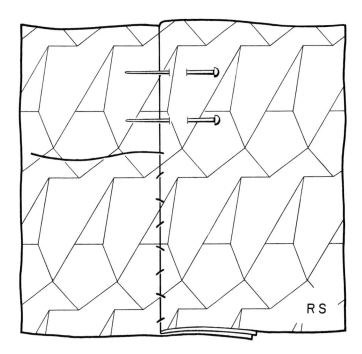

R S

1 *Seaming*

To join curtain widths, use a machine fell seam, or a double machine stitched seam (*see figures 60a–d*). A machine fell seam gives a better finish, as no stitching is visible on the right side, and is suitable for more expensive fabrics. A double machine stitched seam is suitable for the cheaper curtain fabrics used for kitchen, bathroom and some bedroom curtains. The method of making the seams is the same in the preliminary stages, so for either seam begin by following *figures 60a* and *60b*.

Open out the curtain. Fold and tack the prepared turnings *flat* to enclose the raw edge. For a double machine stitched seam, machine close to the folded edge of the turning, (*60c*). For a machine fell seam, use slip-hemming instead of machining, (*60d*).

2 *Side hems*

Prepare the selvedge edges as necessary. For a good finish, make the first and second turnings of the hem equal in width. On light-weight fabric make the finished width 12 mm ($\frac{1}{2}$ in.), and on heavier fabric 25 mm (1 in.). See *figures 61a* and *b*.

If striped fabric is being used, try to leave a complete stripe on all side edges of the curtain, adjusting the hem width slightly if necessary.

3 *The heading*

See heading section, page 92

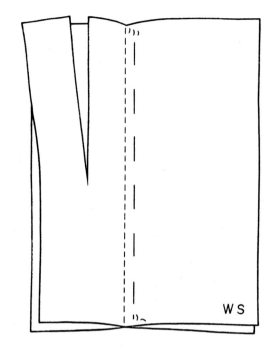

60a   Place fabric with the wrong side outside and the right sides together. Tack and machine 25 mm (1 in.) in from the raw edge. Cut away half the turnings on the side width of the curtain

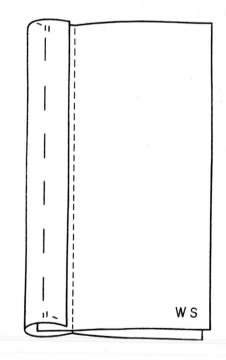

60b   Fold over the single section of the turning, with the raw edge just clear of the machining and tack. Press the seam

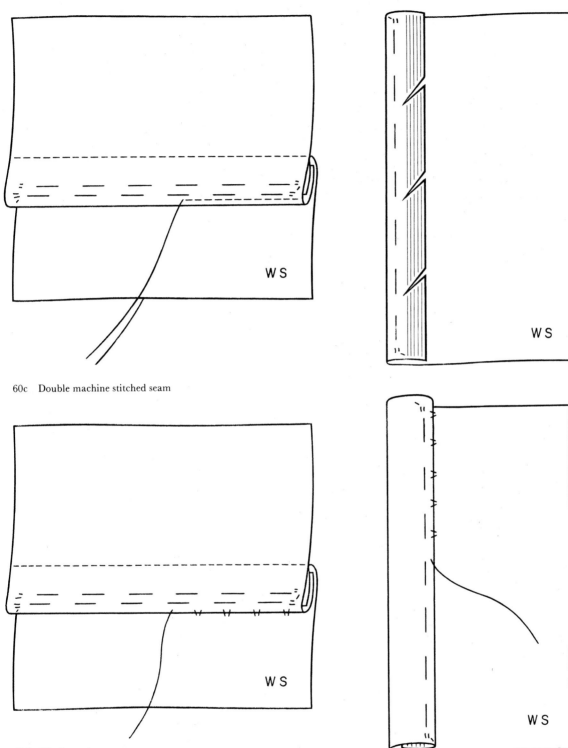

60c   Double machine stitched seam

61a

60d   Slip hemming

61b

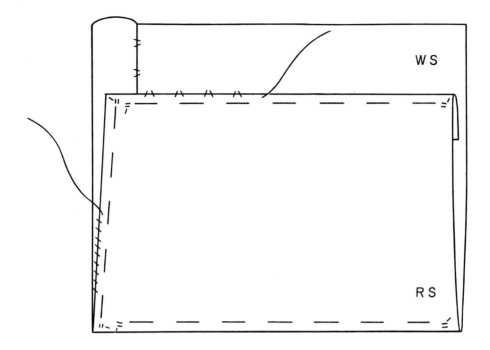

62   Making the hem

4   *The lower hem*

Find the position of the lower edge of the curtain. The amount of hem turning can then be measured and the widths of the first turning and the finished hem decided. The available turning should contain the original 75 mm (3 in.) plus the shrinkage allowance plus any surplus length gained as the curtains hung and dropped with their own weight.

a   Turning a hem with 12 mm ($\frac{1}{2}$ in.) first turning:

Fold back and tack the hem along the lower edge line, making sure that the fold is kept straight with the grain.

Turn in the first turning allowance and tack the hem onto the curtain. Displace the side of the hem slightly to prevent bulk.

b   Turning a hem with a wide first turning:

Fold back and tack the first turning straight with the grain. Fold again straight with the grain along the lower edge line and tack to hold securely.

Tack the upper fold of the hem onto the curtain, displacing the side of the hem slightly to prevent bulk.

c   To finish the hem:

Slip-hem the hem onto the curtain using a slack tension and spacing the stitches 6 mm ($\frac{1}{4}$ in.) apart. Hem the two side edges of the lower hem onto the side hems of the curtain.

Remove the tackings and press the curtain thoroughly before hanging it at the window.

The lower hem may be machined, eg on kitchen and bathroom curtains, but it is inadvisable on fabric which may shrink, as the stitch marks may show when the hem is let down.

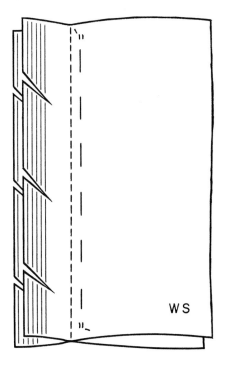

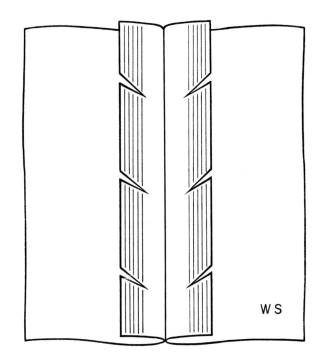

63a and b A plain seam is used as the raw edges will be protected by the lining. The finished width of the seam should be from 12 mm ($\frac{1}{2}$ in.) to 25 mm (1 in.), depending on the weight of the fabric

MAKING LINED CURTAINS

There are two methods of making curtains with the lining attached: curtains with the linings set by hand, and those with the linings partially set by machine. The hand setting is usually chosen for use on better quality fabric, and is certainly the better choice for velvet. The second method is suitable for cheaper fabric or when a quicker finish is required.

Curtains with linings set by hand

1 *Seaming*

Prepare the selvedges by snipping diagonally at 25 mm (1 in.) intervals. Place half widths so that they will hang at the outer edges of the window. See *figures 63a* and *b*.

Join the lining sections with a plain seam, matching the curtain seam in width. This aligns both curtain and lining seams when the two parts are finally joined.

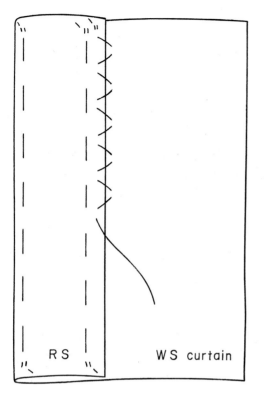

64 Turn the side edges to the wrong side, folding straight with the grain, and to the width required. Tack close to the folded edge, and again 6 mm (¼ in.) above the raw edge. Catch-stitch the turning in place, using a slack tension and a matching thread

2   Side turnings of the curtain

Make the side turnings of the curtain 25 mm to 38 mm (1 in. to 1½ in.), depending on the weight of the fabric. See *figure 64*.

Begin or finish 254 mm (10 in.) above the lower edge of the curtain. This allows for turning up the curtain hem at a later stage.

Press the side turnings of the curtain, and press open the plain seams on both curtain and lining sections.

3   Locking

Locking is a means of joining the curtain and lining sections, at intervals, down their length. Thus held together, the two fabrics hang as one, giving a richer appearance to the folds of the curtains as they hang at the window. Locking also holds the thinner lining fabric in position and prevents it from dropping below the curtain.

The following method gives three lines of locking to each curtain. However, the amount of locking may be adjusted according to the curtain width. For example, when two widths of fabric are joined to make one curtain, it is advisable to lock at the centre and then twice more on either side, giving five lines of equally spaced locking in all. On narrow curtains, two lines of locking are adequate.

Locking a curtain of one and a half widths   Pair the curtain and lining sections. Fold the curtain section in half lengthwise, with the wrong sides together, and fold the paired lining section in half lengthwise, with the right sides together. Press these centre folds lightly.

Open out the curtain section and, with the wrong side uppermost, place it on a large table or on the floor, making sure it is flat.

Place the folded lining section on top, so that the fold is in line with the centre crease line on the curtain section, and the two raw edges are together at the top. If there are seams, check that they are in the same position on both sections.

65 *(opposite)*   The curtain and lining fabrics in position for the first line of locking, which is shown completed

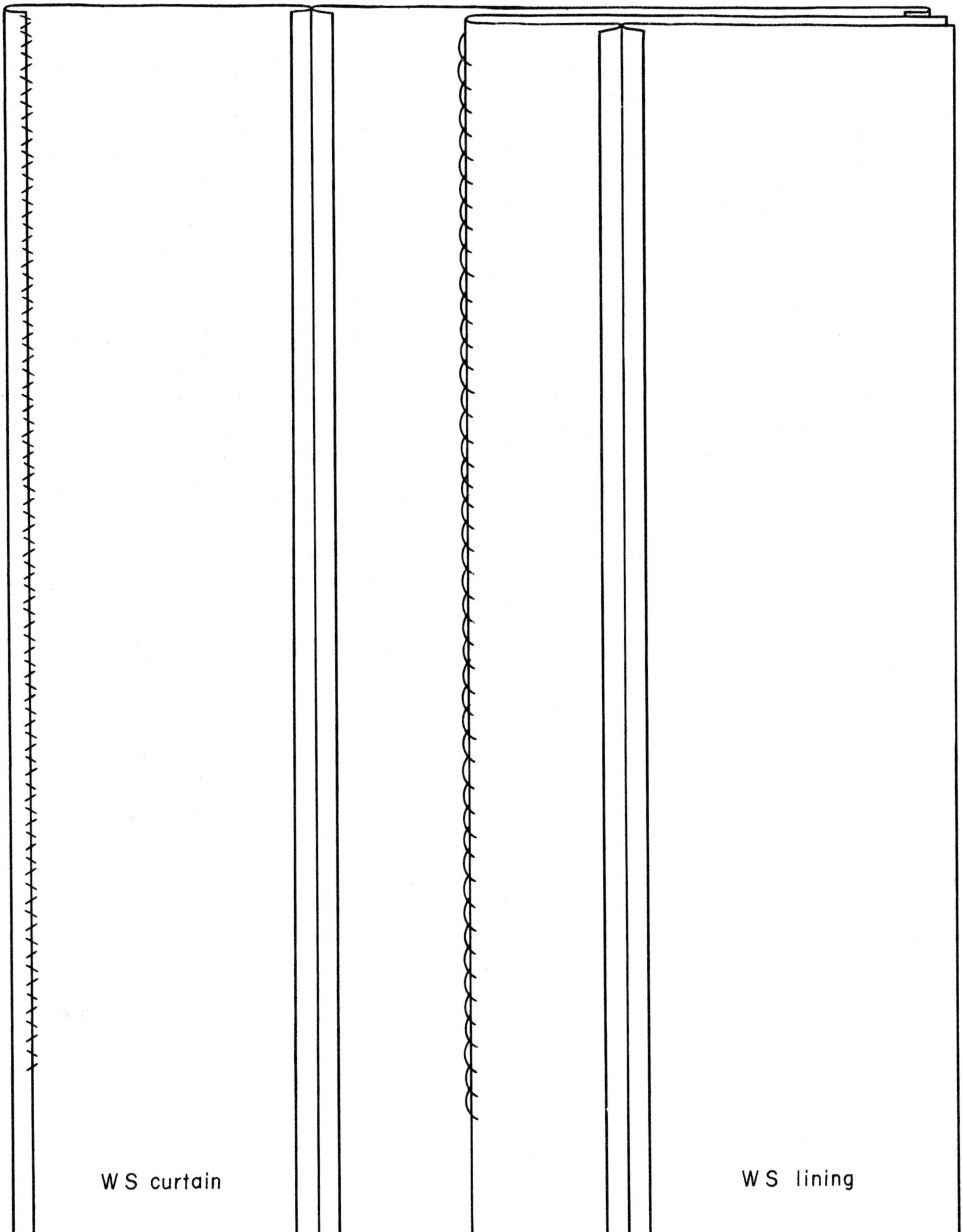

WS curtain

WS lining

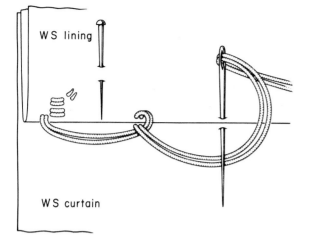

WS lining

WS curtain

Pin through the double thickness of lining fabric and the single thickness of curtain fabric. Pin at right angles to the fold, and at 100 mm (4 in.) intervals down the length.

Lock stitch the two sections together using a double thickness of the thread used for sewing the curtains. Begin or finish the locking 205 mm (8 in.) above the lower edge to allow for turning up the hems at a later stage.

To finish the locking Open out the lining fabric so that the right side is uppermost, and smooth evenly over the curtain. Begin in the centre and tack along the top edge, as far as the seam, to join the two raw edges together at the top, (*figure 67*).

Unfold the lining again and finish tacking the two raw edges together at the top, stopping within 50 mm (2 in.) of the side edge. Fold back the other half of the lining with the distance between the fold and the outer edge the same as that between the seam and the opposite outer edge.

66 *(above)* Lock Stitch. This is an elongated loop-stitch, but when worked, only penetrates the fold of the lining and a single thread of the curtain fabric, so that it will not be visible on the right side. Stitch at 25 mm (1 in.) intervals

67 *(below)* Fold back the lining along the seam line to bring the right sides together. Use short stitches to join the outstanding turning of the lining seam to the corresponding turning of the curtain seam

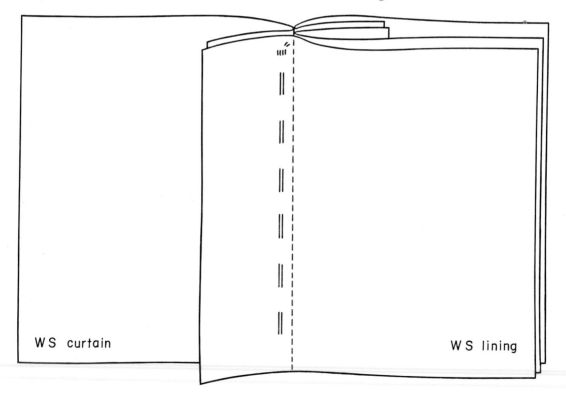

WS curtain

WS lining

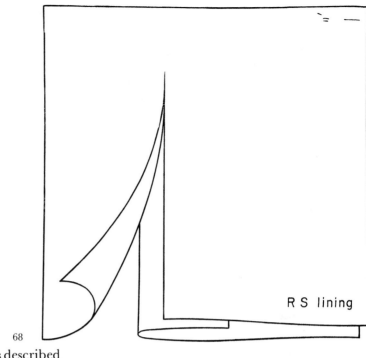

68

Lock stitch the fold to the curtain as described for the central locking. Finish tacking the two raw edges together across the top of the curtain to within 50 mm (2 in.) of the outer edge.

4 *Attaching lining to side turnings*

Trim away the surplus lining fabric at the side edges, so that it is 6 mm ($\frac{1}{4}$ in.) narrower than the curtain, (*figure 68*).

Fold under a 12 mm ($\frac{1}{2}$ in.) turning to the wrong side of the lining, and pin and tack in place onto the side turning of the curtain. The folded edge of the lining will be 20 mm ($\frac{3}{4}$ in.) from the curtain edge.

Slip-hem the lining to the single thickness of the side turning, with the thread used for sewing the curtain, (*figure 69*).

Begin or finish the slip-hemming 254 mm (10 in.) from the lower edge, sew with a slack tension and space the stitches 6 mm ($\frac{1}{4}$ in.) apart. Remove the tacking and press thoroughly.

5 *The heading*

See Heading Section.

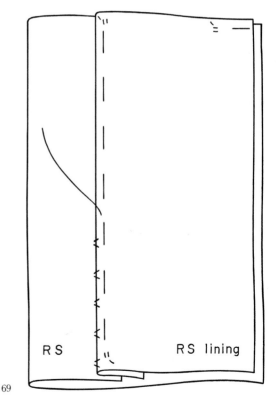

69

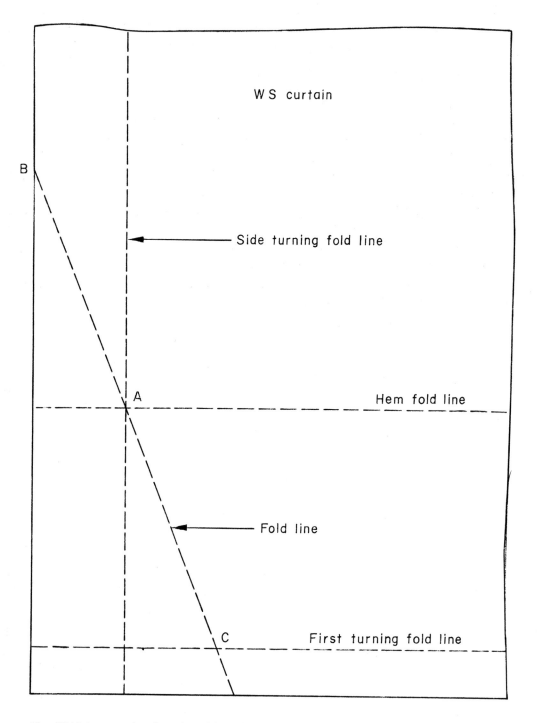

WS curtain

B

Side turning fold line

A   Hem fold line

Fold line

C   First turning fold line

70a   Width between edge of curtain and A equals width
between side turning fold line and C. Measure hem depth
above hem fold line and mark a point B. Tack a guide line to—
join BAC

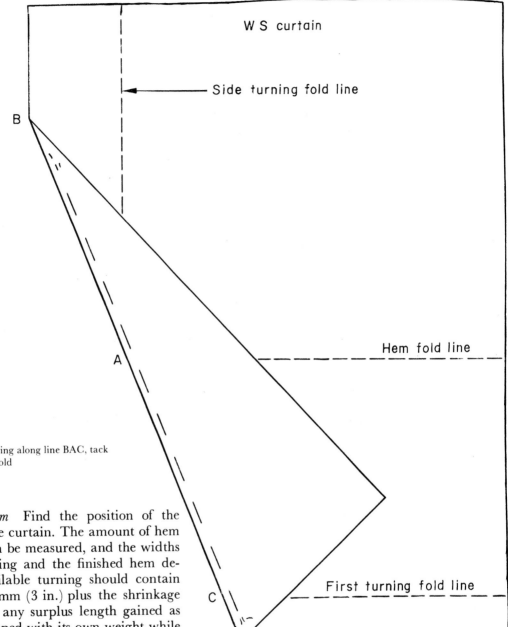

WS curtain

Side turning fold line

B

A

Hem fold line

First turning fold line

C

70b   Fold back a turning along line BAC, tack
and press close to the fold

6   *Hems*

a   The curtain hem   Find the position of the
lower edge of the curtain. The amount of hem
turning can then be measured, and the widths
of the first turning and the finished hem decided. The available turning should contain
the original 75 mm (3 in.) plus the shrinkage
allowance, plus any surplus length gained as
the curtain dropped with its own weight while
hanging.

Fold back the full width of the finished hem
plus turning, folding accurately with the grain
of the fabric, and press this fold line with an
iron. Open back this allowance and press in the
fold of the first turning width, also straight with
the grain.

As the side turning and hem widths are
always different, a mitre cannot be made at the
corner, but a special, angled folding of the
turnings can be arranged, as shown in *figures
70a–d.*

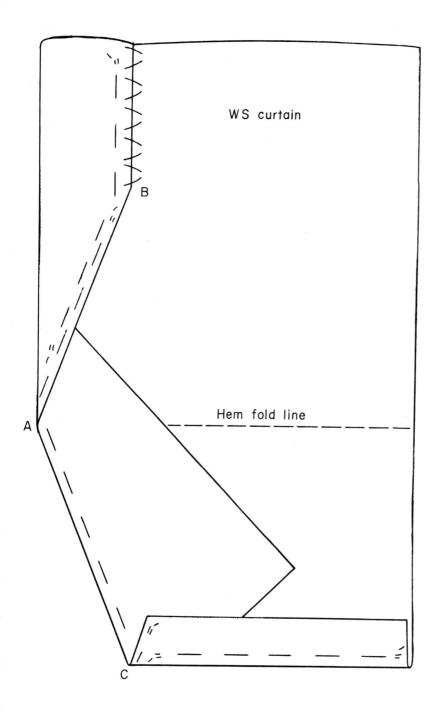

WS curtain

B

Hem fold line

A

C

70c Fold back, tack and finish catch-stitching the side
turning

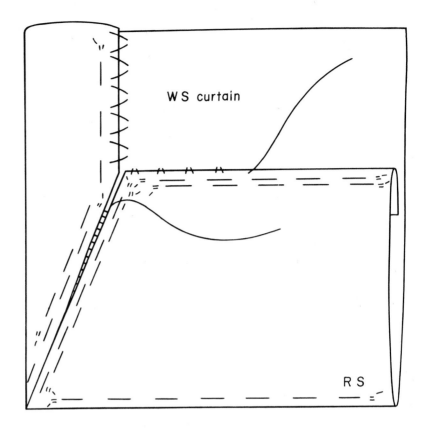

WS curtain

RS

70d   Fold back and track the hem. Slip-stitch the angled
turnings of the hems. Slip-hem the hem

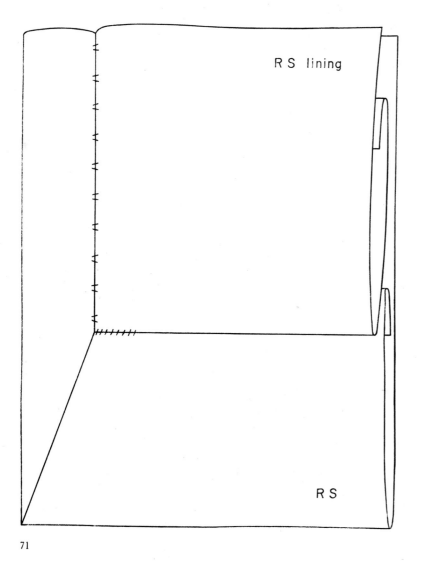

RS lining

RS

71

b *The Lining Hem* Turn up the lining to clear the lower edge of the curtain by 50 mm (2 in.). The hem is then prepared as for an unlined curtain hem.

The lower edge of the lining hem is now 12 mm ($\frac{1}{2}$ in.) below the top of the curtain hem, with the corner on the angled seam.

Finish the slip-hemming on the side edge and hem the lining to the curtain hem for 12 mm ($\frac{1}{2}$ in.), refer to *figure 71*.

If a 38 mm ($1\frac{1}{2}$ in.) turning has been used at the side edges, the lining will need to be set 32 mm ($1\frac{1}{4}$ in.) up from the lower edge, not 50 mm (2 in.) to allow the corner of the lining to meet the angled join.

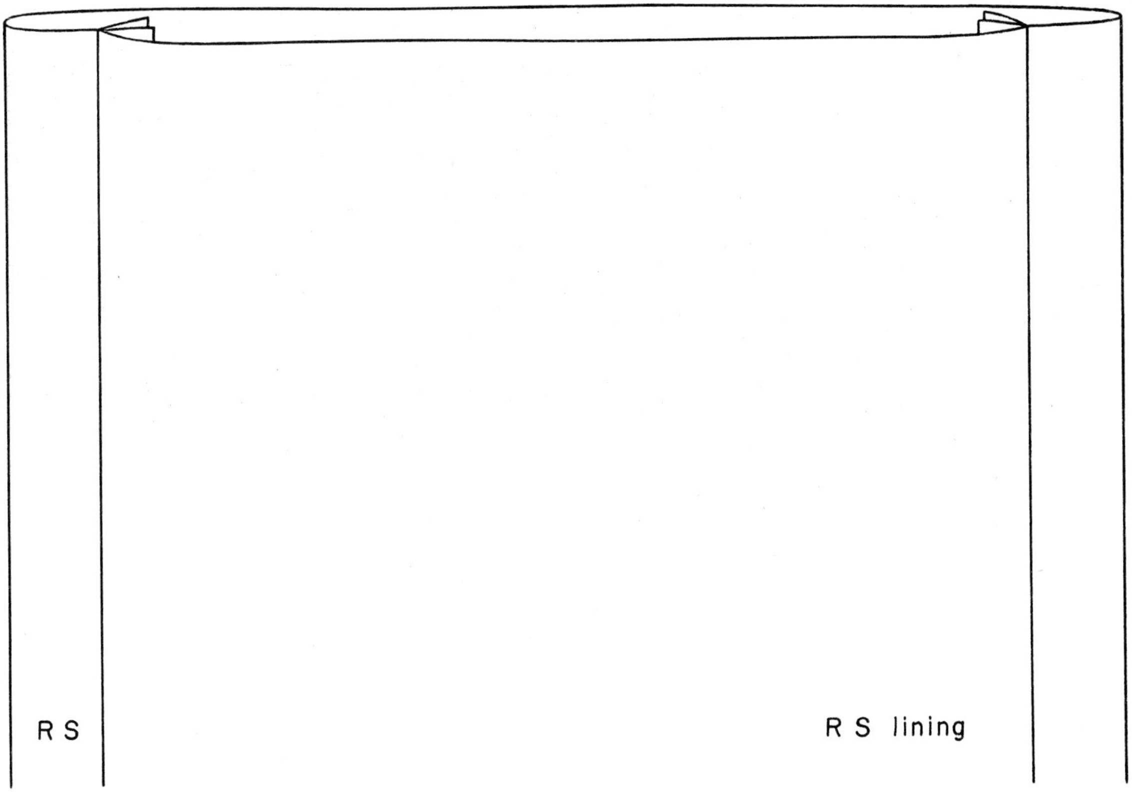

R S

R S lining

72 The lining in position, showing equal width margins of
curtain and fabric

Curtains with lining set mainly by machine

If more than one width of fabric is to be used,
seam curtain and lining widths as described for
the hand method of lining curtains.

1 *Planning width of curtain and lining* There
must be a margin of curtain fabric down each
side of the lining when the curtain is finished.
This margin may vary from 12 mm ($\frac{1}{2}$ in.) to
50 mm (2 in.), according to the weight of the
curtain fabric.

To calculate the width of the lining, decide
upon the required width of margin, and
multiply this measurement by 4. For example,
if a 25 mm (1 in.) margin is chosen, then the
lining fabric should be 100 mm (4 in.) narrower
than the curtain width. If more than one width
of fabric has been used in a curtain, it is important that an equal amount is trimmed away
from each side of the lining, so that the seams of
the lining and curtain fabric will lie, finally, on
top of each other.

W S curtain

W S lining

73 The finished seams, showing the extra curtain width before setting it evenly either side of the lining

2 *Attaching the lining to the curtain* Fold the curtain fabric in half lengthwise with the wrong sides together. Fold the lining fabric in half lengthwise with the right sides together. Press the centre folds lightly.

Spread out the curtain fabric with the right side uppermost. Place the lining fabric on top, wrong side uppermost, with the top edges together, and one side edge of the lining flush with one side edge of the curtain. Pin and tack 12 mm ($\frac{1}{2}$ in.) in from the edge. Lift the lining across until the second pair of side edges meet. Pin and tack as before. Machine the two seams, leaving 254 mm (10 in.) unstitched above the lower edge. This allows for making the hems

later. With the lining side uppermost, begin machining at the top edge if the bulk of the fabric will allow. If the curtain is too bulky, machine the second seam from a point 254 mm (10 in.) above the lower edge. Press the seams towards the centre of the lining.

Turn the curtain through to the right side and, working on a flat surface and with the lining uppermost, line up the centre fold crease lines. There should be an equal margin of curtain fabric showing on either side. (Refer to *figure 72*). Tack first across the top to hold curtain and lining together, and then down the folds of both side edges.

3   *Locking*   This method of construction does not allow the curtain to be locked to the lining in the usual way. However, if locking is desirable, a modified form may be worked. The number of lines of locking can be calculated as for the previous method.

Pin the lining and curtain fabric together down the length at the locking positions.

To work the locking stitch, use a double length of thread which matches the curtains. Fasten on with a double back-stitch at the top edge of the marked locking position.

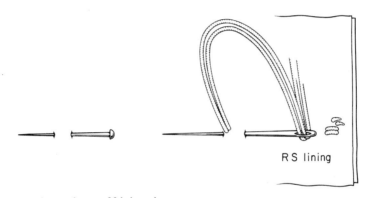

74a   Slide the needle between the two layers of fabric and bring it out 25 mm (1 in.) below this point. Work a small back-stitch, picking up only a thread of the curtain fabric

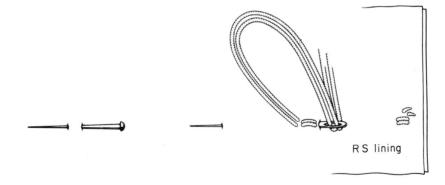

74b   Work a second small stitch over the top of the first, but this time slide the needle between the two layers of fabric and bring it out 25 mm (1 in.) below the last stitch. Continue this stitching to within 254 mm (10 in.) of the lower edge

4 *The Heading* See Heading section.

5 *The hems* Finish the curtain and lining hems as for the hand worked method of lining. If the lining is inset by 25 mm (1 in.), the side turning will be 38 mm (1½ in.) wide. As the lining setting is in a different position from the one described, giving wider side turnings, it will be necessary to set the lower edge of the lining 45 mm (1¾ in.) above the lower edge of the curtain, to bring the corner in line with the angled join. It is worth trying out the corner in paper, with the actual measurements used, to find the correct setting position for the lower edge of the lining.

It is possible to make a detachable lining, but as the calculations of the length depend on the type of heading tape used, the directions for making are on page 119, in the section on the setting of heading tapes.

WEIGHTING CURTAINS

There are two ways of weighting curtains: by fixing round, coin-like weights into the bottom corners of the curtain hems, or by inserting a weighted strip along the length of the hem.

Round weights

These cannot always be bought in soft furnishing departments and, if they are necessary, dress weights from a haberdashery department can be used. Choose weights to suit the weight of the curtain fabric. They help the side edges of the curtain to hang vertically from the track, and are particularly useful for floor length curtains.

To insert weights in a curtain

For each weight make a cotton bag which is just big enough to hold the weight easily. Use calico or a similar fabric which is lighter in colour than the curtains. Scraps of the lining would be ideal if weighting lined curtains.

Insert a weight into each bag, and sew up the fourth side. Sew the bag to the wrong side of the hem allowance, after setting the fold line of the hem. Use cotton to match the curtain fabric. Set the weights as near to the corners of the hem as possible.

Lead-weighted strips

This weighting is sold by the yard, and consists of lead shot or small lead weights inserted at close, regular intervals into a narrow, knitted tube of synthetic fibre which holds them firmly. The strips are available in light, medium and heavy weighting, and are chosen according to the curtain fabric. They are particularly useful for encouraging the straight fall and fluting of curtains made from fabric of a springy nature.

Ideally the strip should be set along the bottom fold of the curtain hem. The disadvantage of this is the difficulty of giving the hem a final press and retaining a sharp edge along the bottom of the curtain. If the fabric will retain a sharp crease, press the lower edge finally before setting the weighted strip and sewing the hem. Sew the strip to the wrong side of the hem turning just above the pressed line. Stitch between two weights at about 25 mm (1 in.) intervals, leaving a loose length of cotton between each stitch. Use cotton to match the curtain fabric. This weighting is washable and dry-cleanable.

The following alternative method can be used when it is desirable to give the hem a final press, just before hanging the curtain and after washing or dry-cleaning. Thread the strip through the hem, making sure that it is not pulled too tightly, and secure it at each end before stitching up the ends of the hem. It can then be removed and reset after washing or cleaning. This is a comparatively easy operation on an unlined curtain, but on a lined curtain involves unpicking the angled join and resetting after replacing the weighting.

VALANCES

Valances give quite an attractive frilling at the top of a window, if this finish is suitable for a room. They are particularly pleasing in a cottage setting with sill length curtains. See *figure 8*, page 23. The first point to decide is the depth, as too long or too short a valance gives an unbalanced appearance. Usually this proves to be about one eighth of the curtain depth, but it is wise to cut a strip of paper, pin or *Sellotape* it in position, and view the effect from a distance. Study the depth suggested by the paper in relation to the window size, and notice whether it seems to cut off too much light. Adjust the depth of the paper until you are satisfied.

The fullness is worked out as for curtains. In fact, a valance is made almost exactly on the curtain principle. It can be either lined or un-lined, and the general rules for curtain making are followed with few exceptions. A narrower heading is adequate on a valance, and a 25 mm (1 in.) hem is made at the lower edge. If a valance is lined, the lining need not be locked to the outer fabric, but if it is not, it must be bar-tacked along the hem edge at 460 mm (18 in.) intervals. Then there will be no shrink-age problem after washing. The valance lining hem should be set 20 mm ($\frac{3}{4}$ in.) above the edge of the valance.

Usually a *Rufflette Standard* tape is used, but an attractive effect is given by using *Rufflette Evenpleat* tape.

PELMETS

The traditional type of pelmet board with its fabric covering is still used and can be made to order if required. It is, however, fast becoming outdated by wooden or hardboard pelmets, and the stiffened, wide heading tapes sold for use with the extensive ranges of attractive but unobtrusive tracks available on today's market.

Wooden or hardboard pelmets are easily cleaned, and can be painted to match any décor. They give to a window a neat, clear-cut finish which suits modern furnishing. See *figures 3, 20* and *25* in the curtain styling section on pages 20, 32 and 34. They are also useful for uniting two or more separated windows into one window unit. See *figure 5*, page 21.

When new curtains are fitted to a window, an existing wooden or hardboard pelmet can be used as it is, if suitable in colour, or repainted to complement the new scheme.

A pelmet is a contradiction to the modern aim of window structure, which is to introduce as much light as possible into all rooms. A narrow wooden or hardboard pelmet does not cause much light obstruction, and can be set partly above the window level, so giving little trouble this way. More decorative pelmets are available in the *Solarbo* range, see page 48.

7 Curtain headings

Various heading tapes are available on the market, and each tape provides an individual style of heading. The following section, with illustrations, shows a selection of some heading styles which can be chosen.

RUFFLETTE STANDARD TAPE

These tapes are made in three different types: cotton, nylon and *Tergal* (polyester). The cotton tape is available in a wide range of colours, but the nylon and *Tergal* tapes are made in white only. They are 25 mm (1 in.) wide, and give a simple, ruffled effect to the curtains.

There are two standard tapes suitable for use with sheer fabrics. They are *Terylene* tape, made in white, which is 15 mm ($\frac{5}{8}$ in.) wide, and *Tervoil* tape, off-white in colour, which is 25 mm (1 in.) wide. *Tervoil* is a stiff tape and, therefore, gives a supported heading to light-weight fabrics.

Standard tapes cannot be used incorrectly as they have no right or wrong side, and are four-way reversible. A suitable tape from this range can be found for use on most fabrics. Curtains headed with these tapes are best hung in conjunction with a pelmet or valance.

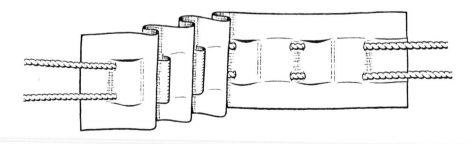

75a   The tape

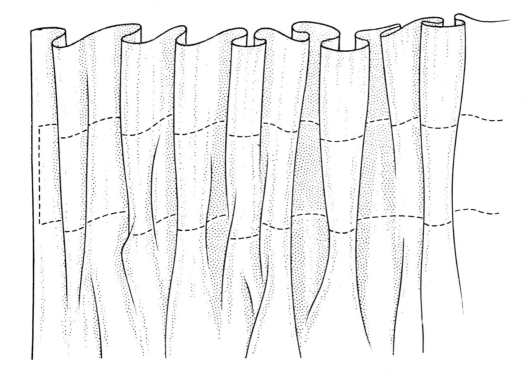

75b The tape in use

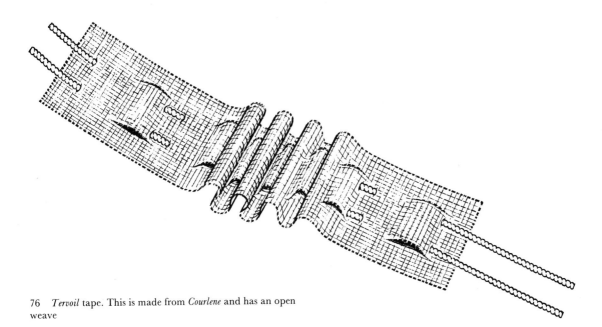

76 *Tervoil* tape. This is made from *Courlene* and has an open
weave

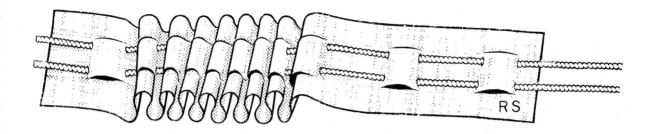

77a   The tape

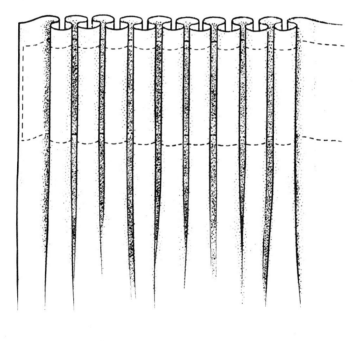

77b   The tape in use with a shallow heading

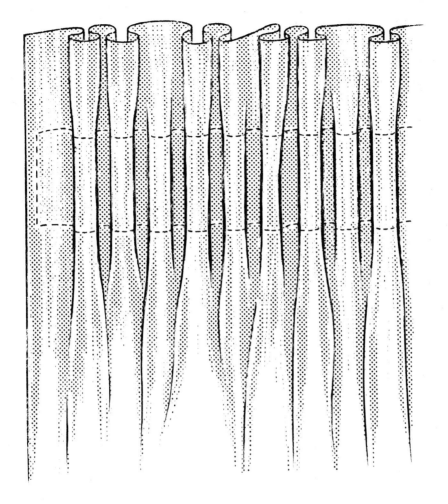

77c   The tape in use with a deeper heading

RUFFLETTE EVENPLEAT TAPE

This tape is made from cotton, and is available in white, natural and beige. It is 25 mm (1 in.) wide, and gives a curtain heading of short, pencil pleats instead of the ruffled effect of the *Rufflette Standard* tapes. Although it resembles the *Standard* tapes in some ways, it has a different arrangement of cords, which form pleats when drawn up. It can be used either way up, but the pocket openings, coming all on one side, form a right and wrong side.

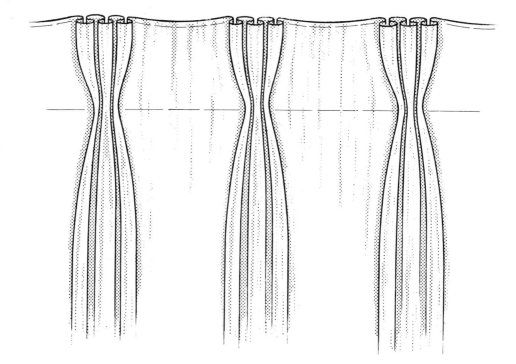

78   The appearance given by using one of these tapes

RUFFLETTE DEEP PLEAT TAPE
KIRSCH EASYPLEAT TAPE

These cotton tapes are available in white only, and are 90 mm (3½ in.) wide. They form deep pinch pleats along the curtain heading. The pleats are quick and easy to form and do not require any stitching. They can be flattened for laundering by removing the hooks. Single, double or triple pleats can be made, and the groups of pleats can be spaced as required. It is necessary to make careful calculation of the curtain width before using the tape.

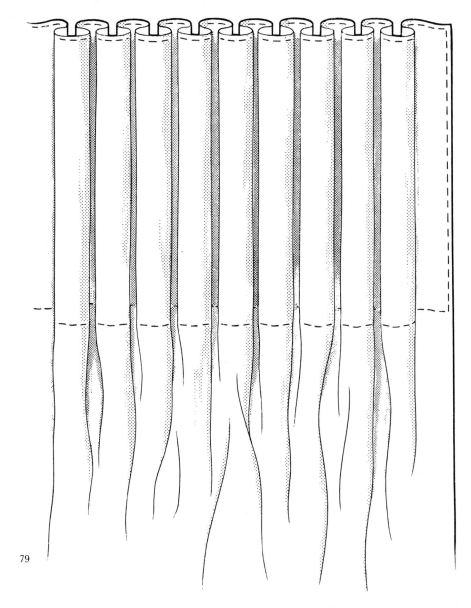

79

RUFFLETTE HI-STYLE TAPE

This cotton tape is made in cream only, and is 75 mm (3 in.) wide. It is provided with three cords which, when drawn up, give a tall, pencil pleated heading to the curtain. These pencil pleats are supported by special hooks.

RUFFLETTE REGIS TAPE

This tape is made in white only, and is 72 mm ($2\frac{7}{8}$ in.) wide. It gives deep, pencil-pleats of similar style to those made by *Rufflette Hi-Style* tape. It differs in character as it is not wholly cotton, being stiffened with a nylon reinforcement. This is an added advantage in shaping the pencil-pleats, although it adds to the price of the tape.

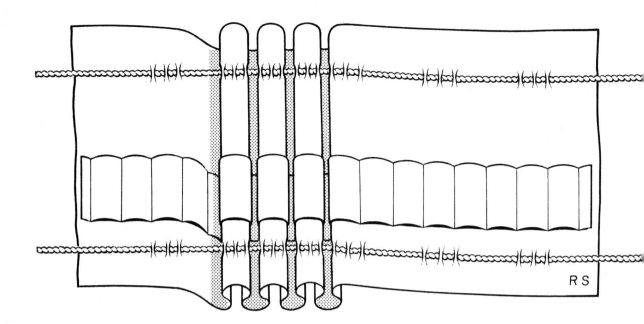

80   Tervoil 60 Tape

TERVOIL 60 TAPE

This tape is made in white only and is 70 mm (2¾ in) wide. It gives deep pencil-pleats of similar style to the previous two tapes. It has a similar arrangement of pockets to *Regis* tape, but the cords are inserted differently. *Tervoil 60* tape is made from *Terylene* and nylon and is, therefore, suitable for use with drip-dry, light-weight fabrics, in particular polyester, acrylic and glass fibre fabrics.

RUFFLETTE TRIDENT TAPE

Another tape which also gives deep, pencil pleats is *Rufflette Trident Tape*. It is available in cream only and is 80 mm (3⅛ in.) wide. It is a strongly woven tape with three cords. The pockets are arranged in three stepped rows to give a choice of suspension point. R60 zinc chromatic hooks are recommended for general use with this tape, but R4 plastic hooks can be used with light-weight fabric.

The tape has a right and wrong side but may be used either way up. It is prepared and applied in a similar way to *Rufflette Hi-Style* tape.

General information

Certain general points, with some exceptions, apply to the preparation of curtain heading tapes. These are listed below and the exceptions noted where necessary.

1. The length of tape required for each curtain is equal to the width of the curtain after the side edges have been finished, plus varying allowances for the finishing of the tape and cords.

The exceptions are *Rufflette Deep Pleat* tape and *Kirsch Easypleat* tape, which require special calculations. For these refer to the section on *Rufflette Deep Pleat* tape on pages 104 and 105.

2. The choice of the tape colour is important. When using the *Rufflette Standard* cotton tape, the nearest colour match to the curtain fabric can be selected. The *Rufflette Standard* nylon and *Tergal* tapes will usually be in contrast to the curtain fabrics, but as the curtain heading is covered with a pelmet or valance, they do not show in use.

The wider tapes may show in use, but they can always be dyed to match the colour of the curtain fabric if the housewife is prepared to take the trouble to do this. It is wise to dye tape to be used on dark-coloured, loose, open-weave fabric, such as some of the acrylics, as the light tape will be visible from the right side.

3. Before setting tape on non-shrink fabrics, eg the acrylics, it is best to soak it in cold water, then dry and iron it. Although the tape is made from pre-shrunk cotton, it may shrink slightly in washing.

The exceptions are *Rufflette Regis* tape, *Tervoil*, *Tervoil* 60, nylon and *Terylene*.

4. The tape ends are prepared differently for each side of the curtain. Decide which edge of each curtain will hang at the centre of the window frame, (remembering that half-widths should hang at the sides of the window) and prepare the tapes for these edges first.

The exceptions are *Rufflette Deep Pleat* and *Kirsch Easypleat* tapes. Refer to the section on

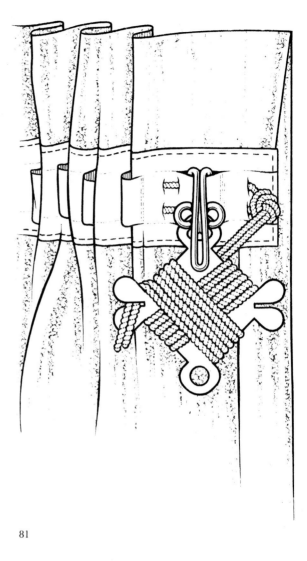

81

Deep Pleat tape on page 104.

5. When the curtains are finished, adjust the fullness on the cords, if corded tape has been used. First pack the fullness to one end of the tape, and then release it until the desired width of curtain is obtained. Tie the free cords loosely to hold the width, and arrange the fullness evenly. Either push the cords into the opening, or wind them onto a cord tidy. See *figure 81*.

A   *Rufflette Standard tapes*

The following set of diagrams shows the hooks to use with cotton tapes:

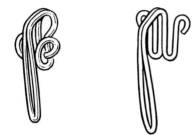

82a   *R7* Solid brass or aluminium standard hook

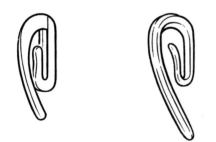

82b *(left)*   *R67* Steel zinc chromate plated hook

82c *(right)*   *R77* Solid brass hook. Recommended for heavy-weight curtains

82d *(left)*   *R5* Nylon hook. Recommended for use with nylon gliders

82e *(right)*   *R4* Plastic hook. Inexpensive. Less strong than either *R7* or *R5*, therefore use with light-weight fabrics only

With nylon, *Tergal* and *Tervoil* tapes use hooks *R5* or *R4*. These tapes are suitable for use on synthetic fabrics and glass fibre.

There is also an *R8* plastic hook which is a little smaller than the *R4*. It is suitable for use with *Terylene* tape.

Heading Allowance   This may be 25 mm (1 in.) for an economical setting, giving a finished depth of 12 mm ($\frac{1}{2}$ in.) or it may be as much as 75 mm (3 in.) for a more controlled finish, giving a depth of 38 mm ($1\frac{1}{2}$ in.).

When preparing curtains to be hung from *Harrison Drape* track, allow 25 mm (1 in.) to 38 mm ($1\frac{1}{2}$ in.) heading allowance, to give a finished depth of 12 mm ($\frac{1}{2}$ in.) to 20 mm ($\frac{3}{4}$ in.). The finished depth should not exceed 20 mm ($\frac{3}{4}$ in.) for this style of track which has hooks attached to the fitment. The hooks form the means of movement along the track and also support the curtain heading. The *Rufflette Standard* tapes and the *Rufflette Evenpleat* tape are all suitable for use with *Harrison Drape* track, as the pockets on these tapes fit over the track hooks.

Calculation of tape length   When calculating the length of tape to buy, an extra allowance of 50 mm (2 in.) on each side of the curtain is required, making an additional 100 mm (4 in.) per curtain width.

Methods of setting   Method A   This is suitable for narrow curtains where there is not much fullness to be adjusted on the cords.

On heavier fabrics it is helpful to prepare the side edges of the heading to reduce bulk and to simplify the machining of the tape. (*See figure 83.*)

Prepare the heading by folding over the top raw edge of the curtain, to the wrong side, for half the depth of the heading allowance. Tack along the folded edge, ensuring that the fold is straight with the fabric grain. At the side, pull in the diagonally trimmed turning to off-set the folded edge. Hem it in place. If the turning allowance exceeds 12 mm ($\frac{1}{2}$ in.), also tack just above the raw edge. See *figure 84.*

Prepare the knotted cord ends first by releasing the cords for 50 mm (2 in.) and cut away 38 mm ($1\frac{1}{2}$ in.) of tape, leaving 12 mm ($\frac{1}{2}$ in.) of the allowance for neatening. Knot the cord ends together securely, stitching the knot if necessary, as it is important that these ends do not pull free. Turn under the 12 mm ($\frac{1}{2}$ in.) allowance, including the knotted cords, so that they are enclosed beneath the tape. Tack the turning in place. See *figures 85a and b.*

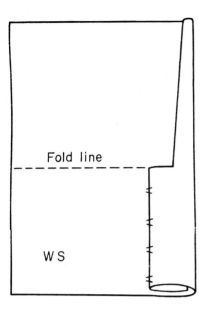

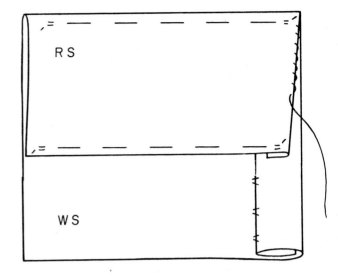

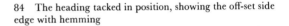

83　On unlined curtains trim the side hems diagonally, as shown, to 3 mm ($\frac{1}{8}$ in.) at the top edge and leaving 6 mm ($\frac{1}{4}$ in.) at the fold line (ie at half the heading allowance below the top edge)

84　The heading tacked in position, showing the off-set side edge with hemming

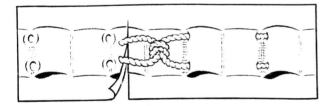

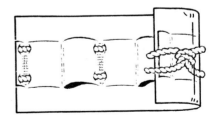

85a and 85b　The knot prepared with tape edge trimmed, and the tape end tacked ready for setting to the curtain

Place the prepared end of tape to the edge of the curtain which will hang at the centre of the window, insetting it slightly so that it will not show from the right side. Overlap the raw edge of the heading by 6 mm ($\frac{1}{4}$ in.) and pin the tape along the curtain, stopping 38 mm (1$\frac{1}{2}$ in.) from the other end. Assess the length of tape required to finish the curtain width and prepare this end of the tape as shown in *figure 86 a and b*. Then finish pinning the tape in place.

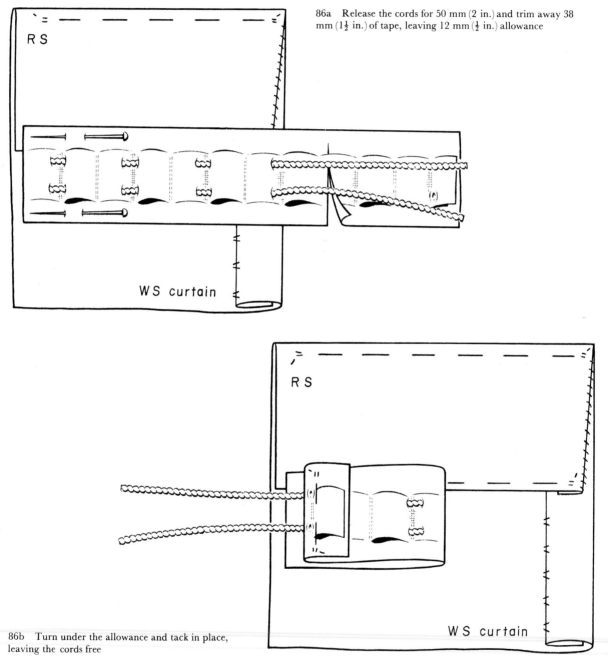

86a   Release the cords for 50 mm (2 in.) and trim away 38 mm (1$\frac{1}{2}$ in.) of tape, leaving 12 mm ($\frac{1}{2}$ in.) allowance

RS

WS curtain

RS

WS curtain

86b   Turn under the allowance and tack in place, leaving the cords free

Beginning at the free cord end, tack and machine along the length of the tape, across the short end, and then along the other side of the tape. The second short end is left open to insert the cord ends after the fullness has been adjusted. However, this may be machined, providing the cords are left free and a cord tidy is used. Press the heading. See *figures 87a and b*.

Never cut off the surplus cord, as it allows the curtain to be pulled out flat to facilitate laundering.

To finish preparing the curtain for hanging at the window, insert suitable hooks into the tape, placing one at each end, and the remainder approximately 75 mm (3 in.) apart, ie, every fourth pocket along the tape.

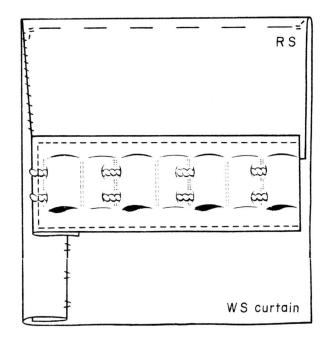

87a and 87b   The tape machined with cord ends secured under tape at edge for centre window position, and the cords left free for winding onto a cord tidy at the outer edge of the curtain. (Machining this short end of the tape must be omitted if a cord tidy is not available.)

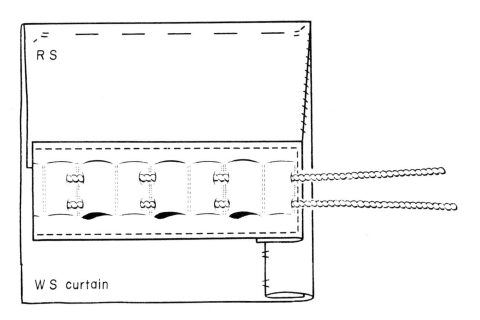

Method B This method is suitable for wide curtains when it is difficult to regulate the fullness if the cords are drawn up from one end. It is best used when the fitment is set above the window frame so that the resulting loose cords are not visible. It does tend to put more strain on the tape.

Prepare the heading as for *Method A*. There is a slight difference, however, when attaching the tape. The second edge, when at the pinning stage, is prepared as the first. As a cord tidy cannot be used with this method, the tape is machined all round. It is important that the cords are stitched firmly at each end of the tape.

Depending on the width of the curtain, adjust the fullness by pulling out the cord at the centre, third or quarter points. Draw up the curtain, proportioning the width as for Method A, and knot the cords loosely to hold the width. The cords will be hidden by the folds of the curtain when they are drawn up.

B *Rufflette Evenpleat tape*

The following hooks can be used with this tape: *R7, R67* and *R77*—metal. *R5*—nylon. *R4*—plastic.

Heading allowance A 65 mm (2½ in.) allowance is required as the tape should not be set more than 25 mm (1 in.) below the top of the curtain. If the heading is made deeper, the beauty of the pleats will be lost.

Calculate the quantity, prepare and apply the tape, as for *Rufflette Standard* tape, making sure that the right side, with the pocket openings, is uppermost.

The curtain should have adequate fullness, and at least twice the width of the curtain track is necessary. Two and a half to three times this width gives a more pleasing appearance.

C *Deep Pleat tapes*

Two makes of this tape are available, *Rufflette Deep Pleat* tape and *Kirsch Easypleat* tape. On

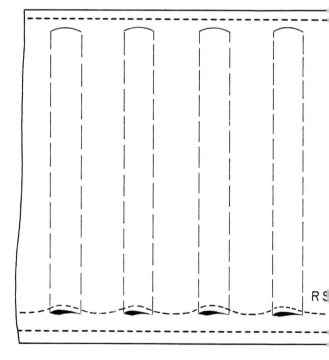

88 *Kirsch Easypleat* tape with approximately 48 pockets per metre (approximately 45 to 46 per yard). It is available in white only

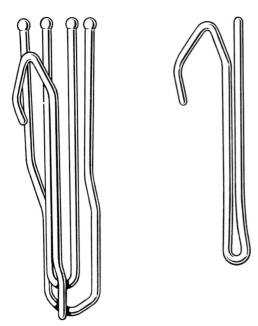

89a and b Long-stemmed *Deep Pleat* hook and end hook. Suitable for a track fitted close to the ceiling

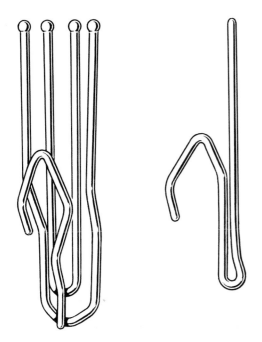

90a and b Short-stemmed *Deep Pleat* hook and end hook. Suitable for a track face fixed to the wall, with space between the track and the ceiling

each there is a coloured line woven in close to the edge. This can be used as a stitching guide if liked, or the stitching can be set a little closer to the edge of the tape. These coloured lines are indicated by stronger lines in the diagrams.

Hooks There is a choice of hooks to suit the proximity of the fitting to the ceiling.

Heading allowance This will depend on the depth of the tape, and whether short or long stemmed hooks are being used.

To calculate the allowance, insert a hook into the tape and measure the distance from the top of the hook to the top of the tape. For loose, open-weave fabric, add the depth of the tape to this measurement. In other cases add on 15 mm ($\frac{5}{8}$ in.).

Deep Pleat tapes have a right and wrong side and an upper and lower edge, so they need to be studied carefully before use. It is important to set the right side of the lower edge in the correct position, or it will not be possible to insert the hooks for hanging the curtain.

Calculation of tape length The quantity of tape to buy must be carefully calculated, as the flat length of tape is considerably reduced by pleating. Enough tape must be bought to accommodate the fitment measurement after the tape is pleated. Sometimes the curtain width may have to be adjusted slightly to suit the necessary length of tape. A helpful leaflet is prepared by *Rufflette* which includes a table to show the reduction of curtain width by various methods of pleating. Insert the hooks to find the most effective arrangement of the pleats. When satisfied, mark the chosen pockets with marking ink. Remove the hooks.

Provision must also be made for neatening the raw edges of the tape, and ensuring that a pocket comes close to each side edge of the curtain, to take a single end hook.

If the curtain width is being determined by the necessary length of tape, it is essential to add the required seaming and side finishing allowances to the tape measurement, to assess the final width of fabric required for the curtain.

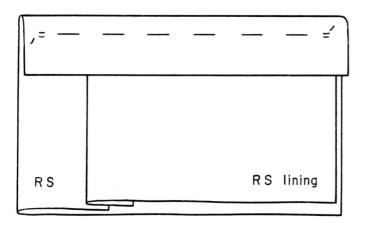

91 A 15 mm (⅝ in.) turning tacked in place on a lined curtain

Preparing the curtain Turn over the top raw edge of the curtain to the wrong side for 15 mm (⅝ in.), making sure that the fold line is straight with the fabric grain. Pin and then tack it in position, (*figure 91*).

Preparing and setting the tape Turn in one raw edge of the tape to the wrong side until a pocket is close to the fold. Tack along the fold and trim back the turning to 6 mm (¼ in.).

Place the tape so that the top edge is just below the fold of the heading, and the pre-pared edge slightly inset from the side edge of the curtain. At this stage check that the right side of the tape is showing, and that the pocket openings come at the lower edge of the tape. If correct, pin in position, and finish the second end of the tape as the first.

Tack the tape in position and machine round all sides of the tape, stitching fairly close to the edge. Be careful not to stitch over the pocket openings. Press thoroughly.

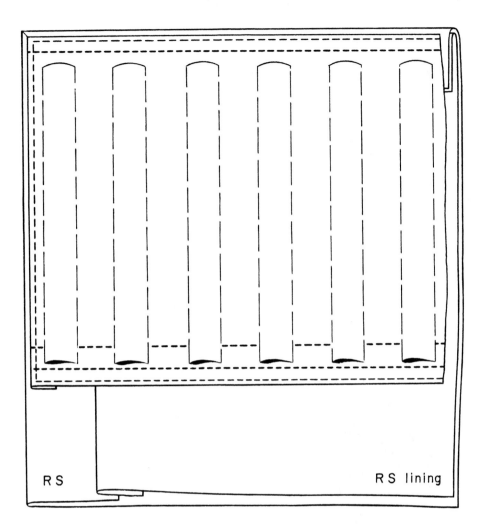

RS

RS lining

92 *Rufflette Deep Pleat* tape machined to a lined curtain. Note that the machining comes below the pockets, leaving them open for inserting the hooks

As this style of curtain is hung without a valance or pelmet, the lines of machining will be visible on the right side. If a more professional finish is desired, the machining may be stitched on the right side, following the fabric grain, and using the lines of tacking as a guide.

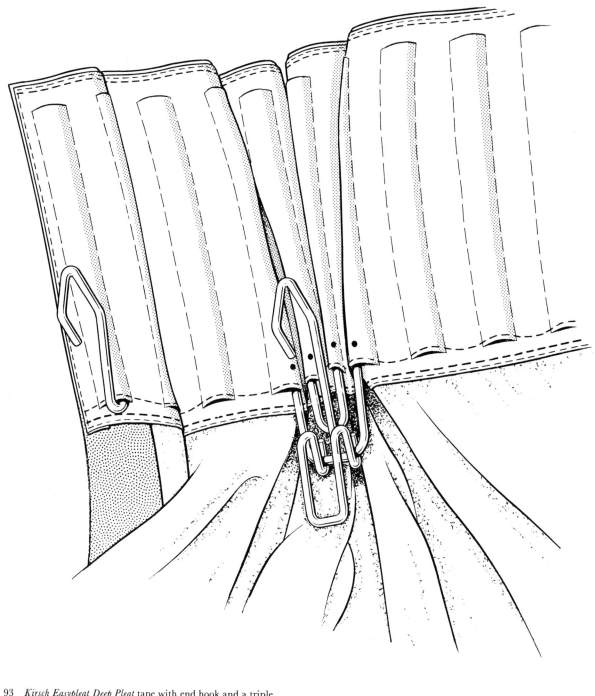

93 *Kirsch Easypleat Deep Pleat* tape with end hook and a triple
pleat being formed. Short-stemmed hooks in use showing a
curtain prepared for a face fixed fitment. Note the locking
device at the base of the hook. This is pushed upwards to set
the pleats

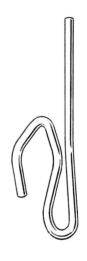

D   *Rufflette Hi-Style tape*

The hook   The special hook designed for use with this tape can be used with a face-fixed track, providing there is 38 mm ($1\frac{1}{2}$ in.) space between the bottom of the runner ring, or glider, and the ceiling.

Heading allowance   It is necessary to take careful measurements before deciding on the depth of heading allowance required, in order to hide the track when the curtains are closed. For a face fixed track, measure the distance from the bottom of the running ring, or glider, to the top of the track, including any fitments which show above the track. For a top fixed track, measure the distance from the bottom of the runner ring, or glider, to the ceiling. If this distance is 38 mm ($1\frac{1}{2}$ in.) the tape should be set flush with the top edge of the curtain. On a face fixed track this measurement may exceed 38 mm ($1\frac{1}{2}$ in.), in which case more heading will be necessary, and the tape may be set up to 12 mm ($\frac{1}{2}$ in.) below the top edge of the curtain to give the required depth of heading.

Calculation of heading allowance   If the tape is set flush with the top edge of the curtain, a 53 mm ($2\frac{1}{8}$ in.) allowance is required. The top of the hook reaches to within 38 mm ($1\frac{1}{2}$ in.) of the top of the tape, therefore 38 mm ($1\frac{1}{2}$ in.) plus 15 mm ($\frac{5}{8}$ in.) turning allowance equals 53 mm ($2\frac{1}{8}$ in.).

If the tape is set 12 mm ($\frac{1}{2}$ in.) below the top of the curtain, a 70 mm ($2\frac{3}{4}$ in.) allowance is required. The top of the hook reaches to within 38 mm ($1\frac{1}{2}$ in.) of the top of the tape, therefore 38 mm ($1\frac{1}{2}$ in.) plus 2×13 mm ($\frac{1}{2}$ in.) for the heading extension plus 6 mm ($\frac{1}{4}$ in.) turning allowance, equals 70 mm ($2\frac{3}{4}$ in.).

Calculation of tape length   The curtains should have adequate fullness, and although twice the width of the curtain track is satisfactory, 2·5 ($2\frac{1}{2}$) to $3 \times$ this width gives a more pleasing appearance, especially with lighter weight fabrics. Allow 150 mm (6 in.) extra tape for every curtain width. The tape has a right and wrong side but can be used either way up.

Preparation of Heading   If the tape is to be set flush with the top edge of the curtain, the preparation is the same as for *Rufflette Deep Pleat* tape. For a deeper pleated heading, the turning will vary from 15 mm ($\frac{5}{8}$ in.) to 20 mm ($\frac{3}{4}$ in.), depending on the previous calculations.

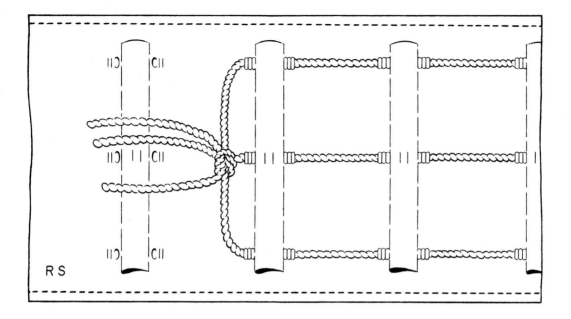

Preparation of tape

95a *(above)* Release the cords for 50 mm (2 in.) to 75 mm (3 in.), and knot them together securely

95b *(below)* Turn under the surplus tape to the wrong side, so that the knotted cord ends are enclosed, and tack along the fold. Trim off the surplus tape to within 12 mm ($\frac{1}{2}$ in.) of the fold

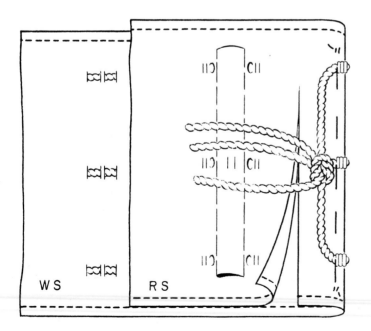

Setting the prepared tape to the curtain   Place the
tape so that the top edge is just inset from the
top edge of the curtain, and with the prepared
side edges also slightly inset. This will prevent
bulk, and make machining easier.

When the turning exceeds 15 mm ($\frac{5}{8}$ in.)
place the tape so that the top edge overlaps the
turning by 6 mm ($\frac{1}{4}$ in.) and the prepared edge
is slightly inset. Pin the tape in position along
the full width of the curtain.

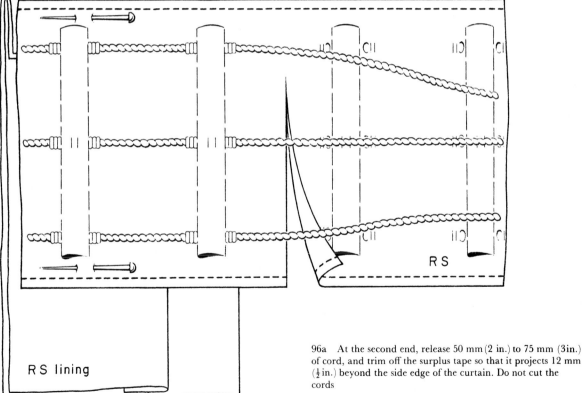

96a   At the second end, release 50 mm (2 in.) to 75 mm (3in.)
of cord, and trim off the surplus tape so that it projects 12 mm
($\frac{1}{2}$ in.) beyond the side edge of the curtain. Do not cut the
cords

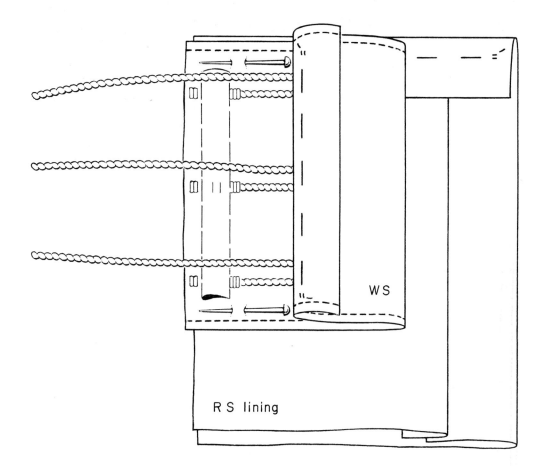

WS

RS lining

96b Turn under 12 mm ($\frac{1}{2}$ in.) turning on the tape edge and tack in place

Tack and machine round the tape fairly close to the edge, beginning at the free cord end, and leaving an opening between the cords, as in *figures 97a and b*. The free cords can be pushed inside the opening when the fullness has been adjusted.

Alternatively, the opening can be closed, leaving the cords free for winding onto a cord tidy.

Insert hooks, one at each end, and then at 75 mm (3 in.) or 115 mm (4$\frac{1}{2}$ in.) intervals along the length of the tape.

97a and b *(opposite)* The tape finally machined in position, showing the setting at each end of the curtain. In this case an opening has been left for the insertion of the cords after drawing up

112

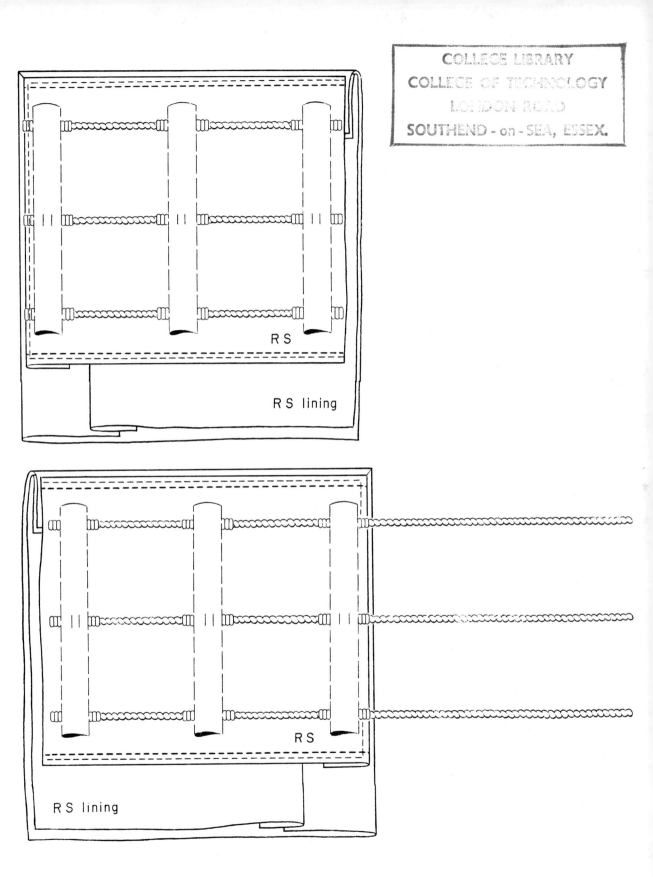

RS

RS lining

RS

RS lining

E *Rufflette Regis tape*

Hooks The hooks required for *Rufflette Regis* tape are *Standard R7, R67* or *R77*.

Heading allowance Careful calculations are necessary before buying the curtain fabric, in order to make the correct allowance for the heading. This varies according to the setting of the track, which may be top fixed or face fixed.

a *Top fixed track* The tape is set flush with the top edge of the curtain, and the pockets come at the top edge of the tape. In this case, 25 mm (1 in.) allowance is required. The hook reaches to within 10 mm ($\frac{3}{8}$ in.) of the top of the tape. Therefore 10 mm ($\frac{3}{8}$ in.) plus 15 mm ($\frac{5}{8}$ in.) turning allowance equals 25 mm (1 in.).

b *Face fixed track*

  (*i*) *Normal pleated heading* When there is a 55 mm ($2\frac{1}{8}$ in.) clearance above the runner ring, or glider, and the ceiling, the tape is set flush with the top edge of the curtain, but with the pockets at the lower edge of the tape. In this case, 66 mm ($2\frac{5}{8}$ in.) allowance is required. The hook is 51 mm (2 in.) from the top of the curtain, therefore 51 mm (2 in.) plus 15 mm ($\frac{5}{8}$ in.) turning allowance equals 66 mm ($2\frac{5}{8}$ in.).

  (*ii*) *Deeper pleated heading* When there is an 80 mm ($3\frac{1}{8}$ in.) clearance, or more, above the runner ring, or glider, and the ceiling, the tape may be set 25 mm (1 in.) below the top edge of the curtain. In this case, 106 mm ($4\frac{1}{4}$ in.) is required. The hook is 50 mm (2 in.) from the top of the tape, therefore 50 mm (2 in.) plus 2 × 25 mm (1 in.) heading allowance plus 6 mm ($\frac{1}{4}$ in.) turning allowance equals 10 mm ($4\frac{1}{4}$ in.).

Calculation of tape length The best effect is achieved with this tape if the curtain has adequate fullness, and 2 to 2·5 ($2\frac{1}{2}$) × the width of the curtain track is recommended.

  Rufflette Regis tape has a right and a wrong side, but may be used either way up depending on the position and style of the curtain track. Allow 165 mm ($6\frac{1}{2}$ in.) extra tape per curtain width.

Preparation of heading For normal setting the preparation is the same as for *Deep Pleat* tape. For a deeper pleated heading the turning must be 32 mm ($1\frac{1}{4}$ in.).

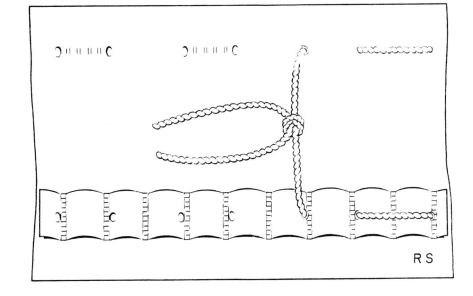

98a *(above)* Release the cords for 75 mm (3 in.) and knot them together securely

98b *(below)* Turn under the surplus tape to the wrong side, so that the knotted cord ends are enclosed, and tack along the fold. Trim off the surplus tape to within 12 mm ($\frac{1}{2}$ in.) of the fold

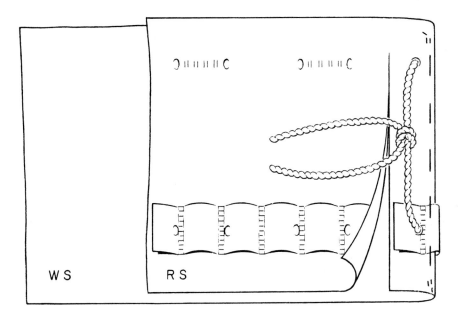

115

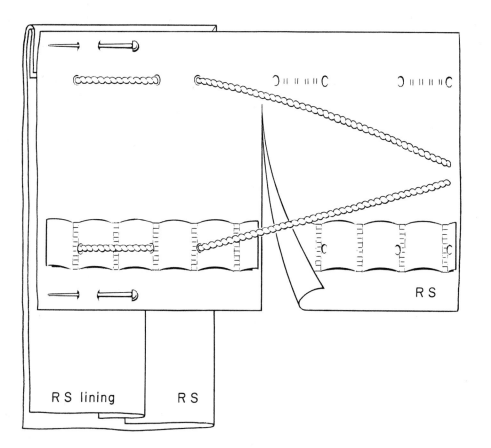

R S

R S lining   R S

Setting the tape   For a normal pleated heading, place the tape so that the top edge is just inset from the top edge of the curtain, and with the prepared side edges also slightly inset. This will prevent bulk and make machining easier.

For a deeper pleated heading, place the tape so that the top edge overlaps the turning allowance by 6 mm ($\frac{1}{4}$ in.), and the prepared side edge is slightly inset.

Pin the tape in position along the full width of the curtain, stopping 25 mm (1 in.) in from the other end.

99a   At the second end, release 75 mm (3 in.) of cord, and trim off the surplus tape so that it projects 12 mm ($\frac{1}{2}$ in.) beyond the side edge of the curtain. Do not cut the cords

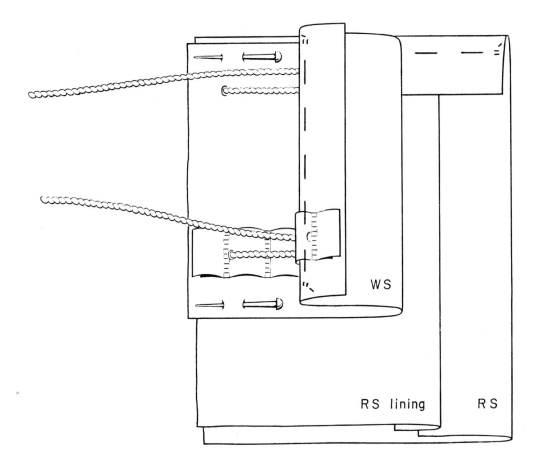

WS

RS lining   RS

99b   Turn the 12 mm ($\frac{1}{2}$ in.) turning to the wrong side and
tack in place

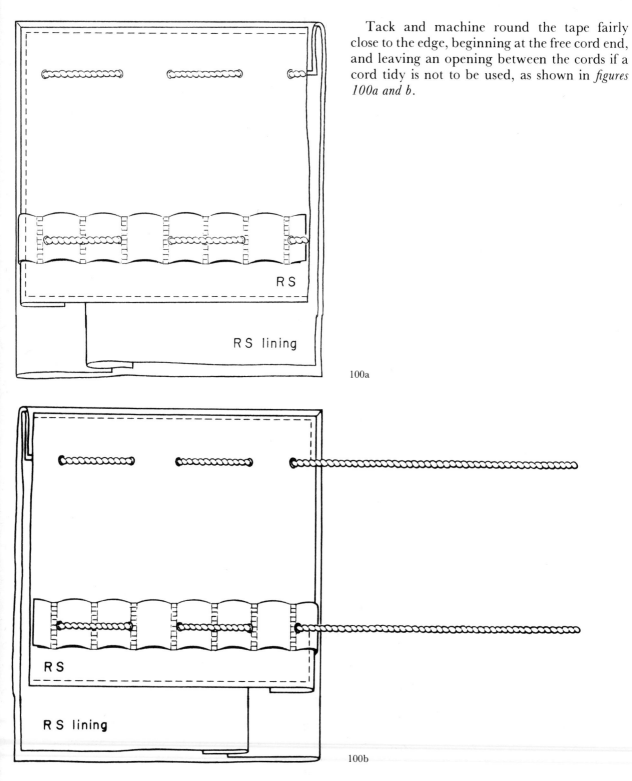

Tack and machine round the tape fairly close to the edge, beginning at the free cord end, and leaving an opening between the cords if a cord tidy is not to be used, as shown in *figures 100a and b*.

RS

RS lining

100a

RS

RS lining

100b

Hooks The hooks required for *Tervoil 60* tape are *R7*, *R5* and *R4*.

Heading allowance
a Top fixed track The tape is set flush with the top edge of the curtain, and the pockets come at the top edge of the tape. In this case, 30 mm (1¼ in.) allowance is required. The hook reaches to within 15 mm (⅝ in.) of the top of the tape. Therefore 15 mm (⅝ in.) plus 15 mm (⅝ in.) turning allowance equals 30 mm (1¼ in.).
b Face fixed track For a normal pleated heading, the tape is set flush with the top edge of the curtain and with the pockets at the lower edge of the tape. In this case 50 mm (2 in.) allowance is required. The top of the hook is 35 mm (1⅜ in) from the top of the tape, therefore 35 mm (1⅜ in.) plus 15 mm (⅝ in.) turning allowance equals 50 mm (2 in.).

The tape has a right and wrong side, but may be used either way up. Calculate length, prepare the heading and prepare and apply the tape as for *Regis* tape, following the directions for the normal pleated heading.

DETACHABLE LININGS

Rufflette lining tape provides a means of making a lining which is not attached to the curtain, although it is hung on the same hooks as those used to hang the curtain from the track. The fullness of the lining is adjusted by the cords in the lining tape, thus making it possible to use the detachable lining in conjunction with any curtain style, despite the fact that the fullness may be adjusted in a different way.

A curtain with lining attached usually has to be dry-cleaned. If it can be laundered at home, it is bulky to handle and difficult to iron. A detachable lining can be removed for laundering or dry-cleaning and, if washable, can be laundered at home even if the curtains need dry-cleaning. This is an obvious economy. In the case of heavy-weight curtains, which may be kept free from dust by occasional vacuum-ing, the lining will need cleaning before the curtain fabric. A detachable lining solves this problem. *Milium* curtain lining fabric must be dry-cleaned because of its aluminium backing and, therefore, should not be attached to washable fabrics. If the insulating quality of this fabric is desired, then a detachable lining will allow for different cleaning treatments for lining and curtain fabrics. This also applies when the fibre content of the lining and curtain fabrics differ, eg a cotton lining fabric used with an acrylic curtain fabric.

During laundering or dry-cleaning an attached lining may shrink more, or less than, the curtain fabric. This will cause the curtain to pucker and will necessitate unpicking and resetting the side edges. A detachable lining overcomes this problem.

Detachable linings have some disadvantages. In the first place the equivalent of two pairs of unlined curtains has to be made, which gives double the work at the side and lower edges, as well as extra tape to be prepared and applied.

A detachable lining cannot support a curtain and enrich its drape in the same way as a lining which is locked and attached to it during construction. Its main function is to protect the curtain fabric from direct contact with sunlight, and to deepen the colour of the curtain fabric from the inside view. They also serve to give an appearance of uniformity to the outside of a house if this is desired.

Unless the loose lining is bar tacked to the curtain, it is likely to show at the side edges. This bar tacking is time taking, and has to be repeated after each washing or cleaning.

Calculating the quantity of lining fabric required

As the lining hangs separately from the curtain, it is not necessary to make it as full as the curtain. The width, however, should be at least 1·5 (1½) × the width of the curtain track measurement, plus 25 mm (1 in.) for seaming if required, and 50 mm (2 in.) for side hems.

As already stated, the lining is hung from the same hooks as used for the curtain. Therefore no heading allowance is necessary. However, the distance from the top edge of the lining, to the suspension point of the curtain, varies according to the style of the tape. The top raw edge of the lining sets below the suspension points by the following amounts:

Standard, Evenpleat and *Regis tapes* 12 mm ($\frac{1}{2}$ in.)
Hi-Style tape   32 mm ($1\frac{1}{4}$ in.)
Tervoil 60 tape   20 mm ($\frac{3}{4}$ in.)
Deep Pleat and *Easypleat tapes*
a   using short stemmed hooks   32 mm ($1\frac{1}{4}$ in.)
b   using long stemmed hooks   58 mm ($2\frac{1}{4}$ in.)

The length of the lining is based on the length of the curtain without any additional allowances. If the lining is to be set 50 mm (2 in.) above the lower edge of the curtain, the length will be calculated as follows:

Standard, Evenpleat and *Regis tapes*   Total deduction from curtain length is 62 mm ($2\frac{1}{2}$ in.)
Hi-Style tape   Total deduction from curtain length is 82 mm ($3\frac{1}{4}$ in.)

Tervoil 60 tape   Total deduction from curtain length is 70 mm ($2\frac{3}{4}$ in.)

Deep pleat and *Easypleat tapes*
a   using short stemmed hooks   Total deduction from curtain length is 82 mm ($3\frac{1}{4}$ in.)
b   using long stemmed hooks   Total deduction from curtain length is 108 mm ($4\frac{1}{4}$ in.)

In all cases 75 mm (3 in.) hem allowance and 30 mm per metre (1 in. per yard) shrinkage allowance must be added.

Lining tape   This is 25 mm (1 in.) wide, and is available in natural and beige. It can be recognised by the double skirt at the lower edge. It has a right and wrong side, and an upper and lower edge, so should be carefully examined before use. Two cords are visible on the right side, but only one on the wrong side. Allow 128 mm (5 in.) extra tape per lining width, to allow for the treatment of the ends.

Preparing the tape

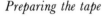

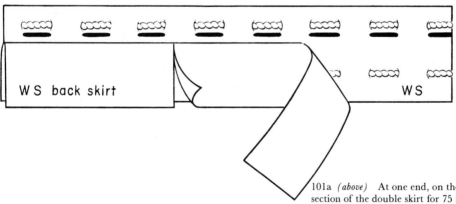

101a *(above)*   At one end, on the wrong side, remove the back section of the double skirt for 75 mm (3 in.)

101b *(below)*   Release the cords for 50 mm (2 in.) and knot them together securely, stitching the knot if necessary

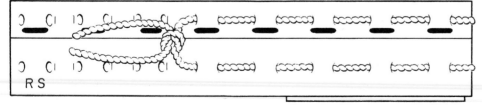

Preparing the curtain and the lining The curtains are made as unlined curtains. Join the lining widths, if necessary, using a double machine stitched seam, see page 74. Prepare the side hems of the lining as for an unlined curtain, but stitch them by machine as a hand finish is unnecessary.

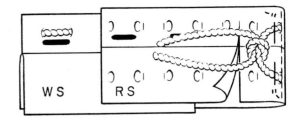

101c Turn under the tape to the wrong side, including the knotted cord ends. Tack and machine close to the folded edge. Trim away the surplus tape, excluding the cords, to within 12 mm ($\frac{1}{2}$ in.) of the fold

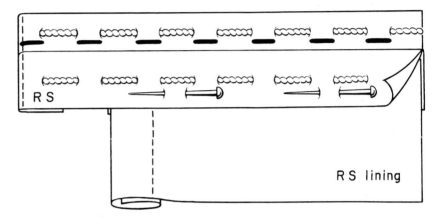

102 With the right side of the tape and lining uppermost, insert the top edge of the lining between the double skirt of the tape so that the side edge of the lining is in line with the trimmed edge of the back skirt. Pin the tape in position to within 25 mm (1 in.) of the other side edge

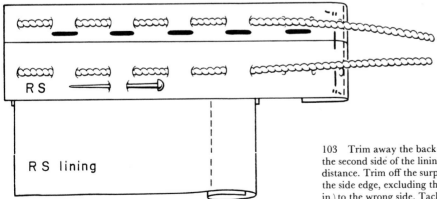

103 Trim away the back skirt, as for the first end, as far as the second side of the lining. Release the cords for the same distance. Trim off the surplus tape to within 38 mm (1$\frac{1}{2}$ in.) of the side edge, excluding the cords, and turn under 12 mm ($\frac{1}{2}$ in.) to the wrong side. Tack and machine close to the fold

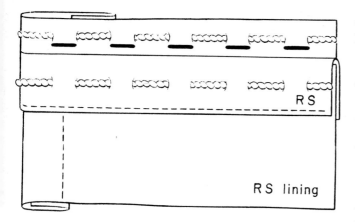

RS

RS lining

Stitching the tape to the lining Tack the tape in place for the full width of the lining. See *figures 104a and b, and 105.*

Adjust the fullness on the cords as previously described, relating the final width to the adjusted curtain width. It is wise to make the lining a fraction narrower than the curtain so that it will not show from the room. Wind the cords onto a cord tidy.

104a and b *(above and centre)* Turn the surplus tape to the wrong side so that the fold lines are in line with the side edges of the lining. Tack in place. Machine along the lower edge of the tape, taking care to include the back skirt

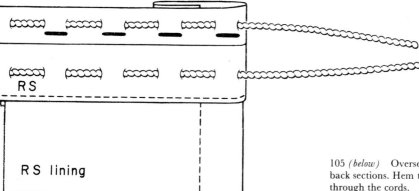

RS

RS lining

105 *(below)* Oversew together the top edges of the turned back sections. Hem the folded edge in place but do not stitch through the cords.

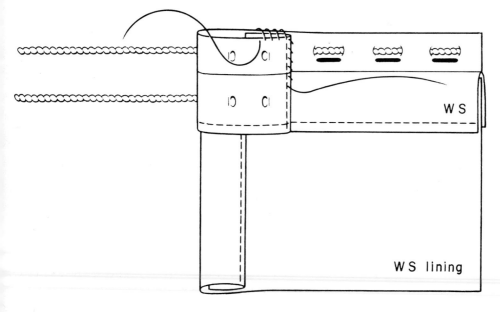

WS

WS lining

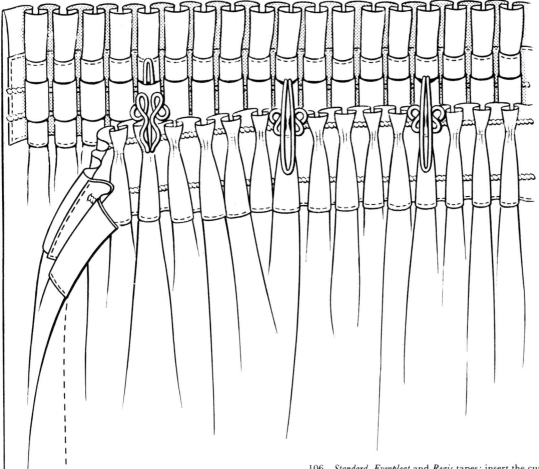

106 *Standard, Evenpleat* and *Regis* tapes: insert the curtain hook through the opening in the upper edge of the lining tape on the right side, and then through a pocket of the curtain tape. Turn the hook over to its final position

To attach the lining to the curtain

a   *Standard, Evenpleat* and *Regis* tapes

b   *Hi-Style* tape   This is the same as for the previous tapes, but the hook does not turn over.

c   *Deep Pleat* and *Easypleat* tapes   The hooks are placed first in the curtain, and then the openings in the lining tape are slipped over the hooks.

The lower hem   Hang the curtains from the curtain track and assess the position of the lining hem. Prepare and stitch the hem as for an unlined curtain, see page 76.

To keep the lining in position, bar tacks may be worked at 150 mm (6 in.) intervals to join the side edges of the curtain and lining. These must be snipped away when the lining needs to be removed for cleaning.

123

8 Café curtains

These are short curtains which are suspended from a rod or pole placed approximately half-way up the window. They are both functional and decorative and can be used on their own or in conjunction with the main curtains. Alternatively, two sets can be made; one hung from the top of the window and one from the halfway position, thus giving a tiered effect. In figure 13, page 27, the lower curtains have been hung from the base of a ranch window to make it appear larger. The lower set would be kept permanently closed in this case. Café curtains can be used to mask an unattractive view, and are sometimes more pleasing than sheer curtains, providing they suit the décor and furnishings of the room.

Café curtains can be made with one of the heading tapes previously described in section 7, such as *Evenpleat*, but they are more often made with an inverted, scalloped heading. The scallops can be separated by straps which form the means of hanging the curtains, similar to a style of curtain popular in the Tudor period. Alternatively, the scallops can be separated by pinch pleats, and the curtains hung from rings placed on the rod or pole. It is no longer necessary to stitch the rings onto the curtain, as rings are available which hold the hooks.

Light to medium-weight fabrics are the most suitable. If a printed fabric is required, it is wise to choose an indistinct or small design. Stripes are suitable providing they fit neatly into the necessary sizing of scallops and straps etc. Sheer and semi-sheer fabrics are not suitable for the scalloped styles.

Although lining is not essential, it does ease the construction of some styles, eg those with a scalloped heading, as it removes the need for a facing.

SCALLOPED AND STRAP HEADING

This gives a neat, sculptured heading, as the curtain is usually hung without fullness. Careful calculations are necessary for planning the width of scallops and straps, so that the curtain will fit the width of the window. The following suggestions give a base for the calculations, but they are bound to be variable according to the required finished size of the curtain. On light-weight fabrics, use a 115 mm ($4\frac{1}{2}$ in.) wide scallop and a 25 mm (1 in.) strap. On medium-weight fabrics, make the straps 32 mm ($1\frac{1}{4}$ in.) wide to facilitate turning it right side out during construction. Remember to calculate for a strap to come at each side edge of the curtain, eg a curtain with eight scallops must have nine straps. The side edges will need 50 mm (2 in.) for turning allowances, so this must be catered for when planning the final width of fabric required.

To calculate width

Measure the length of the rod or pole and divide this measurement by the total width of one scallop plus one strap. This should divide with a remainder equal to the exact width of one strap. If it does not work out like this, the measurement of the scallop and/or strap must be adjusted.

Example A
Length of track   114·5 cm (45 in.)
Width of one scallop plus one strap   140 mm ($5\frac{1}{2}$ in.)
$1145 \div 140 = 8$, remainder 25 mm ($45 \div 5\frac{1}{2} = 8$, remainder 1 in)
This gives the exact requirements, so needs no adjustment, as the 25 mm (1 in.) remainder makes the final strap.

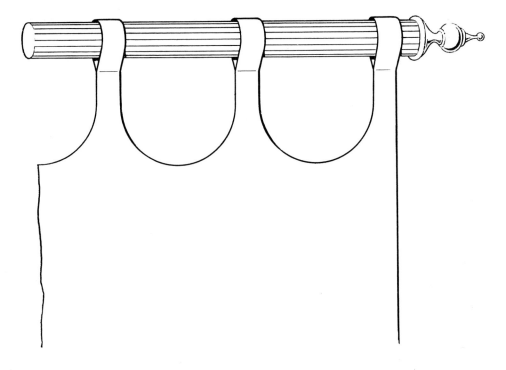

107 Café curtains

Example B
Length of track   91·5 cm (36 in.)
Width of one scallop plus one strap   140 mm
(5½ in.)
915 ÷ 140 = 6, remainder 75 mm (36 ÷ 5½
= 6, remainder 3 in.)
The final strap will use 25 mm (1 in.), so 50 mm
(2 in.) will have to be divided equally between
the scallops to give the curtain an even
appearance.

Add 50 mm (2 in.) (turning allowances) to
the track measurement to find the width of
fabric required. More than one width of fabric
will be necessary if the measurement of the
track exceeds 116·8 cm (46 in.). In this case, it
is best to make two separate curtains. The
method of calculation is the same, but it is based
on half the track measurement for each curtain.

To calculate length

Measure from the base of the rod, or pole, to
the required length, usually the sill. The hem
and shrinkage allowance is the same as for
other curtains (page 65). For the straps an
allowance is made equal to the circumference
of the rod or pole, plus 38 mm (1½ in.).

Calculate the meterage (yardage) in the
usual way, and buy the same amount of lining
fabric.

If two curtains are required, and patterned
fabric is being used, remember to allow for
balancing the design as advised on page 67.

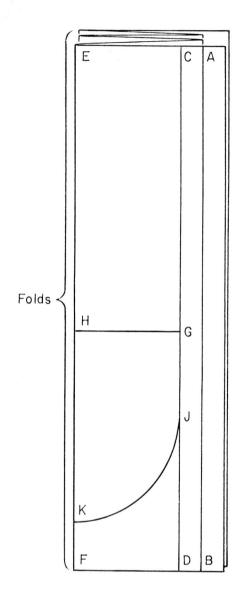

The measurements used in figure 108 are as follows:

Width of scallop	115 mm ($4\frac{1}{2}$ in.)
Width of strap	25 mm (1 in.)
Circumference of rod or pole	115 mm ($4\frac{1}{2}$ in.)

Cut a strip of brown or other firm paper, equal to the track length by 305 mm (12 in.) approximately.

At one end, draw line AB, half the width of the strap, in this case 12 mm ($\frac{1}{2}$ in.), in from the edge.
Draw line CD the same distance from AB.
Draw line EF half the width of the scallop, in this case 58 mm ($2\frac{1}{4}$ in.), from CD. Below C and E measure the circumference of the rod or pole plus 38 mm ($1\frac{1}{2}$ in.), and mark points G and H. Join GH.
Mark point J 50 mm (2 in.) below G.
Mark point K 100 mm (4 in.) below H.
Curve from J to K, making sure that the line is straight for 6 mm ($\frac{1}{4}$ in.) from K. Beginning at line EF, across the width of the paper, draw parallel lines separated by half the width of the scallop plus half the width of the strap. (In this case the lines are 70 mm ($2\frac{3}{4}$ in.) apart.) At the end this should leave half the width of a scallop plus the width of a strap.
Fold the paper concertinawise along these lines, making the first fold along line EF. An amount equal to half the width of a strap will project at each end, giving a full strap width in these positions.
Cut through CGJ and the curve JK, cutting through all thicknesses of paper. When opened out, the full scalloped edge will be formed. Press lightly to remove the fold lines.
Check the pattern against the track to see if it fits.

When making a pattern, the points J and K will never vary, but the other lines and points must be drawn to suit individual curtain requirements.

108   Making the scallop pattern

Making the curtain

Trim the side edge, or edges, of the fabric so that the width is equal to the pattern, ie the track measurement, plus 50 mm (2 in.) for turning allowances. If more than one width is required, trim the two pieces of fabric so that they are each half the length of the track plus 50 mm (2 in.). The necessary amount can be trimmed from one side, but if the fabric is patterned, it may be better to trim equal, or unequal, amounts from the two sides, to retain the balance of the pattern. Trim the lining so that it is 50 mm (2 in.) narrower than the fabric.

On light-weight fabrics it is wise to interface the heading for support. Cut a strip of iron-on interfacing equal in size to the final width of the curtain, by 266 mm ($10\frac{1}{2}$ in.) wide. This width will need adjustment if the straps and/or scallops are made deeper than the suggested measurements. As interfacing is narrower than furnishing fabric, it will be necessary to join the strip. This is best done by overlapping the strips for 12 mm ($\frac{1}{2}$ in.) while applying them. Remember to allow for this when cutting the length.

Join the curtain and lining fabric together at the side edges, using 12 mm ($\frac{1}{2}$ in.) turnings as directed on page 88. Trim the seams to 10 mm ($\frac{3}{8}$ in.) for a 25 mm (1 in.) strap. It is not necessary to trim the seams if the strap is wider than this.

Press open the seams, and then press the two turnings onto the lining. Do not turn the curtain right side out.

Working with the lining uppermost, arrange the lining so that the curtain fabric shows for an equal amount down either side. Pin down the sides and across the top to set the fabric in position. See *figure 109*.

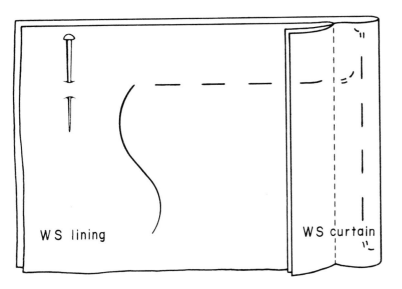

WS lining

WS curtain

109 Tack down the side edges, fairly close to the fold, for approximately 305 mm (12 in.). Tack across the top of the curtain 15 mm ($\frac{5}{8}$ in.) below the top raw edges to hold the two sections together, and to guide the setting of the pattern. Do not press the folded edges

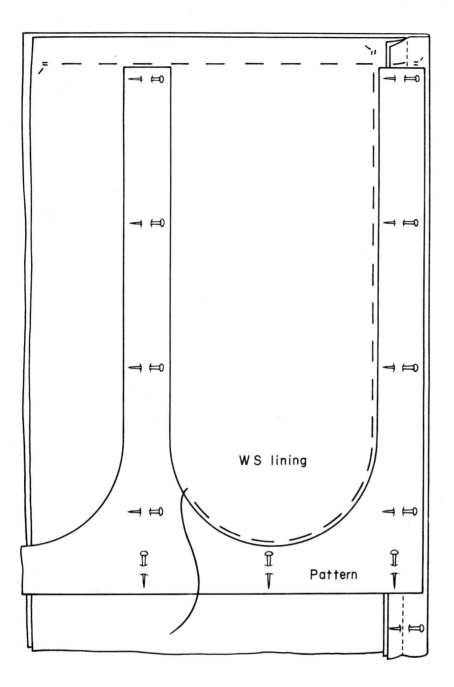

WS lining

Pattern

Place the pattern on the lining side of the curtain with the top edges of the straps in line with the tacking along the top of the curtain.

110   Pin along the top and lower edges, down the straps and round the scallops. Tack the curtain and lining together, following the edges of the straps and scallops

128

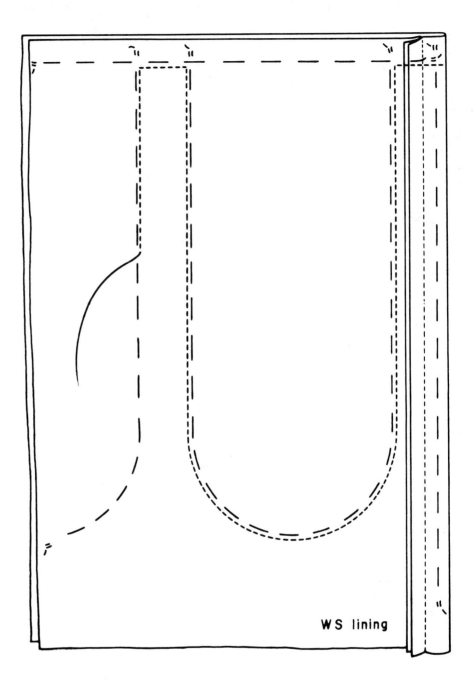

Remove the pattern and also the remaining pins from the side edges of the curtain.

111 Machine along the straps and round the scallops, using the tacking as a guide

129

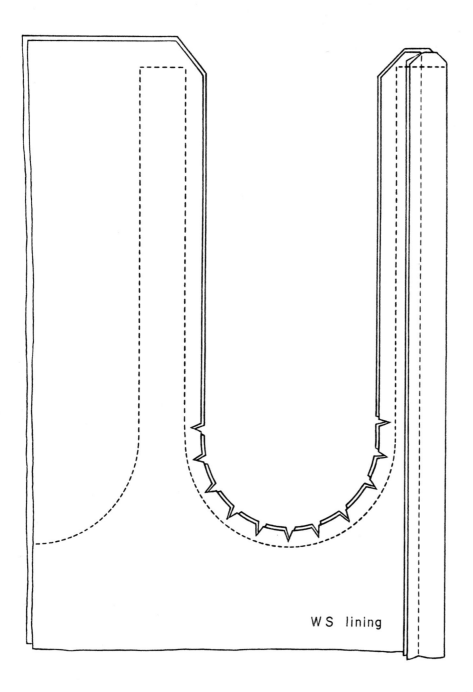

WS lining

112   Trim the turnings and cut away the surplus fabric inside
the scallops, leaving 12 mm (½ in.) outside the machining.
Trim off the corners and snip the turnings inside the scallops
at 12 mm (½ in.) intervals

Turn the curtain right side out, pulling out the shaped sections carefully. Roll the edge between the thumb and finger so that the seam line is exactly on the edge. Tack fairly close to the edge round the straps and scallops and press lightly to set the shaping. Remove the tacking threads and press firmly.

Fold each strap to the wrong side for half the circumference of the rod or pole, plus 32 mm (1¼ in.). Tack each strap in place across the base, and again 25 mm (1 in.) above the base. See *figure 113*.

Remove the tacking threads and press the curtain.

The lining can be locked to the curtain if desired. Follow the directions on page 89.

Hang the curtain to check the length, and finish the hems as directed on pages 82–86.

SCALLOPED AND PLEATED HEADING

Careful calculations are necessary as the fullness is arranged in pleats which must provide a given width of curtain. The curtain, when pleated, should be slightly wider than the fitment. The curtain is made in a similar way to to the previous style, but the curtain is better set 25 mm (1 in.) inside each side edge on the lining side, instead of 12 mm (½ in.). See *figure 114*.

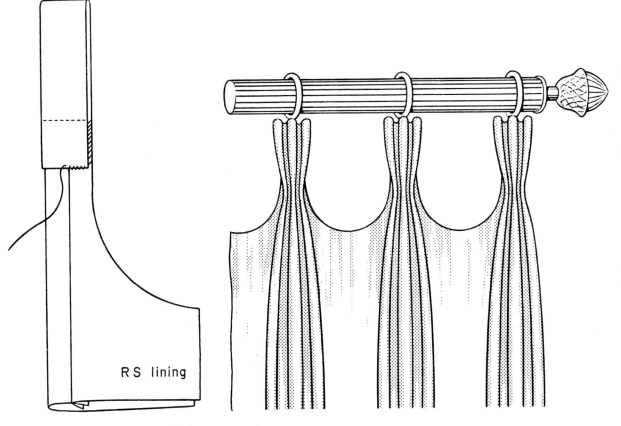

RS lining

113 Machine or stab stitch in line with the upper row of tacking. Oversew one side, hem across the base and oversew the second side.

114 Scalloped café curtains using *Deep Pleat* or *Easypleat* heading tape. This style is best made with triple pleats

131

Calculating the width

A pleated section must come at each side edge of the curtain. Therefore a curtain with eight scallops must have nine pleated sections.

The width of fabric for pleating should be 152 mm (6 in.), to take sufficient tape to form triple pleats. The scallop width may vary from 102 mm (4 in.) to 152 mm (6 in.). The following plans and directions are based on a scallop of 102 mm (4 in.). The width of the fabric will be reduced to slightly more than half the original width when pleated. If twice the length of the track measurement is used for the curtain width, the resulting fullness will improve the drape of the curtain. An extra allowance of 75 mm (3 in.) is required, beyond this measurement, for finishing the side edges.

Divide twice the track measurement by the total measurement of a scallop plus 152 mm (6 in.) (a pleating section). This should divide with a remainder equal to the exact width of one pleating section, ie 152 mm (6 in.). If it does not, the scallop width must be adjusted. Alternatively, the curtain can be made slightly wider to obtain the extra width required for the final pleated section. This will give a little extra fullness which will not detract from the appearance of the curtain.

Example A
Length of track   96·5 cm (38 in.)
$965 \times 2 = 1930$ $(38 \times 2 = 76)$
Width of one scallop plus one pleating section 102 mm + 152 mm = 254 mm (4 in. + 6 in. = 10 in.) 1930 ÷ 254 = 7, remainder 152 mm (76 ÷ 10 = 7, remainder 6 in.)
This gives the exact requirements so needs no adjustment. There will be eight groups of pleats and seven scallops on the finished curtain.

Example B
Length of track   106·7 cm (42 in.)
$1067 \times 2 = 2134$ $(42 \times 2 = 84)$
Width of one scallop plus one pleating section 102 mm + 152 mm = 254 mm (4 in. + 6 in. = 10 in.) 2134 ÷ 254 = 8, remainder 102 mm (84 ÷ 10 = 8 remainder 4 in.)
In this case it is best to make the finished curtain 50 mm (2 in.) wider, and so provide the extra width required for the pleating. This will give nine groups of pleats and eight scallops on the finished curtain.

In most cases more than one width of fabric will be required. Although not generally recommended in curtain making, the seam is best placed, in this case, in the centre of the curtain. This will place the seam in a pleated area, so the seam will be partly hidden by the fullness.

Calculating total width

When the finished width of the curtain has been discovered, add to this measurement 75 mm (3 in) for finishing the side edges plus a seam allowance if more than one width is required.

Calculating the length

Use long stemmed, deep pleat hooks for this style of curtain. To find the length, measure from the suspension point to the desired length, usually to the sill. The hem and shrinkage allowances are the same as for other curtains, page 65.

The heading allowance is the same as for *Deep Pleat* and *Easypleat* tapes, but remember to use the calculations for long stemmed hooks on page 105.

Calculate the meterage (yardage) in the usual way, and buy the same amount of lining fabric. If using patterned fabric for the curtains remember to allow for matching the pattern over the seam.

165 mm (6½ in.) of heading tape will be required for each pleating section. Add on 25 mm (1 in.) to the total measurement to allow for the correct placing of pockets when the tape is cut into the 165 mm (6½ in.) lengths.

Making the pattern

The directions given are for a scallop of 102 mm (4 in.) and a width of 152 mm (6 in.) for the triple pleat. The scallop width can be adjusted easily if necessary.

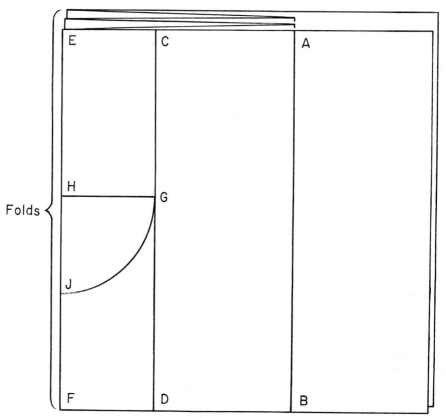

Cut a strip of brown or other firm paper, equal to the finished width of the curtain, by 205 mm (8 in.) wide. See *figure 115*.

At one end, draw 2 lines, AB 75 mm (3 in.), and CD 152 mm (6 in.) in from the edge of the paper.

Draw a third line, EF, half the width of the scallop away from CD, in this case 50 mm (2 in.) Mark points G and H, 90 mm (3½ in.) down from C and E. Join GH.

Mark point J half the width of the scallop below H, in this case 50 mm (2 in.)

Curve from G to J to form a quarter circle. This is best done with a pair of compasses.

Beginning at line EF, draw parallel lines separated by half the width of the scallop plus half the width of a pleated section. In this case the lines are 127 mm (5 in.) apart. An extra 75 mm (3 in.) projects at each end of the pattern to provide one full pleating width at each end of the curtain.

Cut along CG and the curve GJ, cutting through all the layers of paper. When opened out, the full scalloped edge will be formed. Press lightly to remove the fold lines.

On all patterns the spacing of lines AB and CD remains the same, and the points G and H are also constant.

Making the curtain

If necessary, join the two widths of curtain and lining fabric as directed on page 77. Trim the side edge or edges of the curtain fabric so that the width is equal to the pattern plus 75 mm (3 in.). Trim an equal amount from each side of the fabric if it has been joined, in order to place the seam in the centre. On a single width note the points suggested for the previous style. Trim the lining fabric so that it is 102 mm (4 in.) narrower than the curtain fabric. If necessary interface the curtain fabric as directed on

133

page 127. The strip of interfacing needs to be 205 mm (8 in.) wide for this style.

Prepare the curtain as for the previous style, but do not trim the seams. Prepare the shaped top of the curtain, following the previous directions as far as pinning down the sides and across the top to set the fabric in position.

Preparing Deep Pleat tape

Cut strips of tape 165 mm (6½ in.) long, arranging for a complete pocket to come on each edge. This pocket will form the turning allowance, and will make nine pockets, in all, on each strip of tape. One plain strip of tape will be wasted between each section cut.

Fold one pocket to the wrong side on each side edge of the tape sections. This will make the strips slightly narrower than the pleating areas of the curtain. Place the prepared tape so that the top edge is flush with the top of the curtain, and the side edges equally inset from the edges of the pleating area. Pin the tape in position.

Preparing Easypleat tape

Cut strips of tape 165 mm (6½ in.) long, planning the cutting to place seven pockets on each strip, with a plain section of tape at either end to provide a turning allowance. This will cause one pocket to be cut to waste between each strip along the full length of the heading tape.

On the cut edges, fold an equal width turning to the wrong side so that the strips fit the fabric between the scallops. Place the tape with the top and side edges flush with the edges of fabric, and pin in place.

Machining the tape

The curtain and lining can be locked together as directed on page 89.

Insert a hook into each section of tape, setting it into the first and alternate pockets.

Hang the curtain to check the length and make the hems as directed on pages 82–86.

The scalloped headings described for café curtains, can be made on full-length curtains for use with a rod or pole. These can provide an attractive style of curtaining if they suit the décor of a room.

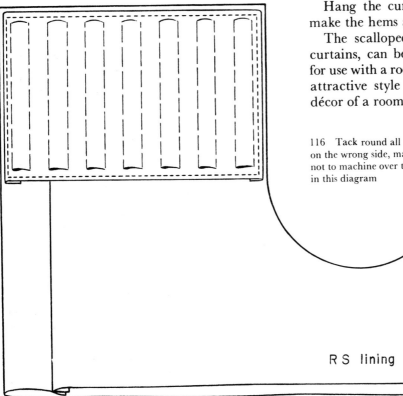

116 Tack round all four sides of the tape sections. Working on the wrong side, machine round the four edges, being careful not to machine over the pocket openings. *Easypleat* tape is used in this diagram

R S lining

9 Sheer and semi-sheer curtains

Sheer curtains are used mainly to give privacy and, therefore, are popular today with the frequently cramped conditions of building and the fashionable large windows. They can also be used to mask an unattractive view, drawing attention to the interior of a room, rather than the outside surroundings.

Sheer curtains may be half or full length, depending on their purpose. They are sometimes called glass curtains because they hang against the glass, and are often subsidiary to the main curtains. When used in this way, they are best kept simple in style. When used on their own, eg in a bedroom, they can be pleasingly decorative, giving a soft, feminine appearance to the window. However, careful consideration should be given before adopting this treatment, as it does not always suit the clean cut lines of modern furniture.

Sheer curtaining is made mostly from polyester fibre because it is strong and resistant to sunlight. Polyester fibre discolours in time, but it yellows less than nylon. Its drip-dry quality makes it easy to launder, and it requires little or no ironing.

The two main types of sheer curtain are known as long nets and short nets. Long nets are sold in standard widths, and the required length is bought; short nets are sold in standard lengths, and the required width is bought.

Long nets can be bought with selvedge or frilled edges, and are available in a range of widths from 91·4 cm (36 in.) to 152·4 cm (60 in.). Occasionally they can be bought in greater widths than this.

Short nets are available in a wide range of lengths from 45·7 cm (18 in.), to 228·6 cm (90 in.), thus catering for most needs.

Sheer curtain fabric is more difficult to handle than most other soft furnishing fabrics, so the inexperienced needlewoman may prefer to buy this type of curtain ready-made, and will find a similar range of widths and lengths are readily available. Although the more decorative type of sheer curtain, such as cross-over drapes and festoons, can be made at home, they are more often bought.

The top and bottom edges of long nets have to be finished in some way, and this allows for variety in style. A casing can be made at either edge, and the curtain attached to the wooden framework of a door or window. In this case the curtain moves with the door or window and provides a useful way of treating a French door which opens inwards, or a pivot window. Alternatively the top of the curtain can be finished with a ruched heading using nylon, *Terylene* or *Tervoil* tape. The curtain can then be hung from a curtain track (see figure 4, page 21), leaving the lower edge free.

Short nets are bought with a casing finish at the top edge, and a plain or decorative hem at the lower edge. This controls the treatment, and the curtains must be hung from some sort of rod or expanding, plastic covered wire.

Vision nets are similar to sheer curtains but the weave is more decorative, and a wider range of colours is available. They are made from cotton as well as polyester fibre, and may be used in the same way as sheer curtains or as room dividers. They are bought as for long nets. Their special characteristic is the arrangement of large holes to form a pattern.

Semi-sheer fabrics have interesting open weaves and textures, and are made in a wide range of colours. They are mostly made from acrylic fibres, although other synthetic fibres, blends and linen are also being used. They are available in widths from 122 cm (48 in.) to 152·4 cm (60 in.). They cut off more light than sheer curtains, but are more pleasing aesthetically, and offer an interesting window treatment when privacy is important. They may be used on their own, or subsidiary to the main

curtains. They, also, make attractive room dividers. However, they do present some problems as the method of construction has to be adapted, and traditional stitches may not always be used.

As these curtains are light-weight, adequate fullness is necessary to ensure an attractive drape. Two and a half to three times the length of the track, or fitment, should be used.

All these fabrics have a degree of transparency, some to a greater extent than others, as indicated by the descriptive names sheer and semi-sheer. Care has to be taken when making hems and headings that turnings do not show in an unattractive way. To counteract this problem, solid hems and headings are made, ie equal width first and second turnings are used for hems. Heading allowances need special calculations which will be dealt with in the sections on headings on pages 138 and 142.

In order to achieve satisfactory results, sheer curtains need special care in handling. They may be made almost completely by machine, and are constructed like unlined curtains with just a few modifications to suit the sheer fabric. It is wise to use a synthetic thread such as *Trylko* or *Drima* when sewing this type of fabric, so that the properties of thread and fabric are similar. The use of fine pins and fine hand and machine needles helps to prevent snagging the fibres while sewing. A short machine stitch and a slightly loose upper and lower tension are necessary to prevent puckering. Tissue paper put under the work while it is being fed into the machine will stabilise the stitching and prevent

the feed dog catching the fabric. The paper can be torn away when the machining is finished.

Sheer curtains rarely, if ever, require seaming as long nets are available in a comprehensive range of widths, and short nets are always bought by the curtain width measurement. If two widths do have to be used, the selvedges can hang together, the fullness concealing the meeting edges. If for any reason a seam is required, use a narrow french seam or a machine fell seam (see pages 74 and 198), making it 6 mm ($\frac{1}{4}$ in.) wide when finished.

a Casing at top and bottom

Calculating quantities:
Length Measure the distance between the suspension point at the top and the fixing point at the bottom of the curtain. The heading is usually 12 mm ($\frac{1}{2}$ in.) to 20 mm ($\frac{3}{4}$ in.), and the casing 12 mm ($\frac{1}{2}$ in.). The casing depth may have to be adjusted to suit the means of fixing. It must allow for the rods, or plastic covered wire, to be inserted easily. Multiply the required heading depth by three, and the required casing depth by two, to find the total allowance necessary. See *figure 117.*

The allowance required for a 20 mm ($\frac{3}{4}$ in.) heading and a 12 mm ($\frac{1}{2}$ in.) casing is 82 mm ($3\frac{1}{4}$ in.). The same amount is required for the

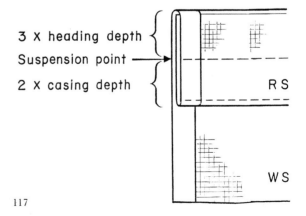

3 X heading depth
Suspension point
2 X casing depth

R S

W S

117

lower edge, so the total length is calculated by adding twice times this measurement onto the measurement taken from rod to rod. This will give the length of net required for one curtain.

Width　Measure the length of the fitment and multiply this by the amount of fullness required. Buy the width of fabric which is the nearest to this measurement. As it is not always necessary to make side hems on long nets, they need not be considered in calculations. If hems are necessary, they will only reduce the width by 50 mm (2 in.), and an adequately full curtain will supply this amount.

If more than one curtain is required, the total length must be multiplied by the number of curtains. If the fabric is patterned, allowance should be made for this. (See previous information on patterned fabric on pages 67–68.)

Construction

1　*Side edges*　If the selvedge is good it may be used as the side edge finish. However, if it is poor, it is best to trim if off and make a hem.

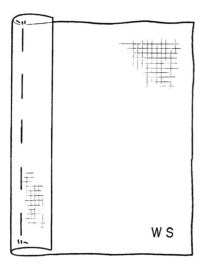

118a　Folding straight with the mesh of the net, turn a 12 mm (½ in.) turning to the wrong side and tack in place

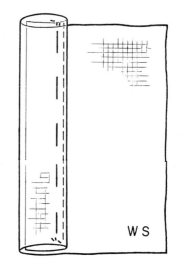

118b　Fold over a second turning of 12 mm (½ in.), to make a solid hem, tack and machine in place

2　*Casing*

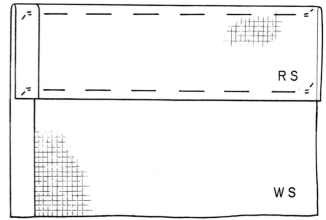

119　To prepare the casing, fold over the trimmed top raw edge, in line with the mesh, for 25 mm (1 in.) for a 12 mm (½ in.) heading, and 32 mm (1¼ in.) for a 20 mm (¾ in.) heading, and tack close to the fold. It is helpful to tack again close to the raw edge to prevent the net slipping

Fold over again for the same amount, tack along the top and lower edges of the hem. A further line of tacking is worked 12 mm (½ in.) above the lower edge of the hem, to stabilise the fabric for stitching the machining which forms the casing. Machine along the

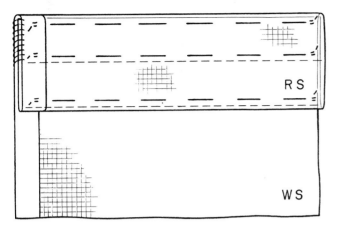

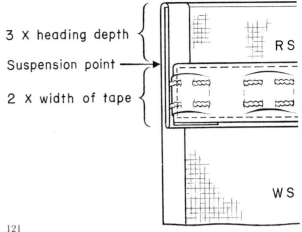

120 The machined casing. Above the casing, the edges of the heading are oversewn

121

lower edge of the hem and again in line with the last line of tacking. Machine just outside the tacking line so that the tacking stitches can be removed easily. Finish off the machine thread ends, but make sure that the ends of the casing are left open. See *figure 120*.

Press the casing and check that the length is correct by hanging the curtains from the top rod. Make the lower casing in the same way.

b Curtains with ruched headings

Calculating quantities:
Length This is estimated as for ordinary curtains. However, the extra allowances differ owing to the solid headings and hems. The depth of the heading may vary, but it is not advisable to use a deep heading because the fabric is too light-weight to support it. With this type of curtain the heading is essentially functional. If a solid hem is made at the top, and the tape is superimposed close to the lower edge of the hem, the three thicknesses of fabric will help to support the heading. Working on this principle, and using *Terylene* tape which is 15 mm ($\frac{5}{8}$ in.) wide, with a heading of 15 mm ($\frac{5}{8}$ in.), an 80 mm ($3\frac{1}{8}$ in.) allowance is required. This is calculated in the following way:
3×15 mm ($\frac{5}{8}$ in.) heading (projection above suspension point) plus 2×15 mm ($\frac{5}{8}$ in.) hem allowance below suspension point, (*figure 121*).

Nylon and *Tervoil* tapes are 25 mm (1 in.) wide, so require 98 mm ($3\frac{7}{8}$ in.) allowance.

The hem, which may vary from 25 mm (1 in.) to 100 mm (4 in.) is best made solid. Therefore twice the finished hem depth will be required for the turning.
Width and meterage (yardage) These are calculated as for the casing style.
Tape Calculate the quantity required as for standard cotton tape. See page 100.

Construction

The order of construction is the same as for the unlined curtains. Prepare the side edges as for the casing style.
Heading If necessary trim the top raw edge straight with the mesh. Fold over the straightened top raw edge for the depth of the heading plus the width of the tape. Tack close to the fold and also along the lower raw edge. See *figure 122*.

The tape is prepared and applied as for standard tape with one exception. In this case the lower edge of the tape is placed in line with the lower edge of the hem, (*figure 123*).
Hem Prepare as for unlined curtains, but with an equal width first and second turning. The hem is best machined in place. The sides of the hem will need to be hemmed by hand onto the side hems of the curtain if the selvedge is not used, (*figure 124*).

138

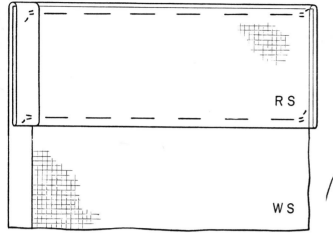

122 Fold over the first turning depth again and tack along the top and lower edges of the hem

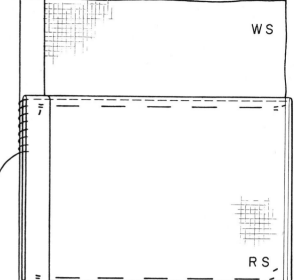

124 If the selvedge has been used at the sides, finish the curtain hem by oversewing

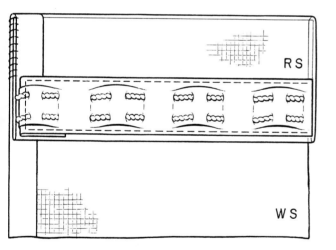

123 The finished heading, showing the oversewing of the edge above the tape

Adjusting and hanging the curtain

The fullness is adjusted on the cords in the usual way. *Nylon R5* or plastic *R4* or *R8* hooks are used when hanging the curtains from a track.

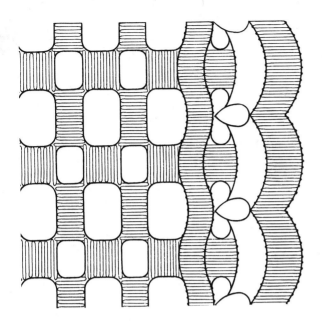

125 *(left)* A cotton vision net with a ready-made, decorative side edge finish

126 *(below)* A *Terylene* vision net showing the fold lines carefully planned to bring the holes on top of one another when the hem is made

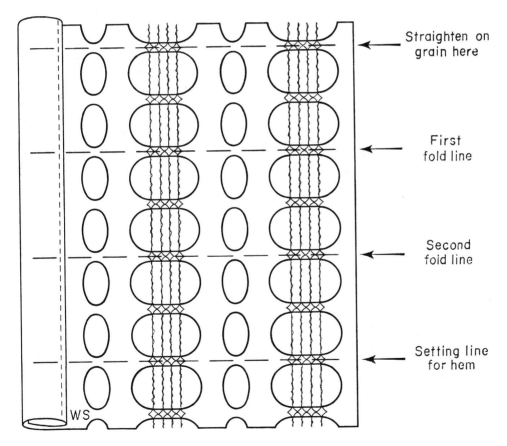

Straighten on grain here

First fold line

Second fold line

Setting line for hem

WS

140

Calculating quantities:
Length   Measure as for ordinary curtains, that is from the suspension point to the desired length position, either sill, apron or floor length. As short nets are made in specific lengths, the measurement must be compared with those available and the nearest measurement bought. If this proves to be difficult, the alternative is to buy the next longest length to the window measurement and remake the casing at the top, after shortening the curtain the necessary amount.

Width   Measure the length of the curtain fitment and multiply this measurement by the desired amount of fullness. The amount required for finishing the side edges will not exceed 50 mm (2 in.). An adequately full curtain will supply this amount, and it need not be considered in the width calculations.

Construction

As these nets are usually bought with a ready-made heading, the side hems cannot be made without some preliminary preparation. The heading must be unpicked for 100 mm to 128 mm (4 in. to 5 in.) at each end to free the fabric, so that a 12 mm (½ in.) solid hem can be made down each side of the curtain. (See page 137). When the side hems are finished the heading can be reset and stitched back in place. It will now be possible to insert a rod, or plastic covered wire, for hanging the curtain.

When calculating the length for cotton vision nets, it is wise to allow for a deeper hem than is required for non-shrink fabrics. This is to provide a shrinkage allowance. Solid hems are necessary on vision nets, so there must be adequate fabric allowed, in the first instance, to provide for another solid hem to be made when letting down the curtain if it shrinks in washing.

Vision nets are made in a similar way to long nets, and may be finished with a casing or a ruched heading. However, it is best to study closely the construction of the net so that it can be used to the best advantage.

Some vision nets have a narrow hem down the sides when bought, but this is usually of a poor finish. If there is an adequate width of close mesh fabric at the sides, this ready-made hem is best trimmed off and a new, solid hem made. Make the new hem as for sheer nets on page 137. If, on the other hand, the vision net has a ready-made, decorative side edge treatment, this can be used as it is. See *figure 125 opposite*.

When preparing the heading and the hem, it may be found that the measurements stated for long nets need adjusting, so that the stitching can come along a firmer part of the mesh, and not across the holes, thus giving a more secure finish. See *figure 126 opposite*.

Most of the heading finishes previously described can be used with these fabrics. The choice will be governed mainly by the method of suspension which is to be used. If the curtains are to be subsidiary to the main curtains, a tall heading is not required. *Rufflette Evenpleat* tape is a good choice as it gives a narrow, well-controlled finish, but use a shallow heading as there is no support apart from the tape and, therefore, a wide heading would not stand upright.

A *Rufflette standard* tape can be used, but the fullness is less precisely controlled. If a standard tape is to be used, nylon or *Tergal* tapes are best with the acrylic fabrics, as they have related properties.

If semi-sheer curtains are to form the main curtaining, a tall heading is effective. *Hi-Style*, *Regis* and *Tervoil 60* tapes are all suitable, and give a similar finished effect. *Hi-Style* being a cotton tape, may not be as satisfactory in this case as *Regis* and *Tervoil 60*. The nylon reinforcement in *Regis* tape provides a good support for light-weight fabrics. *Tervoil 60*, which is made from nylon and *Terylene*, offers properties which are compatible with semi-sheer acrylic fabrics and is specially suitable for these. A deep pleated heading is not a good choice, as semi-sheer fabrics are too loosely woven to form attractive pleats.

Calculating quantities:

Length   Measure as for ordinary curtains, that is, from the suspension point to the desired length. It is wise to use a solid heading for all semi-sheer fabrics to mask the tape. This will mean that the top raw edge, when folded over, will reach the base of the tape, thus giving a double layer of fabric in this area. Having chosen the style, add the applicable heading allowance onto the length measurement.

Heading allowances

a *Standard and Evenpleat tapes* Both these tapes are 25 mm (1 in.) wide. Allow twice times the heading (that is the projection above the tape), plus the width of the tape. The following table gives some guidance:

For a

6 mm ($\frac{1}{4}$ in.) projection, allow 38 mm ($1\frac{1}{2}$ in.)
12 mm ($\frac{1}{2}$ in.)   50 mm (2 in.)
20 mm ($\frac{3}{4}$ in.)   65 mm ($2\frac{1}{2}$ in.)
25 mm (1 in.)   75 mm (3 in.)

b *Hi-Style tape* For the normal setting (that is with tape set flush with the top edge of the curtain), the depth from the suspension point to the top of the curtain tape is 38 mm ($1\frac{1}{2}$in.). Add the width of the tape, 75 mm (3in.). Therefore the allowance is 113 mm ($4\frac{1}{2}$ in.).

For a deeper setting, take twice the projection above the tape, plus the above allowances.
EXAMPLE   a 12 mm ($\frac{1}{2}$ in.) projection requires a heading allowance of 140 mm ($5\frac{1}{2}$ in.).

c *Regis tape* As the pockets can be set either at the top or at the lower edge of the tape to suit the fixing of the track, it is unnecessary to make a deeper heading for this purpose. Therefore always set the tape flush with the top edge of the curtain for semi-sheer fabrics.

For a top fixed track, use the tape with the pockets at the top. From the suspension point to the top of the tape the depth is 10 mm ($\frac{3}{8}$in.), add the width of the tape, 72 mm ($2\frac{7}{8}$in.). Therefore the heading allowance is 82 mm ($3\frac{1}{4}$ in.).

For a face fixed track use the tape with the pockets at the lower edge. From the suspension point to the top of the tape the depth is 50 mm (2 in.), add the width of the tape, 72 mm ($2\frac{7}{8}$ in.). Therefore the heading allowance is 122 mm ($4\frac{7}{8}$ in.).

d *Tervoil 60 tape* For a top fixed track, use the tape with the pockets at the top. From the suspension point to the top of the tape the depth is 15 mm ($\frac{5}{8}$ in.), add the width of the tape, 70 mm ($2\frac{3}{4}$ in.). Therefore the heading allowance is 85 mm ($3\frac{3}{8}$ in.).

For a face fixed track, use the tape with the pockets at the lower edge. From the suspension point to the top of the tape the depth is 35 mm

($1\frac{3}{8}$ in.), add the width of the tape, 70 mm ($2\frac{3}{4}$ in.). Therefore the heading allowance is 105 mm ($4\frac{1}{8}$ in.).

Having worked out the necessary heading allowance, add twice the finished hem depth to estimate the total length required. The hem depth will depend on the weave of the fabric, as it is important that the edge of the hem lies on a firmer part of the weave, in order to have a foundation for stitching the hem. This can only be assessed when the repeat of the weave forming the pattern is known.

Width Measure the length of the fitment, or track, and multiply this measurement by the amount of fullness required. It is unwise to attempt to split a width of fabric, as semi-sheer fabrics are not easily joined, and joins would spoil the overall effect in any case. If the measurement exceeds the buyable width, it is wiser to have more, or less fullness, whichever measurement is nearer to the one taken.

To find the required meterage (yardage), multiply the total length by the number of widths.

Semi-sheer fabrics often have a striped or checked pattern formed by the weave. This should be studied carefully as it is not always immediately noticeable, and it may be necessary to buy extra fabric to balance the stripes or checks across the width. (Refer to the matching of patterns, pages 67–68.)

Construction

As it is unwise to attempt to join half, or full widths, each width should be made up as a separate curtain. If two widths are required for one side of the window, this will not be obvious when the curtains are hung. The light-weight fabric, and the additional fullness, will cause the two free edges to fall into one another and be concealed by the drape of the curtains.

1 Side edges If the selvedge is good, this can be used for the side edge finish. Occasionally a good selvedge does not give a pleasing finish to the edge of the curtain. In this case a single fold can be made to improve the appearance. The width of the turning varies from fabric to fabric. It is important that the edge of the selvedge lies on a firmer part of the fabric weave, to provide a foundation for sewing the turning. Hand-sewing gives a better result than machining as the tension and size of the stitches can be adjusted continuously to suit the irregularities of the fabric weave. In many cases, too, the weave of a semi-sheer fabric is too open to allow for successful machining. However, slip-hemming cannot be used because of the single turning of fabric and the irregular spacing of the weave.

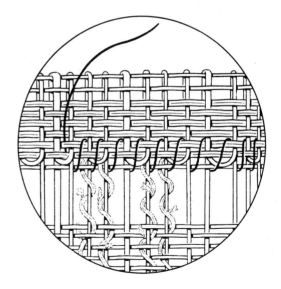

127 Hemming into the weave of the fabric to hold down the turned selvedge edge. In this case the spaces come between the warp threads

Because of the necessary way of sewing the selvedge, it is essential that the sewing thread matches the colour of the warp threads in this area, so that it is inconspicuous.

Although not generally recommended, a very poor selvedge will have to be trimmed off and a solid hem made. The width of the hem must be chosen to suit the fabric, and should allow for the fold line to lie on a foundation of threads to assist in sewing the hem. The hem is stitched as for a turned over selvedge.

2 Heading Turn over the top raw edge, along the fabric grain, for the depth suggested for the style chosen. Apply the tape as previously described, with the lower edge of the tape just covering the raw edge of the heading turning.

a Standard and *Evenpleat* tapes   The following table gives some guidance:

For a

6 mm ($\frac{1}{4}$ in.) projection turn over	32 mm ($1\frac{1}{4}$ in.)
12 mm ($\frac{1}{2}$ in.)	38 mm ($1\frac{1}{2}$ in.)
20 mm ($\frac{3}{4}$ in.)	45 mm ($1\frac{3}{4}$ in.)
25 mm (1 in.)	50 mm (2 in.)

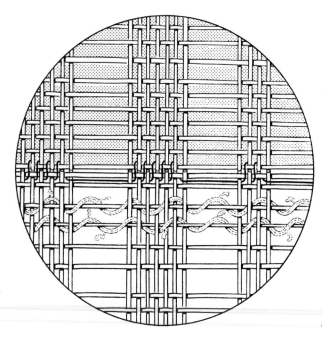

b Hi-Style tape   For a normal setting, turn over 75 mm (3 in.). For a deeper setting, turn over the amount of the projection plus the width of the tape, ie 75 mm (3 in.).

c Regis tape   Turn over the width of the tape, ie 72 mm ($2\frac{7}{8}$ in.).

Careful tacking is essential to keep the fabric on grain, and it is wise to tack close to the fold, and again near the raw edge of the turning. Machining is best worked from the right side so that the grain can be followed. If the tape is tacked in place fairly close to the edge, the machining can be worked just inside the line of tacking to ensure that the tape is held in position. To prevent turning the work, thus causing the bulk of the curtain to pass under the arm of the machine, it will be easier to stitch two separate rows of machining. The sides of the tape can be finished by hand. Either oversew the side folds of the tape to the selvedge, or hem them onto the turning or hem, remembering to leave one side open if a cord tidy is not to be used.

3 Lower Hem This is assessed and turned as for an unlined curtain, but always with an equal width first and second turning. Care should be taken to ensure that there is a foundation of fabric threads near the hem fold to facilitate the stitching, (*figure 128*).

Occasionally the weave is arranged in the opposite way, with the spaces coming between the weft threads. The procedure for stitching the selvedge and hem will have to be reversed.

128   Showing hemming where there is density of weave, and a loose thread stranded across the spaces

Cushions form one of the accessories in an interior décor scheme and, therefore, are usually one of the last things to be considered when planning a room. Cushions supply physical comfort by supporting parts of the body, and visual comfort by being decorative in appearance. They can be used to give just the right touch of colour, pattern or texture that a scheme may lack. A warm, vibrant scheme can be softened and cooled by the right choice of colour for the cushions. A cool scheme can be warmed and enriched by choosing the right contrast in colour. An inconspicuous chair can be made more noticeable by the correct choice of fabric for the cushion.

Patterned fabric, or the pattern supplied by embroidery, may be used for cushions, but with discrimination. Existing pattern in the scheme should be studied before further pattern is added. Otherwise the scheme will become disjointed and restless. If more pattern is suitable, and the curtain fabric is patterned, it will be better to use this for the cushion rather than introduce an additional pattern. As already mentioned in the section on pattern, geometric patterns can be mixed more easily than the naturalistic ones. A design motif should be centralised on a cushion and, if more than one cushion is to be made, the motifs should be centralised on each cushion so that they have a balanced appearance. Even if different design motifs are selected, they should be centralised, and the shape of each cushion related to its own design.

The texture of the fabric is also an important consideration. For example, a satin fabric would be out of keeping for a cushion to be used on a tweed covered chair. It would, however, be suitable for a velvet covered chair as it would enhance the already existing sheen. A warm colour and matt, slubbed fabric can be combined in the cushion cover to add warmth to the cold appearance given by leather and vinyl upholstery.

Making cushions at home can be an economical outlet for originality and creativity. Ready-made cushions are expensive to buy, and it is often difficult to find the exact requirement of colour, texture and pattern to suit the room.

Cushions can be divided into three main types: scatter cushions, shallow seat-pads and boxed cushions. Whatever the type, cushions often attract notice and, therefore, should be made with careful attention to detail.

The equipment required for curtain making is used with some additions. A pencil, ruler and paper will be required for pattern making. Carbon paper and a tracing wheel can be used for marking fitting lines on inner covers. A Stanley knife may be useful if a pad needs special shaping. A zipper or cording foot for the machine is necessary for making a piped cushion.

Cushions can be of varied size and shape according to their purpose. They may be as small as 305 mm × 305 mm (12 in. × 12 in.) for scatter cushions, or as large as 610 mm × 965 mm (24 in. × 38 in.) for boxed cushions. Measurements vary although scatter cushions do not generally exceed 457 mm (18 in.). The furniture will usually dictate the size of shallow seat-pads and boxed cushions, although boxed cushions used as floor seating are currently popular.

The shape of a scatter cushion is largely a matter of taste, but the furniture will obviously dictate the shape of a pad or boxed cushion.

FILLINGS

The purpose of a cushion will generally govern the choice of filling. A scatter cushion requires a soft filling whereas a boxed cushion needs a firm pad. Down and feathers are declining in popularity because of the introduction of synthetic fillings. Feathers are cheaper to buy than down so are more often used for cushions, but the choice of the inner cover is important as it must be feather-proof. Feathers offer a light, resilient filling which will retain the shape of the cushion after use. Kapok, one of the seed fibres, has been used for some time as a filling, but, although soft and light in weight, it has the disadvantage of lumping in use. However, although it is not generally recommended, it is an inexpensive filling and can be used for cushions which are essentially decorative. Unlike feathers, it does not work through fabric, so cheaper coverings may be used. *Terylene* fibre filling is now more readily available on the retail market. It is light in weight, soft, non-absorbent, resilient and washable. It is more expensive than kapok, but its properties compensate for this. It is often used for pillow fillings. Chips and crumbles made from Latex and plastic foam are inexpensive but not as satisfactory as *Terylene* filling as they tend to give a lumpy finish to the cushion. However, they are adequate for children's fun cushions.

Latex and plastic foam pads are suitable for boxed cushions and can be reversed in use. They are obtainable in square, rectangular and round shapes, and can be cut to irregular shapes if required. *Dunlopillo* is also frequently used for boxed cushions. Its structure does not allow for the reversing of the cushion in use, but it retains its shape very satisfactorily. A limited range of shapes and sizes is available, but they can sometimes be supplied to fit a special piece of furniture, eg *Ercol* dining chairs. Whatever type of pad is used for a boxed cushion, the inner cover must be closely fitting to give a professional result.

THE INNER COVER

It is usually wise to make the cover removable for laundry or dry-cleaning purposes. Because of this, the filling used for the cushion needs an inner cover to contain it. This may be made from featherproof ticking or cambric, calico, sheeting or remnants of dress fabric. Down-proof cambric should be used for down, featherproof ticking for feathers, and it is wise to use a drip-dry fabric for *Terylene* fibre, foam chips and crumbles if the cushion is to be washed. Care should be taken when using dress remnants as strongly coloured and patterned fabrics may show through the outer cover.

THE OUTER COVER

This need not be a furnishing fabric. Dress fabrics can be used, and often provide a more subtle range of colours. When choosing fabrics for scatter cushions, there is no real limit, except that it is best to choose a crease resistant fabric and one which will wear well. A non-transparent fabric should be used, unless the cover is to be interlined. Pads and boxed cushions, however, need a strong, evenly woven fabric, as well as one that is crease resistant. If the cushion is to be piped, slubs in the weave of the fabric will cause irregularities in the piping, and a loosely woven fabric will reveal the piping cord.

When preparing the pattern for a cushion to fit a specific piece of furniture, it may be found that two opposite sides of the seat are not quite evenly matched, as one edge of the seat may not follow exactly the same curve or slope as its opposite edge. This will necessitate cutting the cushion with these two edges not equally balanced to the fabric grain. In this case it is unwise to choose a striped or patterned fabric, or one with a very clearly defined grain, as this would emphasise the lack of balance.

For all types of cushion, a fabric which can be laundered at home is convenient, and a drip-dry, minimum-iron fabric obviously will be an advantage as it will save labour.

It is necessary to have an opening in all cushion covers, but the opening need not always be made with a permanent means of fastening. In some cases the opening may be slip-stitched, and appear to be part of the seam in which it is placed. This is the simplest opening to handle, and is a suitable treatment for covers which do not require frequent laundering. It is particularly suitable for circular scatter cushions, as it is difficult to make an opening with fastenings in a circular shape, and the opening may distort the shape if attempted. This opening can be unpicked to allow the cover to be laundered without the pad.

When an opening with a permanent fastening is required, extra fabric is provided for it by extending the width of the seam turning in the opening area. This type of opening is suitable for scatter cushions which have at least one straight edge, and is best fastened with press studs or hooks and bars. When the opening is left in a seam, zips, although fairly expensive, form a useful fastening. A zip closure can be used on both scatter and boxed cushions and is, in fact, the best form of opening for boxed cushions.

If a shallow seat-pad or boxed cushion is made to be tied onto a chair or stool, a wrap and facing opening on the under section is a good choice because it is flat. This is best fastened with press fasteners.

The position of the opening is important, and the least conspicuous place in the cushion cover should be chosen. This will be determined by the purpose of the cushion.

The opening should be long enough for the pad to be inserted and removed easily. Too short an opening will cause undue strain on the cover, particularly at the ends of the opening. Suggested opening lengths are given for the various styles of cushion.

These are the simplest cushions that can be made. They do not involve difficult openings and fastenings, and can be attempted by an inexperienced needlewoman. Scatter cushions are based on geometric shapes, and can be square, rectangular, triangular or circular in shape.

Making the patterns

Nett patterns are made, ie ones without turnings. These can be allowed when cutting .out, which simplifies the marking of the fitting lines close to the pattern edge. Use brown paper for the patterns, or any other clean, strong paper. Decide on the size of the cushion and make sure that the paper is big enough for the size of cushion required.

The triangle

Fold the paper in half.

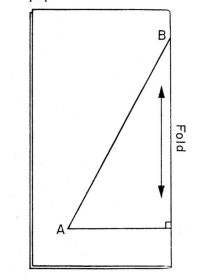

129   At right angles to the fold, measure half the base measurement to point A. Join A to the fold. Mark B on the fold for the required measurement. Join AB. Mark a grain line parallel to the fold

Cut along the two lines but do not cut the fold. Open out the pattern and press lightly.

The circle

Fold the paper in four and mark a point A at the folded corner. Mark off points at regular intervals from A, making them equal to the radius of the required circle.

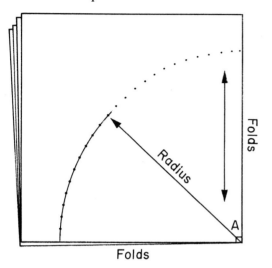

Folds

130 Link these points to form a smooth curve, thus forming a quarter of the circle. Mark a straight grain line parallel to one folded edge

Hold the pattern firmly on the table with one hand, and cut along the marked curve through the four thicknesses of paper. The pattern will open out to a full circle. Press lightly to remove the fold lines.

The inner cover

An inner cover is essential for a cushion with a constructed opening, but it is not as important for a cushion made by the quick method. However, it is better to have a container for the filling as it improves the shape and the cover can be replaced eventually by a new one without having to handle the filling. If an inner cover is not used, both the fabric and the filling should be drip-dry.

For a well-shaped cushion, the inner cover needs to be 6 mm ($\frac{1}{4}$ in.) bigger all round than the cushion.

Press the inner cover fabric and straighten

one weft edge. Fold the fabric in half with the fold parallel to the selvedge and with the weft threads in alignment.

For a square or rectangular cushion, mark out the fitting lines of the shape using tailor's chalk. Keep the chalk lines in line with the fabric grain and mark the shapes 12 mm ($\frac{1}{2}$ in.) larger than the desired finished size. Allow 15 mm ($\frac{5}{8}$ in.) turnings all round. These can be marked with chalk outside the fitting lines, and give a guide for accurate cutting.

For triangular or circular cushions, pin the outer cover pattern onto the fabric with the grain line parallel to the selvedge. Mark the fitting lines with tailor's chalk 6 mm ($\frac{1}{4}$ in.) outside the edge of the pattern. Then mark a 15 mm ($\frac{5}{8}$ in.) turning allowance outside the fitting lines. Cut out the inner cover and unpin the pattern.

Construction

Keep the two pieces of fabric together, as cut out, so that the grain is aligned. Pin, then tack round the marked fitting lines, leaving approximately 150 mm (6 in.) open in the centre of one straight side, or in part of the circumference of a circle.

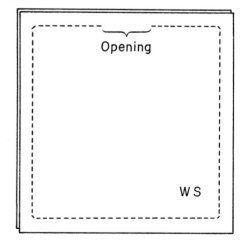

131 Machine on the fitting line. At each corner, turn the fabric on the machine needle, make a stitch diagonally across the corner, turn the fabric on the needle again, and proceed along the next side. This gives a good final shaping to the corner

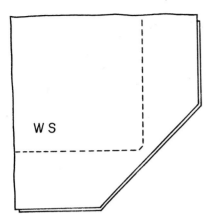

132 Trim off the corners of the square, rectangular and triangular shapes to within 3 mm ($\frac{1}{8}$ in.) of the stitching to reduce bulk

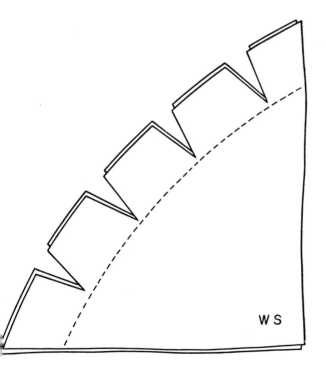

133 On a circular cover, notch the turning allowance as far as the fitting line at 25 mm (1 in.) intervals

The turnings are notched by cutting away V-shaped sections of fabric. This is done when the turnings have to lie, finally, within a smaller area than their original size. The notches allow the turnings to close in and lie flat without giving bulk to the finished edge.

At the opening, fold the turning allowance to the wrong side on the fitting lines and tack in place. Turn the cover to the right side, pushing it out well along the seam line, and press to set the shape. Stuff with a suitable stuffing, being careful to use enough, but not too much.

Pin and then tack the two prepared edges of the opening together and slip-stitch securely in place. Remove the tacking threads, and the pad is ready for use.

The outer cover

When using patterned fabric, it is best to cut out the two sides of the cushion separately so that the design motif can be seen and balanced more easily.

If the cushion is to be made without an inner cover, follow the directions for making the inner cover, but use the required finished measurements of the cushion. Unless the fabric frays badly, it is unnecessary to neaten the raw edges as they will be permanently enclosed.

When making a cover to be used over an inner cover, follow the directions for the inner cover, but use the required finished measurements of the cushion. Allow 20 mm ($\frac{3}{4}$ in.) turnings and leave a larger opening to allow the pad to be inserted easily. The size of the opening will depend on the size of the cushion. On a square cushion leave almost the whole of one side open, beginning and finishing the stitching 25 mm (1 in.) from the corners on the opening side. This prevents straining the corners when the pad is inserted. The base of a triangle, and one short side of a rectangle are treated in the same way. On a circular cushion leave a quarter of the circumference measurement open.

As the cover will be removed for laundering or dry-cleaning, it is wise to neaten the raw edges by zigzagging on a swing-needle machine, or overcasting by hand.

Insert the pad and close the opening as for the inner cover. This stitching will have to be unpicked to remove the cover for washing. Therefore it should not be so secure that unpicking is impossible, although it must be neat and strong for satisfactory use.

Openings with fastenings

Extended turning opening with press fasteners　This opening is suitable for cushions with at least one straight side, and is fastened with press fasteners or hooks and bars. It is not suitable for use on thick fabrics as it would be too bulky.

It is helpful to make a pattern for the cushion so that the correct extensions are allowed.

Draw out the required shape on suitable paper, drawing accurately the right-angled corners of a square or rectangular cushion, and the angled corners of a triangular cushion. The opening is placed on one side of a square, on one short side of a rectangle, and on the base of a triangle.

134 The fitting line indicates the finished edge of the cushion. The width of the extension allowance is shown outside the fitting line. The straight grain is at right-angles to the opening

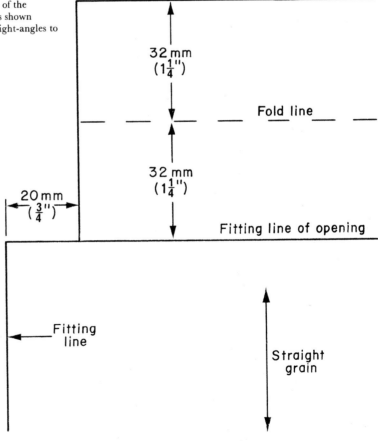

32 mm
$(1\frac{1}{4}")$

Fold line

32 mm
$(1\frac{1}{4}")$

20 mm
$(\frac{3}{4}")$

Fitting line of opening

Fitting line

Straight grain

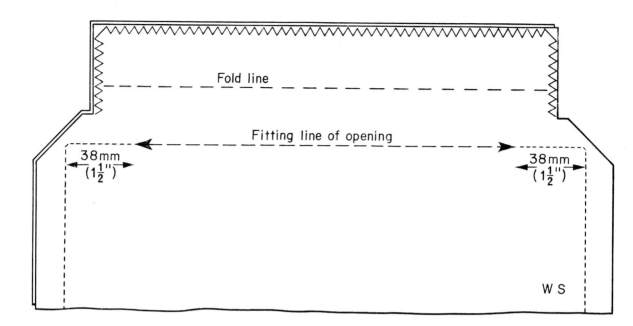

Fold line

Fitting line of opening

38mm
$(1\frac{1}{2}")$

38mm
$(1\frac{1}{2}")$

W S

135a *(above)* If selvedge edges have not been used, neaten the raw edges of the extension separately, using either machine zigzagging or hand overcasting. Trim off the corners of fabric

135b *(below)* On one side fold over the extension edge to the wrong side, so that it meets the fitting line of the opening. Tack close to the fold and again just above the lower edge. Machine close to the fold to hold it flat

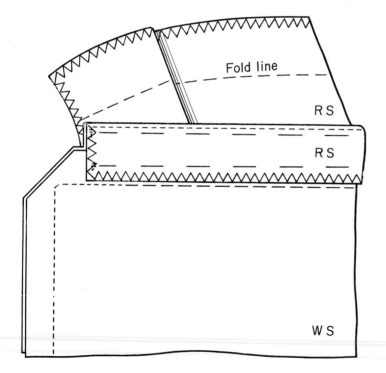

Fold line

R S

R S

W S

Prepare the fabric and pin on the pattern as previously described. On plain fabrics the grain line may be placed on the weft grain, and the edge of the extension along the selvedge. This will save neatening this edge at a later stage. Mark the turning allowance round the edge of the cushion, beginning and finishing at the opening extension. No turnings are required on the extension. Cut out, and mark the fitting lines all round the edge of the cushion, including the opening position.

Construction

With the right sides together, pin and tack along the fitting lines, beginning and finishing 38 mm (1½ in.) in from the corners on the opening side. Machine along the tacked fitting lines. See *figures 135a and b opposite.*

Prepare the second side of the opening in the same way. See *figure 136 below.*

Neaten any fraying edges. Sew on the press fasteners, or hooks and bars, at approximately 38 mm (1½ in.) intervals along the opening. Sew them close to the fitting lines, and stitch through the double thickness of the opening extensions.

136   To hold the extension in place, tack and machine the two prepared edges together from A to B

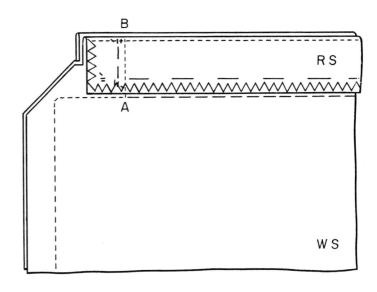

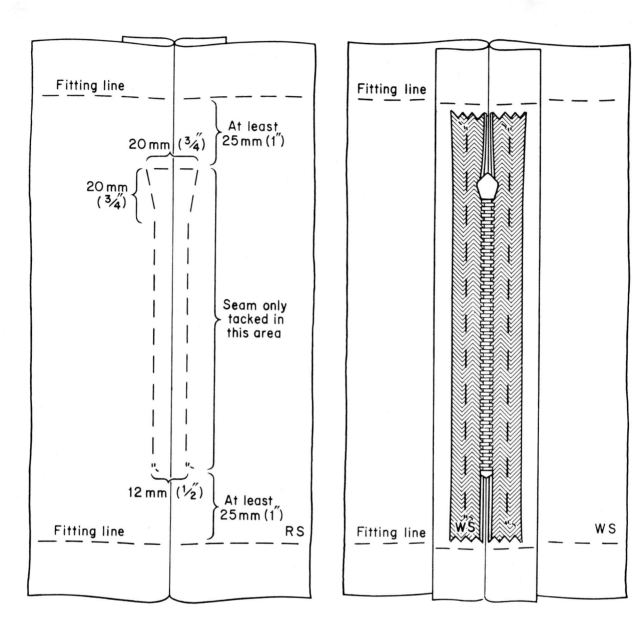

Fitting line

At least
20 mm (¾″) 25 mm (1″)

20 mm
(¾″)

Seam only
tacked in
this area

12 mm (½″)

At least
25 mm (1″)

Fitting line   R S

Fitting line

Fitting line   W S   W S

137a   Working on the right side, and with a contrasting
thread, tack the turnings in place 6 mm (¼ in.) either side of
the opening fitting line. This is to guide the final machining.
Shape one end as shown, to accommodate the zip slide when
the zip is set

137b   Place the right side of the zip to the wrong side of the
opening with the slide at the specially shaped end. The centre
of the zip must come exactly over the opening fitting line. Pin,
and then tack the zip in position, using a different coloured
tacking thread. Take the stitches through to the right side

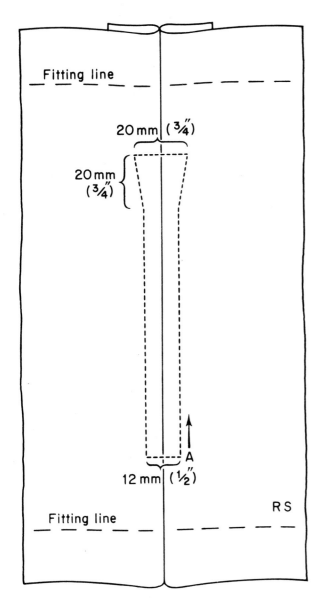

Fitting line

20 mm (¾")

20 mm (¾")

12 mm (½")

A

R S

Fitting line

137c Using a piping foot on the machine, stitch on the right side along the guide tacking line, beginning at point A and working in the direction of the arrow

Scatter cushion with zip fastened opening

Cut out the two sections of the cover and mark the fitting lines as before. Refer to page 150 for the length of the opening, and mark its position on the cover. Pin and tack along the fitting lines on either side of the opening. This makes two short seams on the opening side of the cover; the remaining sides are left open until after the zip is set. Using running stitches and a contrasting thread, join the fabric together along the fitting lines of the opening. Strong stitching is necessary as there is strain on it when the zip is machined in position.

Machine the seam on either side of the opening, but do not stitch beyond the corners. Press open the turnings, including the opening area. See *figures 137a, b and c.*

Remove the tacking and the running stitches down the seam fitting line to free the zip for use. Neaten the wrong side by joining the zip tape to the turning allowance either by machine zigzagging or by hemming.

Open the zip. Smooth the two right sides of the cover together and pin and tack along the remaining fitting lines. Begin machining 20 mm ($\frac{3}{4}$ in.) from one corner on the opening side. Turn the corner and machine round the cushion, continuing the machining for 20 mm ($\frac{3}{4}$ in.) beyond the last corner. This will make a double row of machining to strengthen the first and last corners. Trim off the corners as previously described, and neaten the raw edges. Turn the cover to the right side and press to set the shape. Insert the pad and close the zip.

Setting an Alcozip within a seam

1 Tack mark the fitting lines of the seam.
2 Tack the seam together, beginning at the top position for the zip and continuing on below the zip area.
3 Press the tacked seam flat, giving particular attention to the zip area.
4 Study the sewing-in instructions given with the zip, and follow them for setting the zip and for stitching the seam below the zip. It is

155

important to begin sewing the zip level with the top stop A.

5   Remove all tacking stitches.

6   Close the zip, then pin and tack together the seam fitting lines above the top stop of the fastener.

7   Open the zip and insert the tacked seam into the machine, still using the zipper foot.

8   Lower the needle carefully, setting it into the top of the machine stitch made at top stop A in the first place. Check that the two tapes will not get caught into the stitching.

9   Machine the seam along the fitting line and remove the tacking stitches.

10   Close the zip to check that the last line of machining has not impeded its full closure. If necessary, unpick the first one or two stitches of the seam, but do not cut the threads.

11   Knot the two machine thread ends tightly together, thread them into a needle, and sew them in securely.

12   Press the seam open flat.

Open the zip and make up the cushion as described on page 155.

PIPING

Piping gives a neat, tailored finish to seams on some articles of soft furnishing, eg the edges of scatter cushions, seat pads and boxed cushions. It is made by covering cord or twine with strips of cross-cut fabric. An edging of 6 mm to 12 mm ($\frac{1}{4}$ in. to $\frac{1}{2}$ in.) can be made from self or contrasting fabric, but if the latter, it should be similar in weight and fibre content to the main fabric for purposes of wear and cleaning or washing.

Preparing crossway strips

As no straight thread pulls along its length, the crossway of fabric is pliable and elastic. A strip of fabric cut parallel with the crossway will stretch sufficiently to lie in a smooth line along a curve, or turn a corner without puckering.

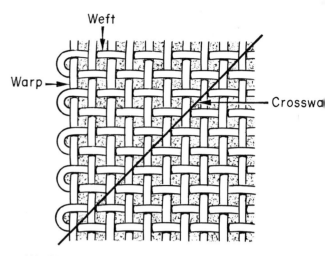

138   Magnified drawing, showing that the warp and weft threads meet at right angles along the crossway, which cuts across the grains with a diagonal slope

a   *Folding and cutting on the cross*

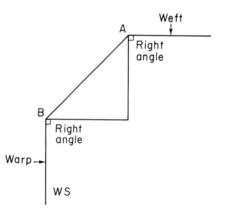

139   To obtain a crossway fold, take a straight warp edge, a selvedge is suitable, and fold it over so that it makes a right angle with itself and lies along a weft thread. Cut through the fold from A to B, pulling the blade of the scissors right up into the fold. This gives a straight, clean cut

b   *Cutting the strips*

As the strips stretch easily, they always tend to lose a little width with handling. It is wise, therefore, to cut them 6 mm ($\frac{1}{4}$ in.) wider than required.

156

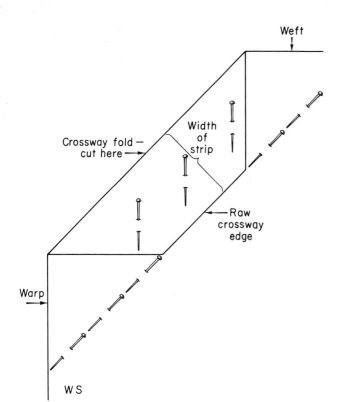

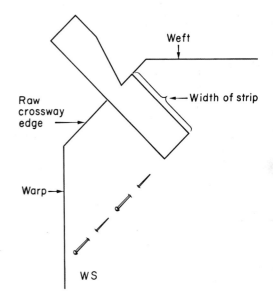

140a   Method 1. Fold over the newly cut crossway edge for the width required, and pin it in place. Mark the cutting line with pins beyond the edges of the raw crossway edge, to guide the cutting. Cut through the fold, and along the raw crossway edge, thus cutting two strips at once. Repeat this until the required number of strips has been cut

140b   Method 2. This method is useful for fabric which frays easily or is slippery. Measuring from the raw crossway edge, for the width of the strip, mark the cutting line with pins. Cut along this line, following it very accurately

c *Trimming the strips*

Each strip must be a perfect parallelogram. The long edges are cut parallel along the crossway of the fabric. The width edges must be trimmed with a straight grain so that they, too, are parallel Width edges always make satisfactory joins if trimmed with the warp grain, but there is no reason why they should not be trimmed with the weft grain providing it gives a flat, inconspicuous seam. A fabric with vertical stripes, however, should always be trimmed with the warp grain, and one with horizontal stripes with the weft. The important thing to remember is that all the joins must be made with the same grain throughout all strips prepared for use on any one article. If this is not done, the joins will be conspicuous, as they will vary in appearance according to the grain used.

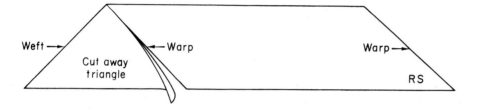

141a Place the strips right side up, pull out a warp or weft thread as a guide and cut along this line. Check the trimmed edge to ensure that it is straight with the grain

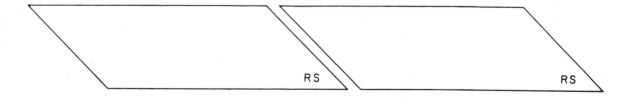

141b When the width edges have been trimmed, the strips will fit together into a straight line, with all warp or weft edges parallel

d *Joining the strips*

Place the right sides of the strips together with the width edges level, but allow the sharp points to project at each end to give a turning width of 10 mm to 12 mm ($\frac{3}{8}$ in. to $\frac{1}{2}$ in.) This width of turning is required because of the weight and fraying habit of furnishing fabrics. See *figure 142*.

Machine along the fitting line of the join, using a short stitch. This is necessary to give a strong join which will not open and allow the piping cord to show through. Remove the tacking threads and press the seam open. See *figure 143*.

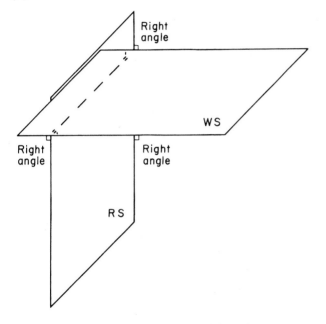

142 The fitting line runs between the two right angles formed by the two pointed projections. Pin and tack along the fitting line

The strips, prepared as described, have the warp and weft threads crossing each other at right angles along the length of the strips. This arrangement of the weave provides strips with the maximum stretchability which are, therefore, pliable to handle and will set readily round corners and curves.

When a sufficiently long strip has been made, rub a finger along the length to remove a little of the stretch. This will cause the strip to curl a little and will give a closer covering of the cord.

Unfortunately, in a few cases, the appearance of the fabric on the cross is unattractive, and spoils the look of the finished piping. This problem is particularly apparent with twill and some basket weaves. These weaves form a noticeable, diagonal line on the fabric which does not run in line with the crossway direction. On a close inspection of the fabric, this diagonal line will be seen to lie on the bias, that is, on a diagonal somewhere between the straight grain and the crossway. In this case, strips cut on the crossway will give an unprofessional look to the finished piping. Twill and basket weaves are more pliable than most weaves, and it is worth making a sample to see if the piping is successful with the strips cut on the bias, ie in line with the diagonal formed by the weave. If it does not set satisfactorily, it may be better to use a contrasting fabric for the piping, make a plain seam or edge the cushion with a bought trimming.

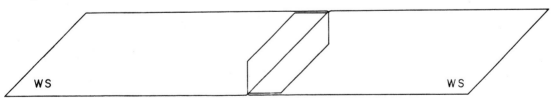

143 The finished join on the wrong side with turnings pressed open flat, and the protruding sharp points cut away. The join slopes across the strip in line with a fabric grain. If there are several joins in a strip, they must all be parallel

Piping cord

Cotton piping cord is available in a range of sizes, but sizes 2, 3 and 4 are the most suitable for cushion making. As this cord is made from cotton, it should be preshrunk by soaking it in water before use. An allowance should be made for this when calculating the length required, as it will shrink up to 75 mm per metre (3 in. per yard). Assess the length required accurately as it is unwise to make more than the final join in the cord. The length needed will be equal to the length of crossway strip after joining, and must be calculated with the shrinkage allowance in mind. Directions for calculating the quantity of piping required will be given with each style of cushion.

Preparing the piping

With the prepared crossway strip wrong side uppermost, place the cord in the centre of the strip. Fold the strip over the cord and set the top edge 3 mm ($\frac{1}{8}$ in.) above the lower edge to prevent bulk. Tack fairly close to the cord to hold it in position ready for machining. Replace the machine presser foot with a zipper or cording foot. See *figure 144*.

Do not stitch too closely to the cord at this stage as a further two rows of machining are worked before the piping is completely enclosed in the cushion seam. The two rows are worked progressively closer to the cord.

When the machining is finished, remove the tacking stitches except at the two ends which have not been machined. The piping is now ready to be applied. It is wise to mark the fitting lines on the cushion sections with tacking stitches to give an accurate guide for applying the piping.

PIPING SQUARE, RECTANGULAR OR TRIANGULAR SHAPES

Calculating quantities

Length of crossway strip   this equals the measurement of the perimeter of the shape plus
150 mm to 205 mm (6 in. to 8 in.) for ease
75 mm (3 in.) to use for the final join
20 mm to 25 mm ($\frac{3}{4}$ in. to 1 in.) for each additional join.

Crossway strips usually need joining to provide the full length required, but the positions of joins should be planned carefully. Avoid having a join near the two ends of an opening or near a corner.

The length of piping cord after shrinking, should equal the perimeter measurement plus the allowances given above for ease and the final join.

Width of crossway strip   this is equal to the circumference of the cord or twine, plus 2×15 mm ($\frac{5}{8}$ in.) for turnings. The width usually varies from 38 mm ($1\frac{1}{2}$ in.) to 50 mm (2 in.) according to the thickness of the cord.

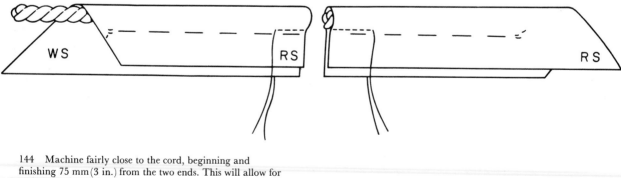

144   Machine fairly close to the cord, beginning and finishing 75 mm (3 in.) from the two ends. This will allow for accurate joining when the piping has been applied

Applying the piping

Set the prepared piping onto the right side of the upper section of the cover. Begin in the centre of one side, and lay the machined line of the piping strip over the cover fitting line, with the raw edges facing in the same direction. The piping crosses the opening as it is set along the fitting line.

Pin accurately along the fitting line, easing the piping slightly, to within 50 mm (2 in.) of the corner. Then allow more ease up to the corner point. This extra easing at the corner enables the piping to set well, with a sharp corner shaping, when the corner is finished and turned through to the right side. Without this ease, the finished corner becomes rounded instead of squared. See *figure 145*.

Begin 75 mm (3 in.) from the end of the piping and tack it in place up to this point, so that the end of the piping is left free for making the final join. Turn the piping round the corner, giving extra ease for 50 mm (2 in.). Continue to apply the piping with a little ease to within 50 mm (2 in.) of the second corner. Give extra ease and snip the turnings of the piping as for the first corner. Tack the piping in place up to the second corner. Continue to ease, pin and tack the piping, and snip it at the remaining corners until arriving within 75 mm (3 in.) of the starting point. Remove the tacking from the ends of the piping to allow for making the final join. See *figure 146*.

Make the join as previously described and press it open flat

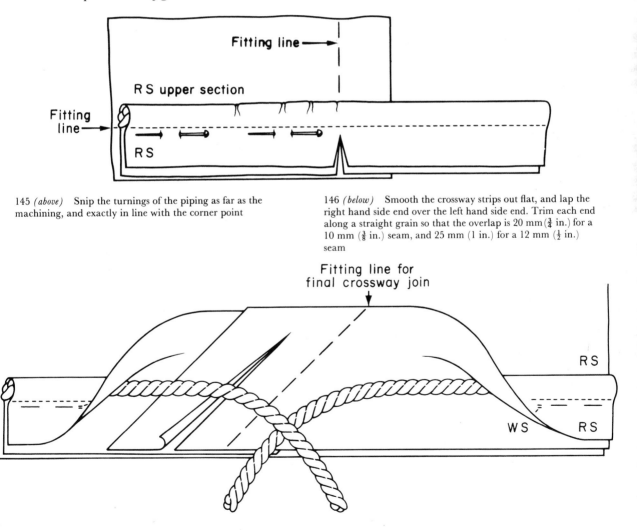

145 *(above)*   Snip the turnings of the piping as far as the machining, and exactly in line with the corner point

146 *(below)*   Smooth the crossway strips out flat, and lap the right hand side end over the left hand side end. Trim each end along a straight grain so that the overlap is 20 mm (¾ in.) for a 10 mm (⅜ in.) seam, and 25 mm (1 in.) for a 12 mm (½ in.) seam

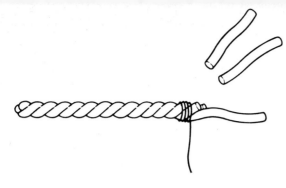

147a   25 mm (1 in) in from each end of the cord, wrap and secure a length of thread, but leave the ends hanging. Cut two strands of cord from one end and one strand from the other end

147b   Splice the three remaining cords and wind first one thread and then the other round the join to hold it firmly in place. Fasten off the threads securely

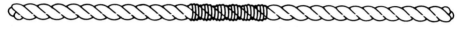

Joining the cord

Arrange for the cord join to come under the seam in the crossway strip. This will make the piping smoother in finish, as the turnings of the crossway seam will compensate for the slight loss in thickness which the join causes in the cord.

Cut the cord ends so that they overlap for 25 mm (1 in), arranging the centre of the overlap in line with the centre of the crossway seam.

See *figures 147a and b* then *148 and 149*.

This position of the machining will make the cover slightly smaller than the pad, and will ensure a good fit on a seat-pad and on a boxed cushion. On a scatter cushion the width of the piping will compensate for the slight loss in size.

Trim the piping turnings narrower than the cover turnings, layering them to reduce bulk.

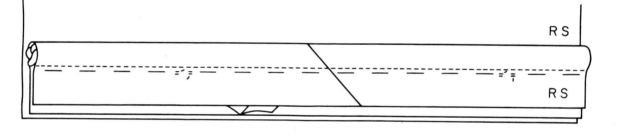

148 *(above)*   Fold the crossway over the join and finish the stitching to enclose the cord. Pin and tack the piping onto the cover across the final join

149 *(right)*   Machine the piping in place, stitching just inside the machining which is holding the cord within the crossway. Begin machining in the centre of a side

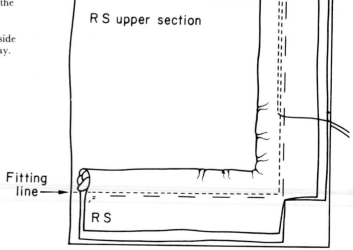

PIPING A CIRCULAR SHAPE

Calculating quantities

Length of crossway strip: this equals the measurement round the circumference of the circle plus 100 mm (4 in.) for ease
plus 75 mm (3 in.) to use for the final join
plus 25 mm (1 in.) for each additional join.

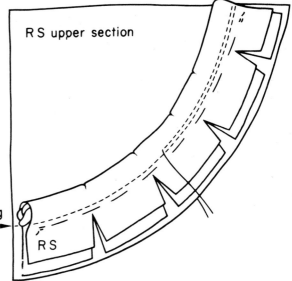

150   Machine the piping in place stitching just inside the machining which is holding the cord within the crossway

To prevent bulk, arrange for the crossway joins to come away from seams or the two side edges of an opening.

Width of crossway strips: as for square and rectangular shapes.

The length of piping cord after shrinking, should equal the circumference of the circle, plus the allowances given for ease and the final join. To ensure flat setting round the circular shape, the turnings of the piping must be prepared according to the style of cushion being made. For a scatter cushion notch the turnings, see page 149. For a boxed cushion the turnings are snipped. The snipping allows the turnings to open out and lie flat, during the first setting of the piping, while the piping turning has to lie flat on the turning of the circular shape. Finally the piping turnings are pressed onto the boxing,

and the snipping allows the turnings to close up and set smoothly inside the boxing.

Set the prepared piping onto the right side of the upper section of the cover. Begin clear of seam or opening. Snip or notch across the turnings of the piping at a point 75 mm (3 in.) in from one end, and begin setting it to the cover fitting line from this point. Continue snipping or notching the turnings at 25 mm (1 in.) intervals as the piping is applied. Ease the piping evenly round the circumference of the circle, but pin and tack in position as described in the previous section. The final join of the strip and the cord are made as shown in *figures 146, 147a and b*. Snip or notch the turnings across the final join and finish applying the piping as shown in *figure 148*. See *figure 150*.

If necessary, trim the piping turnings narrower than the cover turnings, to reduce bulk.

Inner curves require different handling as the curve decreases in size outside the fitting line. The turnings of the piping are always snipped.

151   The piping lying on the turning of the inner curve. When applying the piping, stretch it slightly in this case. Machine the piping to the upper section of the cover as already described

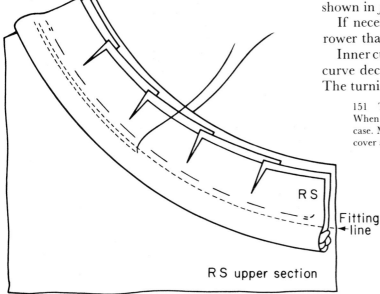

PIPED SCATTER CUSHION WITH A SLIP-STITCHED OPENING

The method used for applying the piping makes the cover 3 mm ($\frac{1}{8}$ in.) smaller all round. However, the piping on the right side will compensate for this loss of size. The pad should be made 3 mm ($\frac{1}{8}$ in.) larger all round instead of 6 mm ($\frac{1}{4}$ in.) larger as directed for the inner cover.

Decide on the shape and cut out, preparing the pad as for the plain scatter cushion on page 148, but with the above exception.

The outer cover

Cut out and mark the cover sections as for a plain cover, see page 150. It is also necessary to mark warp grain lines on square and circular shapes so that the two sections are in alignment when the cover is finished. This keeps uniformity in appearance and prevents twisting after washing or cleaning. On a square shape, choose the central warp line across each section and mark it with about 50 mm (2 in.) of tacking at either end. On a circular shape, mark the warp diameter in the same eay on each section.

Apply the piping to the upper section of the cover, following the directions which apply to the chosen shape. See pages 161–163.

Place the piped upper section of the cover, right side uppermost, on the table. With the wrong side uppermost, place the under section on top, matching the marked grain lines. Line up the fitting line of the under section with the row of machining which holds the cord in the piping. This places the two fitting lines together. Pin along this line to join the two sections, but tack just inside the line. This will place the tacking in line with the second row of machining worked, ie the row which shows on the wrong side of the upper section. This is an important stage, and should be carried out carefully to achieve an accurate result. Leave an opening in one side, or in part of the circumference of the circle, as directed for a plain cover on page 150.

Using a zipper or cording foot on the machine, place the cover in the machine with the wrong side of the upper section on top. Begin and finish the machining at the edge of the opening. See *figures 152a and b*.

152a and b   Machine the two sections together, stitching just inside the visible line of machining

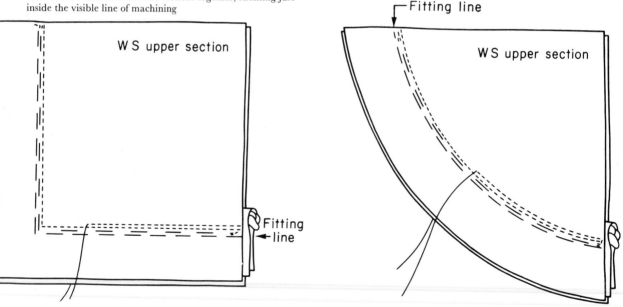

In all, three lines of machining are stitched into a piped seam.

1 to hold the cord into the crossway strip
2 to set the piping to the upper section of the cover, and
3 to join the two sections of the cover.

As each line of machining is worked, the stitching is set progressively closer to the cord, and slightly inside the fitting line. This gives a closely covered cord and a well-fitting cover. If this procedure is followed, it will ensure that no machining is visible on the right side of the cover.

When the machining is finished, trim off the corners of a square, rectangular and triangular shape as in *figure 153*. This is necessary to reduce bulk in the corners when the pad is turned right side out.

Neaten the turnings of the opening separately with machine zigzagging or overcasting by hand. Except for the opening area, join the cover turnings together with the chosen neatening stitch. This will enclose the turnings of the piping. On badly fraying fabric, strengthen the raw edges of the corners with loop or buttonhole stitch.

153 The corner trimmed

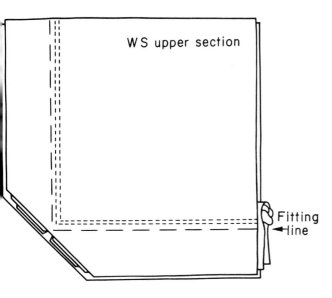

WS upper section

Fitting line

On a circular shape, the turnings of the cover should be notched after the piping turnings have been trimmed and before neatening is done.

On the under section, fold the turning allowance of the opening to the wrong side, so that the fold line is in line with the row of machine stitching joining the two sections together, and tack it in place. This will set the fold line approximately 3 mm ($\frac{1}{8}$ in.) inside the fitting line. Turn the cover to the right side and press to set the shape. Insert the pad and then set the prepared, folded edge of the opening so that it just overlaps the two rows of machining on the piping. Pin, tack and hem the folded edge in place.

Buttoned finish for a scatter cushion

Scatter cushions can be finished with buttons stitched in the centre of each side. One thread is used, and the buttons sewn simultaneously, thus pulling together the two sides of the cushion.

If a buttoned finish is desired, the button, the inner and outer cover fabrics and the filling, should all be washable. The whole cushion can then be laundered without removing the buttons.

An opening with a fastening is not required and the opening closed with slip-stitching is most suitable.

Mark the centre of the two sections before beginning to make the cushion. Cover two button moulds, using self or contrasting fabric. The size of the moulds varies from 20 mm to 25 mm ($\frac{3}{4}$ in. to 1 in.), depending on the size of the cushion.

'Trim' moulds are suitable and the directions for covering them are clearly set out on the card.

If a flatter finish is required, a cheap, plastic button can be covered as follows:

1 Measure the diameter of both the front and back of the button. Cut two circles of fabric, making one with a diameter 12 mm ($\frac{1}{2}$ in.) to 20 mm ($\frac{3}{4}$ in.) larger than the front measure-

ment, and the other with a diameter 6 mm ($\frac{1}{4}$ in.) to 12 mm ($\frac{1}{2}$ in.) larger than the back measurement, depending on the weight of the fabric.

2 Stitch a gathering thread 3 mm ($\frac{1}{8}$ in.) inside the raw edge of the larger circle. If liked a thin layer of wadding or thin Latex foam can be placed over the front of the button to give a softer finish. This may increase the size of the button and should be taken into consideration when cutting the front circle.

3 Place the front of the button in the centre of the wrong side of the larger circle, draw up the gathering thread tightly, and fasten it off securely.

4 Fold a 3 mm to 6 mm ($\frac{1}{8}$ in. to $\frac{1}{4}$ in.) turning to the wrong side of the smaller circle, tack it in place and press the prepared circle. Hem it in place, thus enclosing the raw edges of both circles.

When sewing on this type of button, stitch through the under fabric as there is not a shank. Use a long darning needle with a strong thread, such as button thread, and work with a double strand in the needle. Fasten on in the centre of one side of the cover, pass the needle through the shank, or fabric, of one button and then through the cushion to the other side. Pass the needle through the shank or fabric of the second button and back through the cushion. Repeat once, pull the thread tightly and fasten off firmly.

PIPED CUSHION COVER WITH
EXTENDED TURNING OPENING

Prepare the pattern as for the plain cover on page 151.

To calculate the amount of piping required, refer to the square shape instructions on page 160.

Cut out two sections, and mark the fitting and grain lines as for the piped cover on page 164.

Prepare and apply the piping to the upper section as for the square cover on page 160. The piping is applied to the fitting line all round the shape, including the opening area.

Trim off the upper turning of the piping to 6 mm ($\frac{1}{4}$ in.), and the under turning to 10 mm ($\frac{3}{8}$ in.). See *figure 154, opposite.*

Join the upper and under sections together, following the principles outlined for the square shape on page 164. Begin and finish the machining 38 mm ($1\frac{1}{2}$ in.) in from the corners on the opening side.

Finish the cover as previously described on page 152.

When the extension is turned to the wrong side, the fold line may need adjusting slightly, so that the raw edges meet the fitting line. This is because of the slight loss in size caused by the application of the piping.

SHALLOW SEAT-PAD

A shallow seat-pad is made to fit a particular chair. It is suitable for wooden chairs as it makes them more comfortable, and more attractive in appearance. Old wooden chairs can be renovated by repainting them and furnishing them with a seat-pad of matching or contrasting colour. These make useful kitchen chairs and, with suitable fabric for the pad, they can also be used as occasional chairs for a bathroom or bedroom. The pads can be made quite plain, or they can be given a more tailored appearance by the addition of piping round the edge. Although not essential, an opening can be made on the underside of the cover and the inner pad removed for laundering purposes. It is wise to have an opening on a piped pad to give a clean edge to the piping. The pad is held firmly to the chair seat with tape loops and a tie.

The outer fabric should be medium-weight and should have a drip-dry finish if the inner pad is to be permanently enclosed. If the pad is to be piped, the fabric should have the qualities required for a piped box cushion (page 146).

For the tape loops use tape, or ribbon seam binding, in a colour matching the chair, so that the tape is inconspicuous when tied.

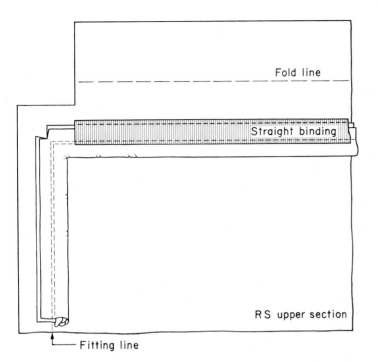

Fold line

Straight binding

R S upper section

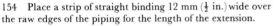

Fitting line

154   Place a strip of straight binding 12 mm ($\frac{1}{2}$ in.) wide over the raw edges of the piping for the length of the extension. Tack and machine close to the edge along both sides of the binding

It is necessary to make a pattern of the chair seat, so that the cushion will fit well when made. Check the measurements of the seat to find out whether it is the same on both halves, ie symmetric. If it is, then only half the pattern need be drawn out. This is best done on folded paper, with the centre, from back to front, coming along the fold. Mark the grain line along this fold. The two halves can then be cut together, thus making them identical, and the pattern opened out to its full size when used.

Pad with a slip-stitched opening

With a symmetric pattern and plain fabric, pin the pattern onto double fabric, lining up the grain, and cut out allowing 15 mm ($\frac{5}{8}$ in.) turnings all round. With a patterned fabric it may be necessary to cut out on single fabric in order to place the pattern over a suitable design motif. Cut out the upper section first, and later reverse the pattern for cutting the under section. Allow 15 mm ($\frac{5}{8}$ in.) turnings. When the cutting out is finished, mark out the fitting lines.

The tape loops

Cut four pieces of tape or ribbon seam binding equal to the measurement of the seat depth, plus half the width of the seat, plus 65 mm ($2\frac{1}{2}$ in.) seam allowance. The position of the loops is determined by the arrangement of the back struts and the legs of the chair. Both pairs of loops may be placed on the side of the pad, or one pair on the sides and one pair on the back. Choose the position which will give the best control. If all four tape loops are to be placed on the sides, set them sufficiently far in from the corners to avoid the legs when the loops are drawn to the underside of the chair. If only two loops are to be set in the sides, place them near the two front corners. In this case the back loops are also set just inside the corners to avoid the back legs.

167

Construction

Place the tapes in the chosen positions, on the right side of the under section, with one raw edge in line with the raw edge of the fabric, and the length of the tape directed inwards. See *figure 155*.

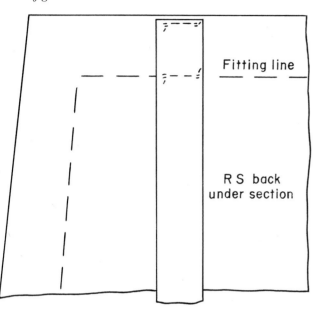

Fitting line

R S back
under section

155   Tack the tape securely on the fitting line and again close to the raw edge

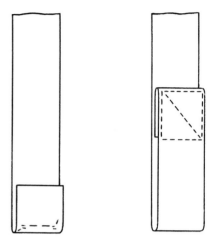

156a and b   Fold over one raw edge of each tape, towards the underside of the pad, for 12 mm ($\frac{1}{2}$ in.) and tack. Fold over again for 38 mm ($1\frac{1}{2}$ in.) and tack to form loops. Machine in a square and once across the diagonal to secure the first turning

Place the upper section of the cover on top of the under section, right sides together, and construct as for a scatter cushion (page 148), leaving the opening at the back. When tacking the two sections together, be careful not to catch in the free ends of the tapes. Trim off the corners, and snip or notch the rounded areas as required.

Cut a piece of 12 mm ($\frac{1}{2}$ in.) *Latex* foam sheeting, 6 mm ($\frac{1}{4}$ in.) smaller all round than the pattern. (Normally an inner pad is made slightly larger than its cover. This gives a full looking scatter cushion, and a close fitting boxed cushion. However, the depth of the foam is not catered for in the seat-pad cover, so allowance has to be made for this.) Insert the pad into the cover, and close the opening with secure slip-stitching. See *figures 156a and b*.

Set the pad on the chair with the tape loops hanging in position. Thread a long piece of narrow tape through the four loops, and draw them tightly to the underside of the chair. Tie the tape firmly to hold the pad in place. To give a neat finish, wrap the loose ends of the narrow tape round the loops.

The pad can be given a buttoned finish, but a flat, plastic button must be used. For the method of covering and sewing on the button, refer to pages 165 and 166.

168

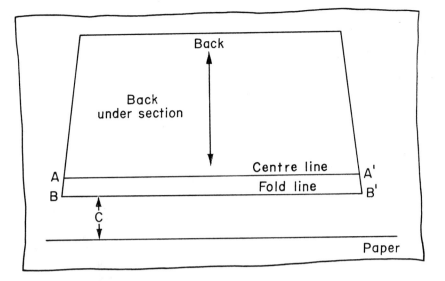

157 (above) Continue the pattern line for a further 20 mm (¾ in), mark points B and B1 and, with a ruler, join BB1 for the fold line of the opening. Draw another line parallel to BB1, 45 mm (1¾ in) away from it. (Distance shown by C). Cut away the paper along this line

158 (below) Fold back the paper along BB1 and trim up the sides of the pattern to make the final shape

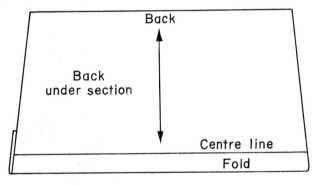

Cover for a seat-pad with an opening

In this case a second paper pattern is required for the underside of the pad. This pattern is made in two halves, bringing the opening across the centre of the pad from side to side. It is made in the form of an under and over wrap, and fastened with press studs.

On the original pattern mark a straight grain line down the centre from back to front. At right angles to the grain line, draw the opposite central line from side to side. Mark it A A1 and cut along this line. Pin the back half of this prepared pattern onto another piece of paper, with space beyond the central line. Draw round the back seat pattern. Remove the pattern. See *figure 157, above.*

Beyond the central line there is now a 20 mm (¾ in.) allowance to form an underwrap for the opening, and an additional 45 mm (1¾ in.) to fold back and support it. See *figure 158, above.*

Repeat this drawing of the opening extension on the front half of the seat-pad pattern, but this time, of course, it is the overwrap of the opening which is provided.

169

Making the cover

Take the two parts which comprise the under section of the pad, and neaten the raw edges of the opening. Prepare the front section first by tacking a 12 mm ($\frac{1}{2}$ in.) wide tape close to the fold line as in *figure 159*. This will act as a support for the fastenings when they are sewn on later.

Instead of using tape, a strip of iron-on interlining can be applied over the full width of the extension before the raw edge is neatened.

Prepare the back section in the same way, but omit the taping or interfacing. The fastenings can be sewn through the double thickness of fabric on the under side of the opening.

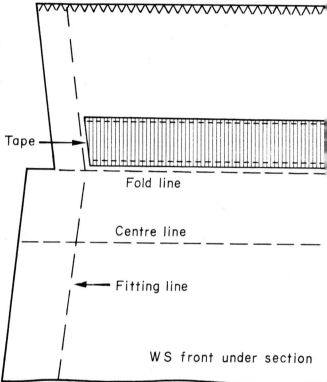

Tape

Fold line

Centre line

Fitting line

WS front under section

159 *(above)*   Machine close to the two edges of the tape and trim the side turning of the extension to prevent bulk

160 *(below)*   Fold the turning to the wrong side along the fold line. Tack close to the fold and again fairly close to the neatened raw edge

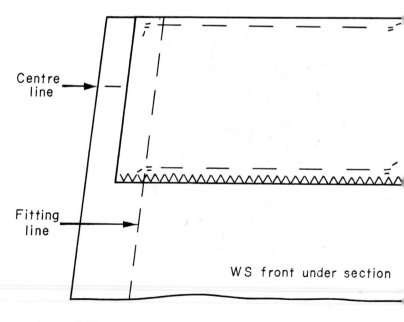

Centre line

Fitting line

WS front under section

170

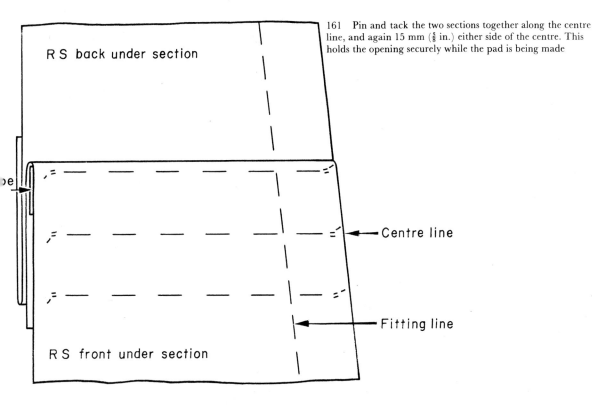

161 Pin and tack the two sections together along the centre line, and again 15 mm ($\frac{5}{8}$ in.) either side of the centre. This holds the opening securely while the pad is being made

RS back under section

be

Centre line

Fitting line

RS front under section

162 *(below)* The layered turnings

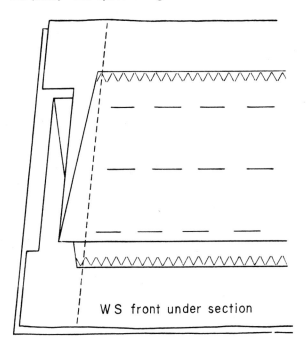

WS front under section

With the two sections right side uppermost, place the back section flat on the table, and lap the front section over it, bringing the centre lines on top of one another.

Apply the tape loops and join the two sections together as previously described, but do not leave an opening. Trim off the corners, layer the turnings at the opening as in *figure 162*, and neaten the seams if the fabric frays badly.

Unpick the tacking threads from the opening, press the finished edges and turn the cover right side out. Sew press fasteners onto the wrong side of the opening overlap, placing them 38 mm ($1\frac{1}{2}$ in.) apart, and 6 mm ($\frac{1}{4}$ in.) in from the fold. Stitch through the fabric turning and tape (or interfacing) only, so that the stitching will not come through to the right side. On the underlay of the opening, the fastener sockets can be sewn through both layers of fabric.

Press the cover, insert the pad and close the opening.

Piped cover for a shallow pad

Prepare the opening on the under section, and attach the tape loops as described on pages 168 and 170. Prepare and apply the piping to the upper section as for the square shape, see pages 160 and 161. Join the two sections together as for the piped scatter cushion, but do not leave an opening. Trim the corners and neaten all the seams as described for the scatter cushion on page 165.

Complete the pad as previously described, but cut the *Latex* foam 10 mm ($\frac{3}{8}$ in.) smaller all round to allow for the reduction in size caused by the method used for applying the piping.

BOXED CUSHIONS

Boxed cushions are usually piped, although this is not essential. Both the upper and the under sections require piping, and this must be remembered when calculating the length of piping required. The opening is usually placed in the boxing strip so that the cushion can be reversed. However, if the cushion is to be tied onto a chair or piece of furniture, in a similar way to a shallow seat-pad, the opening is best placed in the under section.

A SQUARE BOXED CUSHION

The inner cover

Paper patterns can be made for the sections of the cushion, but this is not essential as the shapes can be marked out onto the fabric, marking straight with the two grains for all sections. Allow 15 mm ($\frac{5}{8}$ in.) turnings on all edges. The following shapes are required: two squares equal to the size of the pad, four boxing strips equal in length to one side of the square by the depth of the pad in width.

The warp grain running parallel with the width of the strip, gives the most economical cutting, but it may be placed in the other direction if preferred. The grain should run in the same direction on all four boxing strips.

Cut out the shapes remembering to add the turning allowances if they have not been marked out. If necessary, mark the fitting lines.

Making the boxing

Pin the four boxing strips together, along the short sides, matching the fitting lines and with the right sides facing. Tack along the fitting lines.

Press the seams open flat.

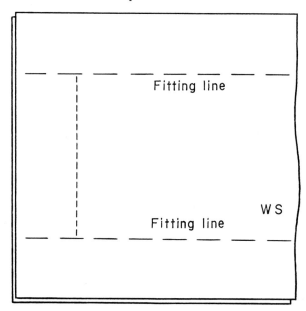

163 Machine the boxing strip seams for their finished length, leaving the turning allowance free at either end

Joining the inner cover

With the right sides facing, pin the boxing onto one square section, matching the fitting lines, and setting the seams of the boxing exactly in line with the corner points of the square. The unstitched turnings at either end of the seams will allow the corners to be turned easily. See *figures 164a and b*.

The second square is applied in a similar manner except that an opening must be left for the cover to be turned through to the right side and the pad inserted. When machining, work with the boxing uppermost and begin 12 mm

$(\frac{1}{2}$ in.) before one corner. Machine round the fitting lines of the square, and finish 12 mm $(\frac{1}{2}$ in.) beyond the fourth corner. Trim the corners and seam turnings as before.

At the opening, fold the turning of the boxing to the wrong side along the fitting line, and set the fold along the fitting line of the square. Tack and slip stitch it in place.

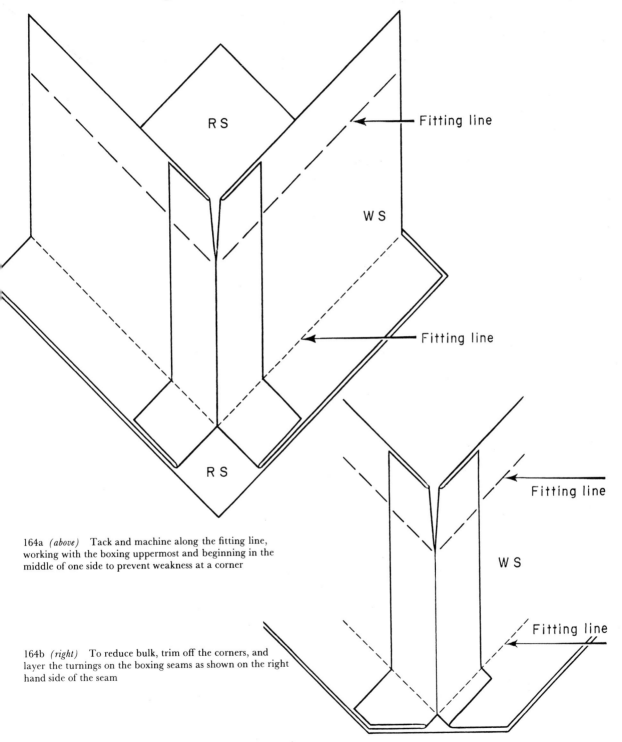

RS

Fitting line

WS

Fitting line

RS

164a *(above)* Tack and machine along the fitting line, working with the boxing uppermost and beginning in the middle of one side to prevent weakness at a corner

Fitting line

WS

Fitting line

164b *(right)* To reduce bulk, trim off the corners, and layer the turnings on the boxing seams as shown on the right hand side of the seam

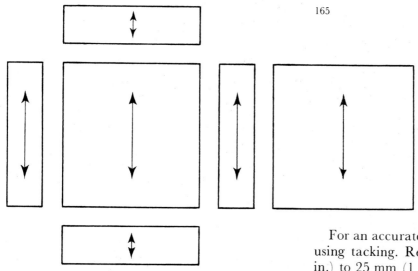

The outer cover

The pattern pieces for the outer cover are the same as for the inner cover, except that five boxing strips are required, the extra one being used when making the opening. The warp grain may be placed in line with either the width or the length of the boxing strips.

In some cases it is advisable to cut two boxing strips one way and two the other, thus allowing the grain to follow all round the cover in each direction, as in *figure 165*.

The fifth strip can be cut either way, but must be paired with a matching piece when making the opening. This method of cutting is often the best treatment for striped fabrics and for fabric which shades.

It is wise to make a cutting plan before buying the fabric, to ensure that sufficient is bought to allow for cutting the crossway strips. These are best cut as long as possible to avoid too many joins. To calculate the length of crossway required, refer to page 160, remembering that both the upper and the under sections are piped. See *figure 166*. If patterned fabric, including stripes and checks is chosen, allow extra fabric for matching the pattern.

For an accurate result, mark out the sections using tacking. Remember to allow 20 mm ($\frac{3}{4}$ in.) to 25 mm (1 in.) for turnings between the sections. Cut out and mark the warp grain as directed on page 164. On badly fraying fabric neaten the raw edges as this will prevent loss of turnings during construction.

The opening

The opening, which is made in one side, is best fastened with a zip fastener. An *Alcozip* may be used if desired, but it is only available in a limited range of sizes. The zip should be 50 mm (2 in.) shorter than the side into which it is to be set. This will prevent the ends of the tape adding bulk to the boxing strip seams at the corners of the cover. Buy the zip with the nearest length to this measurement.

Inserting the zip fastener

With the right sides facing, place together two boxing strips from the three with matching grain. (Any two strips can be used if all five have been cut on the same grain.) Join the two strips together down the centre of one long side, using running stitches and a contrasting thread. For a semi-concealed zip setting, machine the two end sections, leaving the running stitches uncovered in the centre for the length of the zip-teeth and slider. See *figure 167*.

Set the zip as on page 154. For setting an *Alcozip*, follow the directions on page 155.

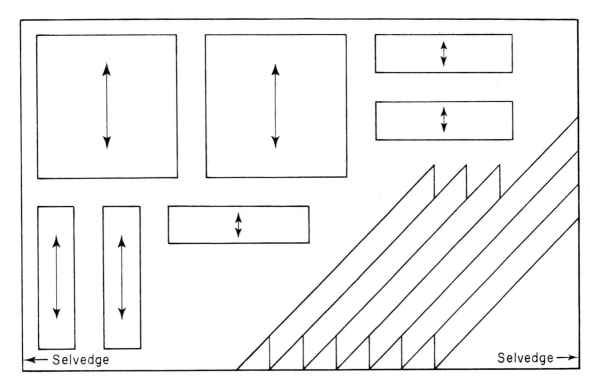

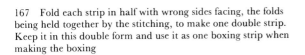

166 A scaled cutting plan for use on corded fabric. The cushion is 305 mm (12 in.) square, with a depth of 75 mm (3 in.). The plan shows two boxing strips cut with the warp grain running along the length, and three with the weft grain in this direction. Nett patterns are shown. There is adequate length for the crossways to be cut with only three joins, including the final join, on each piping. The exact length of fabric used is 73·7 cm (29 in.). The nearest buyable quantity is 75 cm ($\frac{7}{8}$ yd). The extra fabric will allow for straightening the weft edges

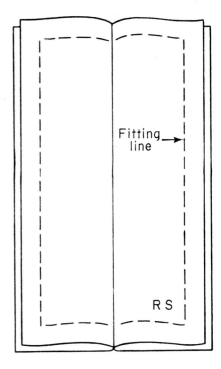

167 Fold each strip in half with wrong sides facing, the folds being held together by the stitching, to make one double strip. Keep it in this double form and use it as one boxing strip when making the boxing

175

Making the boxing

Join the four boxing strips together as for the inner cover, but machine just inside the fitting line. This will reduce the size fractionally and will compensate for the slight loss in size when the piping is applied to the upper and under sections. Neaten the seams if necessary and press them open.

Piping and joining the cover

Apply the piping to the upper and under sections as directed on page 160.

With right sides together, place one edge of the boxing strip on top of the upper section and line up the fitting lines. Make sure that the seams of the boxing are exactly in line with the corner points of the upper section. Pin, tack and machine the strip in place, following the principles already given for a piped scatter cushion on page 164.

Open the zip and apply the second edge of the boxing to the under section of the cover. Be careful to place the marked warp grain points over each other so that the grain is aligned on both sides of the finished cover. Trim off all eight corners, and layer the turnings of the boxing seams. Neaten all the seams following the directions given for the scatter cushion on page 165, thus enclosing the turnings of the piping. Even if the sections were neatened before construction, this last stage is advisable as it helps to set the turnings when the pad is inserted.

Press the cover, pressing the turnings towards the boxing. Turn the cover right side out, insert the pad and close the zip.

A RECTANGULAR BOXED CUSHION

The inner cover

This is similar to the square shape except that the pattern pieces are slightly different. Two rectangular shapes are required, and two boxing strips equal in length to the longer sides and two equal in length to the shorter sides of the rectangle. The width of all strips should equal the depth of the pad, and be cut with the warp grain.

Allow 15 mm ($\frac{5}{8}$ in.) turnings all round each section. With a small pad, leave the opening in one short side; with a large pad, leave it in one long side for easier insertion.

The outer cover

Leave the opening on one short or one long side, depending on the purpose and size of the pad. An extra boxing strip will be required for the opening side. Make the cover following the method outlined for the square cover.

A BOXED CUSHION WITH AN OPENING IN THE UNDER SECTION

Make the opening following the principles outlined for the shallow seat-pad with this type of opening. See pages 167–171. The tape loops are set in position on the under section before it is piped. The pad is then made following the directions which apply to its shape.

A CIRCULAR BOXED CUSHION

The pad

It is not always possible to buy a circular pad of the required size. However, a square pad, equal to the diameter of the circle, can be cut to on page 148. Place it on one side of the square pad and mark round it carefully. Repeat this shape. Make a pattern of the circle as directed on the other side of the pad. Using a Stanley knife, or any suitable, sharp knife, cut round the shape penetrating to half the depth. Repeat this on the other side of the pad. Trim rough edges with a medium sized pair of sharp scissors.

The inner cover

If a pattern has not been made for the pad, it will be necessary to make one for the cover. The boxing strip is equal in length to the circumference of the circle, and in width to the depth of the pad. For economy, the width should be cut in line with the warp grain. If the length of the strip exceeds the width of the fabric, the strip may be split and two sections cut and joined. Remember to add turning allowances all round the two sections. Cut out two circles and the boxing strip, allowing 15 mm ($\frac{5}{8}$ in.) turnings on all edges. Mark the fitting lines.

Place the two short edges of the boxing strip together, right sides facing, and pin and tack along the fitting line. Machine and press the seam as for the boxing on the square pad. See *figures 168a and b overleaf*.

Prepare the second edge of the boxing in the same way and apply it to the second circle, but leave open a quarter of the circumference. Layer the turnings of the boxing as in figure 168b. Press open the seams and then press them towards the boxing. Turn the cover right side out and insert the pad.

At the opening, fold the turning of the boxing to the wrong side along the fitting line, and set the fold along the fitting line of the circle. Tack and slip stitch it in place.

The outer cover   The opening

Decide on the length of the opening, usually a quarter of the circumference measurement. If necessary, adjust the length to suit the nearest buyable length of zip fastener. The total length of the opening is equal to the length of the zip plus 50 mm (2 in.) to allow for the ends of the zip tapes.

The pattern for the outer cover

The following pattern pieces will be required:
2 circles equal to the size of the pad
2 boxing strips equal in length to the total length of the opening by the depth of the pad

1 boxing strip equal in length to the circumference of the circle minus the length of the short boxing strips
Allow 20 mm ($\frac{3}{4}$ in.) to 25 mm (1 in.) turnings on all edges. Example:
For a pad with a diameter of 35·5 cm (14 in.) circumference of 111·8 cm (44 in.)
depth of 75 mm (3 in.)
buy a zip of 305 mm (12 in.), as a quarter of the circumference equals 280 mm (11 in.).
Plan the pattern pieces in the following way:
2 circles of 35·5 cm (14 in.) diameter.
2 short boxing strips of 35·5 cm (14 in) × 75 mm (3 in.) (for setting the zip).
1 long boxing strip of 76·2 cm (30 in.) × 75 mm (3 in.)

To calculate the length of piping required, refer to page 163, remembering that two circles will be piped.

Making the cover

Plan the lay, cut out the sections and mark the fitting and warp grain lines. Set the zip into the two short boxing strips as directed for the square pad on page 174. Join the short and long boxing strips together as explained on page 176.

Apply the piping to the upper and under sections as outlined for the circular shape on page 163. Prepare one long edge of the boxing as for the inner cover and apply it to the upper section following the principles outlined for the circular scatter cushion on page 164, but in this case, take care to set the centre of the short strip opposite to a marked warp grain point.

Open the zip fastener and prepare and apply the second edge of the boxing to the under section of the cover. Be careful to place the marked warp grain points over each other, so that the grain is aligned on both sides of the finished cover.

Trim the turnings of the boxing seams and neaten all raw edges if necessary. Press the cover, pressing the turnings towards the boxing. Turn the cover right side out, insert the pad and close the zip.

168a On one long side of the boxing, snip the turning allowance, at regular intervals, to within 3 mm ($\frac{1}{8}$ in.) of the fitting line

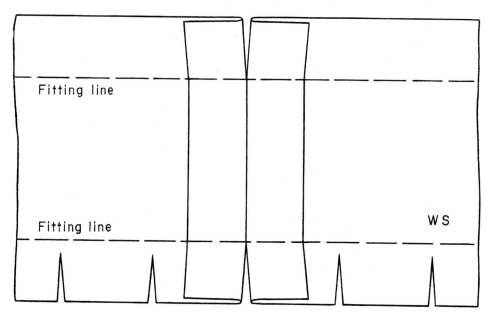

168b Place the prepared edge of the strip on one circle, with right sides together, and pin and tack in place. Working with the boxing uppermost machine along the fitting line. Trim away part of the seam turning as shown on the left-hand side of the seam

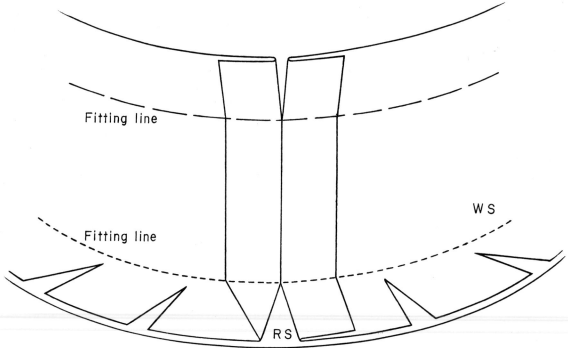

IRREGULAR-SHAPED BOXED CUSHIONS

If the pad is not a traditional cornered or round shape, its treatment should be assessed before handling it. Use the principles already given for judging the lengths of crossway strip and piping cord to prepare. Apply the piping round corners, outer curves and inner curves as previously described. When the cover has been finally joined together, the turnings should be treated on straight edges and at corners as for square shapes, and on outer curves as for the round shape. On inner curves, the turnings should be snipped before neatening.

BOXED CUSHIONS WITHOUT PIPING

A boxed cushion is usually piped, but this is not essential. If the cushion is to be made with plain seams, the pattern for the cover should be made 6 mm ($\frac{1}{4}$ in.) smaller than the pad to ensure a good fit. A plain outer cover is made in the same way as the inner cover, except that an opening must be included. As there is no piping, the stitching of the seams should always be worked on the fitting lines.

A BOLSTER CUSHION

The inner cover

Make a pattern for the circular end shape as directed on page 148. The rectangle, which will be referred to as the strip, is equal to the length of the pad by the measurement round the circumference of the circle. The warp grain may run either with the width or the length of the strip, whichever is the most economic. Cut out two circles and one strip, allowing 15 mm ($\frac{5}{8}$ in.) turnings all round each section. Mark the fitting lines.

The opening

An opening of approximately 150 mm (6 in.)

should be marked in the centre of the strip seam.

Making the inner cover

Fold the strip in half lengthwise with the right sides facing, and match the fitting lines of the seam. Pin and tack the seam, leaving it open between the marked points. The seam has to be machined in two sections in order to leave the opening free. Begin one section at the circular end fitting line and finish the other to match, thus leaving the two end turnings unstitched. Press the seam turnings flat, pressing open the machined sections. Press back the opening turnings along the fitting lines and tack them in position as pressed.

Set the strip to the two circles as for the circular pad on page 177, but do not leave an opening, and remember to snip the turning allowance of the strip. Press the seams as for the circular pad, and turn the cover right side out. Fill the cover firmly with the chosen filling, and slip stitch the opening securely.

The outer cover

The pattern pieces required will be the same as for the inner cover. The strip may be cut with the warp grain running with either the length or the width, according to the fabric. To calculate the length of piping required, refer to page 163, remembering that both circular ends are piped.

Fold the strip in half lengthways, with the right sides facing, and match the fitting lines of the seam. As the pad is more easily inserted if the opening is left closer to one end of the strip, mark a point 50 mm (2 in.) from the fitting line at one end of the seam, and a second point the length of the opening away from the first point. The length of opening varies according to the size of the pad, as it is usually half the length of the strip. Prepare and make the seam, and insert the zip, as directed for a scatter cushion on page 154, unless an *Alcozip* is to be used, when the seam is prepared and the zip applied as on page 155.

Apply the piping to the two circles as directed on page 163. Attach the strip to the two piped circles and finish the cover as outlined for the circular pad.

Bolster cover with gathered ends

The ends of the cover can be gathered for a more decorative effect. Choose light to medium-weight fabric for this style, as heavy fabric is too bulky to give a satisfactory finish at the gathered ends.

The pattern, pad, cover strip and piping are prepared and made as for the previous bolster.

The gathered ends

The gathered ends of the bolster are made from rectangles of fabric equal to the circumference of the circle × the radius. Allow 20 mm ($\frac{3}{4}$ in.) to 25 mm (1 in.) turnings on one long side and on both short edges of each rectangle. Neaten all four edges of each rectangle with machine zigzagging or overcasting, and join the short edges with a plain seam pressed open flat. Along the edge without a turning allowance,

work two rows of gathering, placing the first row 3 mm ($\frac{1}{8}$ in.) inside the edge, and the second row 3 mm ($\frac{1}{8}$ in.) below the first row. Apply the piping to the other edge.

The prepared bolster strip is now joined to the two piped sections, placing the seams in line with each other. Neaten the piped seam, turn the cover right side out and insert the pad.

Draw up the gathering threads as tightly as possible and fasten off the ends securely. There will be a circular space left in the centre. Fasten on a length of double thread to the gathered circle, pass the needle across the space and through the fabric opposite the starting point. Pass the needle back across the space and bring it out 6 mm ($\frac{1}{4}$ in.) away from the starting point. Pulling the thread tightly with each stitch, continue stranding across the circle in this way, gradually stitching round the circle and drawing the raw edges together.

Cover a 25 mm (1 in.) to a 32 mm ($1\frac{1}{4}$ in.) button as directed on page 165. Cover the raw edges of the drawn up centre with the button and hem it carefully in place, making sure that all the raw edges are concealed.

Lampshades are one of the last items to consider when planning interior décor as, along with cushions, they are accessories to the scheme. Although they are useful decorative features, supplying perhaps the right touch of colour, pattern and/or texture, they are also functional. The shades can be used to 'warm' or 'cool' a colour scheme, or add, together with the cushions, a necessary touch of contrasting colour. The illuminative quality of the shade is an important consideration and should not be overlooked. A green or blue shade, although perhaps right for a colour scheme, will give a cold light. The lamp may, therefore, suit the décor admirably during the daytime, but give an unfortunate appearance of coldness at night. If a shade is to be lined, a pale pink, peach or lemon lining will give a more pleasing light. When a coloured lining is to be used, check its effect on the cover fabric, both with and without a light behind it, to discover the two different appearances it will have. If possible, the effect of the illuminated colour should be tested against the colour, or colours, which will surround it. The use of patterned fabric requires careful consideration as some printed fabrics look dull with light behind them, whereas others become more attractive. Apart from the light factor, the size and the type of design require thought, as they must not only suit the shape and size of the shade, but also merge harmoniously into the general décor.

Although table lamps may be chosen for their decorative qualities, it is wise not to choose a fabric which is so opaque that no light is transmitted through the shade. This will cause a harsh light to be directed both upwards and downwards, which can be displeasing. It is better to choose a fabric which will diffuse some of the light, thus softening the effect. Remember that hanging lights are usually functional and so the shade should transmit the maximum light. Unless the shade completely conceals the bulb, it is best to choose a pearl bulb to avoid harsh light and glare.

Lampshades of quality are very expensive to buy, and it is sometimes difficult to find the exact requirements. Lampshade making is also valuable in that it provides an opportunity for originality to those interested in embroidery and fabric printing. For these reasons lampshade making is, perhaps, the most economic and rewarding aspect of soft furnishing.

Firm drum shades are easy to make and are a good starting point for the inexperienced worker. Stretched and pleated shades need more skill, but with care, time and patience, a satisfactory standard can be achieved by the average needlewoman. The standard of workmanship is important as any defects will be very noticeable when the shade is illuminated.

Lampshade making supplies an opportunity for originality which is valuable in an age of mass production. It is an outlet for those interested in embroidery and fabric printing, and these are positive ways of achieving originality. Drawn thread, drawn fabric and Hardanger embroideries are examples of types of embroidery which are suitable for lampshades. Some of the open-weave acrylic fabrics can be made even more interesting in appearance by the addition of hem-stitching. Machine embroidery, including machine appliqué, is also suitable. A shade decorated with appliqué motifs cut from printed fabric is more effective, and certainly more original, than one made from printed fabric itself.

The first consideration for a table lamp is the base. It is not necessary to buy an expensive base as, with a little imagination, containers such as vases and bottles can be converted into interesting and original ones. For example, an acid bottle filled with pebbles makes a good

169 *(left)*   The base is made up of a series of cylindrical shapes, so the drum shade is the best choice to complement these shapes

170 *(centre)*   This shows a china base with a less angular line than the previous sketch, and so requires a different shade. A pleated shade which narrows towards the top is suggested, as this is in keeping with the line of the base

171 *(right)*   In this lamp the shade is much taller than the base but, because it tapers, it gives a pleasing whole, and the circular shape of the base is retained

base for a large table lamp. The pebbles add weight to the base, are attractive in daylight and gain in attraction when illuminated. Conversion units are readily available, those with a strip of cork, perhaps, giving the most satisfactory results. The cork can be cut to the required length to give a secure fitment and acts on the same principle as a normal cork in a bottle. The cork supplied with the fitment is

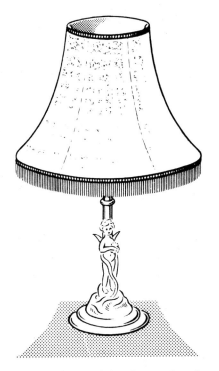

172 This base suggests a period setting, so a bowed, empire shade has been chosen to suit both the décor and the base of the lamp

very important items. Drum shades usually suit modern settings, whereas stretched or pleated shades are more often suited to period settings.

The shape of the base will often suggest the shape of the shade, and these compliment each other in a lamp of pleasing appearance. For example, a round base is complimented by a round shade; a base which tapers usually looks best with a shade which is slightly narrower at the top than at the bottom. An inexperienced person would benefit from making a critical study of the lamps displayed in a good store, as this helps to develop an appreciation of line and proportion. The sketches give some examples to guide the choice of base and the frame for the shade.

As a general rule the height of the shade is the same or slightly less than the height of the base. The height of the base is taken from top to bottom, excluding the fitment. The width of the shade is not quite as easily established. There is no hard and fast rule, but it is usually slightly more than the height. Cut-out shapes in brown paper will help to establish the required shape and size. If possible place the base where it will normally stand in the room. If this is not possible, try to set it at the right height from the ground. The paper shapes should then be held above the base and be viewed from a distance. Obviously help is required for this, and a second opinion is often an advantage.

The size, and in some cases the shape, of the frame will be affected by the fabric chosen for the shade. Light colours will make the shade appear larger, and dark colours will make it appear smaller. Striped fabrics can create an illusion; vertical stripes seeming to give more height and horizontal stripes more width. Therefore it is wise to have the cover fabric in mind when planning the shape and size of the shade. Once a suitable shape and size have been found, the measurements of the height and width can be taken from the cut out shape. This is an important stage, and should not be hurried, as once the frame has been bought, the size of the shade cannot be adjusted. The

inadequate for a vase or bottle with a large opening, but 3 mm ($\frac{1}{8}$ in.) cork sheeting can be bought from most garages and can be cut to the required size.

The base of a lamp must be sufficiently stable to support the shade. Light-weight bases are knocked over easily, resulting in damage to the shade and often to the base as well. Pebbles have already been suggested as an effective and practical form of weighting. Opaque vases and bottles can be weighted with ball bearings. Some bought bases are very light in weight and, on examination, will prove to be hollow with a layer of felt fixed across the bottom. If the felt is removed carefully, weighting can be added and a thin piece of hardboard, cut to shape, stuck in place before replacing the felt.

Having chosen the base, the frame and covering fabric are the next considerations.

The shape and size of the frame are both

only possible adjustment, in fact, is the height of a drum shade if two rings are being used for making it. Consequently, if a wrong decision has been made, it will mean extra expense. When buying the frame for a table lamp it is wise to take the base to the shop to make a final check.

Frames of all shapes and sizes are fairly easily available, and some handicraft shops will make frames to order, if the desired shape and size cannot be found. It is not advisable to use an old frame unless it is in very good condition.

All frames are jointed. Sometimes the joints are soldered, but welded joints are more satisfactory. Examine the joints to see that they are secure. If the frame has struts, these should not project too far, or they will wear through the lining and/or covering fabric.

There are four types of fitting which are used to attach the frame to its holder or to the bulb. A pendant fitting is usually used for frames which are suspended from the ceiling, but is sometimes used for table lamps. A gimbal fitting allows for adjusting the angle of the shade and is the most suitable for table lamps. A butterfly fitting, which consists of two circular wires which clip onto the bulb, has a limited use and is suitable only for small shades. It should be used with a low wattage bulb, as the fabric covering is very close to the bulb and the heat will quickly damage it. A duplex fitting is suitable for a very large table lamp or a standard lamp. A gimbal is attached to the stand or base, and the duplex ring is placed over it.

When buying a frame check that the frame has not been distorted in any way; when buying a pair of rings for a firm drum shape, check that the two rings are the same size and that each one is an accurate circle.

White plastic-covered frames are available. These are a little more expensive than the plain metal ones, but eliminate one of the stages in making a shade.

The frame has to be bound to give a foundation for the stitching which attaches the cover to it. Special lampshade tape, white or cream in colour, is available for this purpose. This is satisfactory for lined shades and for some firm shades which are unlined. If a shade is unlined, it is important that the binding matches the inside of a shade in colour, and because of this, the special tape is not always the best choice. If sufficiently soft, strips of cover fabric can be used for unlined soft shades, otherwise bias binding is the best choice.

The length of tape or binding required is equal to twice the measurement of the length of wire to be covered. This varies with the style of shade, as it is not always necessary to bind the whole of the frame. The method of binding is dealt with in the section on the preparation of the frame.

There is no real limit to the choice of cover fabric, and often interesting and original shades can be produced by the use of unusual fabric. Certain shapes, such as the empire, however, do require fabric with particular qualities. In this case it must be soft and flexible so that it will stretch tautly over the frame without wrinkling. Suitable fabrics for an empire shade are crêpes, crêpe-backed satin, voile and fine lawns. Pleated shades require soft fabric with good draping qualities such as silk chiffon. Nylon chiffon is unsuitable as it will not retain the pleating.

Straight-sided, firm shades offer more scope, as the range of suitable fabrics is much wider. Remnants of both furnishing and dress fabrics can often be found which provide interesting ideas for lampshades.

When choosing fabric for a table-lamp or a standard lamp, consider the base as well as the room décor, and the background immediately behind the lamp. The base influences the colour, pattern and/or texture of the fabric. For example, an alabaster base will require a different fabric from an unglazed pottery base. Pleated chiffon would suit the alabaster, but would be out of keeping with the pottery.

Although, perhaps, one of the most difficult to make, a lined soft shade gives a professional finish. This type of shade is particularly suitable for a light suspended from the ceiling, as the lining hides the struts. A light coloured lining increases the amount of reflected light if a dark cover fabric has been chosen and, as already stated, a blue or green shade will give a warmer light if the lining fabric counteracts the cold colour of the shade. The fabric used for lining a shade should be lightweight, strong and disinclined to fray. Crêpes, the reverse side of crêpe-backed satin and soft satins are all suitable. Fabric which splits easily and pin-marks, such as taffeta, is unsuitable.

The choice of trimming is important as it can make or mar the final shade. It is both decorative and functional as it gives the finishing touch to the appearance of the shade and also covers up the stitching which shows on the right side. On a plain coloured shade, choose a trimming which either matches exactly or is a pleasing contrast. If the shade is made from fabric of more than one colour, select one colour which can be suitably emphasised for the trimming. The texture of the trimming is important and should complement the cover fabric. For example, a rayon braid with a sheen would be suitable for a shade covered with satin, but would be quite out of keeping on a hessian shade. In this case a cotton braid with a matt finish would be a better choice.

There is a wide range of trimmings available on the market including braid, bobble braid, fringing, ribbon and lace edgings. Suitable trimmings can be found in both haberdashery and soft furnishing departments. If a fringe is chosen for a table-lamp shade, remember that it will add height to the frame and, as it probably will hang below the fitment, it will reduce the apparent height of the base. These two points must be considered when planning the size of the shade.

Despite the range of trimmings available, a suitable one cannot always be found. Hand-made edgings can be attractive in both crochet and tatting and provide suitable trimmings for some shades. The cover fabric can be used to make a trimming for some firm drum shades, and directions for this are given on page 194. The quantity of trimming required is stated with each style of shade.

Lampshade making is a craft in its own right and, as there is so wide a variety of styles of shade, it is impossible to cover all types. Directions are given for five styles requiring different techniques, and it is hoped that those interested will be able to use the basic principles for further experimentation.

The equipment used for curtain and cushion making is also used for making lampshades. Any additional equipment depends on the style of shade chosen. For a drum shade, spring clothes pegs are required, and a set square will be useful for making right angles. Glass headed pins are helpful when making stretched shades. Clear adhesive is required for most shades.

PREPARING THE FRAME

Painting

A frame which is not plastic covered should be painted with quick drying coloured enamel, or cellulose paint, to prevent rusting and to give a better finish. Paint the frame and fitment according to the following directions:

1 An unlined, firm shade: paint the frame and fitment to match the cover fabric or the card stiffening.

2 An unlined, soft shade: paint the frame and fitment to tone with the cover.

3 A lined shade with:

a An opaque cover: paint frame and fitment to match the lining

b A transparent cover: paint the frame to tone with the cover, and the fitment to match the lining

Binding

This is a very important stage and should not be hurried as the tightness of the binding determines the success of the shade. A slack binding will slip when the cover fabric is stitched to it, causing a loss of tautness. A stretched cover fabric will wrinkle and a pleated cover will sag. On a firm shade, slack binding will cause instability of the cover fabric. If the first attempt at binding is not satisfactory, it is well worth the time and effort required to rebind the frame.

The specially woven lampshade tape gives the firmest binding and should be used when possible. If the cover fabric is to be used, cut 12 mm ($\frac{1}{2}$ in.) wide strips on the weft grain. The weft grain is used as it has a little more give than the warp grain and will, therefore, set more smoothly round the wire frame. Fold over one long, raw edge to the wrong side for 3 mm ($\frac{1}{8}$ in.) and press in place. If bias binding is being used, press out one of the turnings as this gives a flatter finish.

Binding the rings

This must be done as a continuous operation as, if left in the middle, the binding will unwind itself. Prepare a strip of binding material equal in length to twice the circumference of the ring, as it is not possible to join the binding while working. To prevent tangling in use, wind the binding round a strip of card, and trim the free end diagonally.

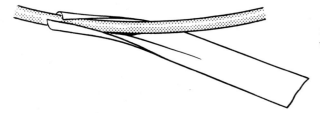

173a   Stick the trimmed end round the wire using clear adhesive, eg *Uhu*

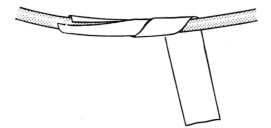

173b   Wind the tape firmly round the wire, overlapping the edge by approximately one third of the tape width

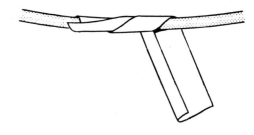

173c   If woven fabric, or bias binding, is being used, work with the folded edge to the left. As the wire is bound, the folded edge overlaps and conceals the raw edge

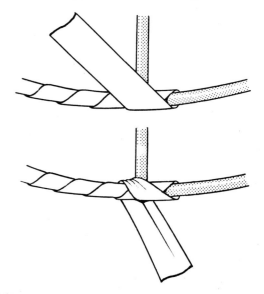

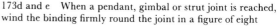

173d and e   When a pendant, gimbal or strut joint is reached, wind the binding firmly round the joint in a figure of eight

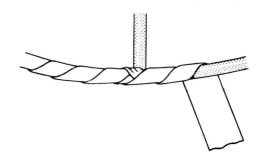

173f   Continue binding the ring until the starting point is reached

Trim the end of the binding diagonally and stick it in place. Test the tightness of the binding by passing the finger and thumb along the bound frame in both directions.

Binding the struts

If the cover and lining fabric are to be stretched over the frame, it is necessary to bind two opposite struts, choosing the two which come nearest to the joints of the pendant or gimbal fitting. (This is not necessary for a firm drum shade.) The binding in this case, is only temporary and will be removed once the stretching is finished. Cut a length of binding equal to twice the length of the strut, and prepare it as for the rings.

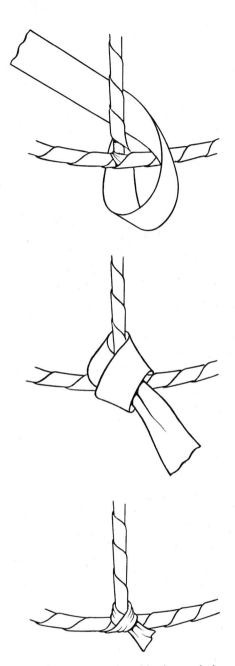

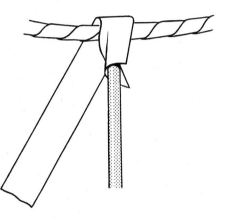

174a   From the left-hand side, pass the prepared end of the binding behind the top of the strut, and then pass it over the top of the ring

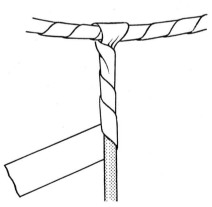

174b   Continue to bind the strut until the lower ring is reached

174c, d and e   Finish the binding with a knot at the base of the strut and trim off the surplus binding

Stitch the two joins to prevent their moving during use, but remember that the stitching will be unpicked later, so it should be clearly visible.

Straight-sided drum

This is the easiest type of shade to make, and is suitable as a hanging lamp and as a table lamp. Two rings of the chosen diameter are required, one of which must have a pendant or gimbal fitting. A drum shade must have a firm cover fabric. Milliner's buckram, which is white, and thin pelmet buckram, which is burnt orange in colour, are both suitable and make simple but effective shades. Covered lampshade card, or lampshade card which can be covered with fabric to meet particular requirements can be used, and allow for a choice of colour. The prepared lampshade card, which is fairly expensive, is available in a limited range of widths, so wastage is almost inevitable, and the range of covering fabric is also limited. The plain lampshade card, the slightly rough side of which is adhesive when heat is applied, offers more scope. Light to medium-weight fabrics can be applied to this, thus giving a much wider range. The card can also be used for the foundation of an embroidered cover if desired. This card is white, and is 99 cm (39 in.) wide. It is economic for shades with a circumference up to 91·4 cm (36 in.), as an amount equal to the height measurement of the shade can be bought, which also provides a test strip.

Prepare the two rings as directed on page 186.

Preparation of cover fabric

Milliner's buckram: pelmet buckram: bought covered lampshade card Place a pin through the binding on the outside of the ring, to mark a starting point, and measure round the circumference with a tape measure. Cut a rectangle equal to the circumference of the ring plus 15 mm ($\frac{5}{8}$ in) × the height of the shade. If possible use a set square when marking out the rectangle, to ensure right angled corners.

Plain lampshade card Cut a rectangle of card to the above measurements. Cut a rectangle of the chosen fabric to the same size. Make sure the edges are straight with the fabric grain, but place the warp grain in line with either the width or the length of the rectangle according to the desired effect. If the fabric frays badly, it is wise to overcast the two edges which will come at the top and bottom of the shade, to prevent loss of size during handling. Do not use machine zigzagging for this neatening as it may stretch the edges. Overcasting should not be deeper than 6 mm ($\frac{1}{4}$ in) so that it will be masked by the edge trimming. The other two edges do not require neatening as they are dealt with quickly.

a Covering with light-weight fabric To check for shine marks and to see if the fabric will adhere satisfactorily to the card, make a test sample to find the temperature of iron required. Cut a small piece of spare card, and place it, adhesive side uppermost, on the ironing board. Place a piece of the covering fabric on top, right side uppermost, and iron with a moderately hot iron. If the fabric does not adhere very well, follow the directions for the medium-weight fabric. If shine marks appear, protect the fabric with a thin pressing cloth when ironing it in place.

Press the prepared rectangle of cover fabric.

With the adhesive side uppermost, place on the ironing board the end of the card which will form the depth of the shade. With the right side uppermost, place the fabric on top so that it overlaps this edge of the card for 10 mm ($\frac{3}{8}$ in.), *see figure 175*, and is flush with the other two edges. Keep the fabric grain aligned with the cut edges of the card.

Iron the fabric to the card, moving the iron slowly over the surface. Move the card forward and continue to iron the fabric in place, section by section. This should be done slowly, and care should be taken to prevent distortion of the grain. The card should be left uncovered for 10 mm ($\frac{3}{8}$ in.) at the end to provide width for making a neat final join. See *figure 175*. Unless the fabric stretches during application, this extension of card will be inevitable owing to the overlap at the beginning. If necessary trim away any unwanted cover fabric, cutting straight with the grain.

Place the covered card on a flat surface and allow to cool. See *figure 176.*

b   Medium-weight fabric   Usually the adhesive on the card is not strong enough to hold the fabric securely in place. This can be discovered by testing with a small section of card and cover fabric.

The method of applying the cover fabric is the same as for light-weight fabric, except that thin lines of adhesive are placed between the card and fabric to give better adhesion. This needs to be done very carefully as too much adhesive is likely to mark the fabric. It is wise to try this before beginning to work on the shade itself.

Place the card ready for ironing as described in the previous section and apply the lines of adhesive over the area of the card on the ironing board. Lay the fabric in position as before, and iron it to the card. Move the card forward and fold back the fabric so that the adhesive can be applied to the next section of card. Lift the fabric back into position and iron it to the card. Care is necessary to keep the fabric on grain and to avoid wrinkles between each section. Continue in this way until all the fabric has been stuck to the card. Treat the two ends as for light-weight fabric. See *figures 175 and 176.*

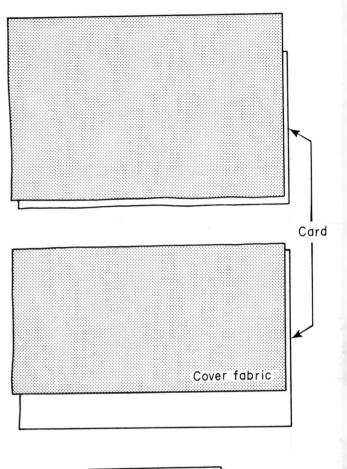

Card

Cover fabric

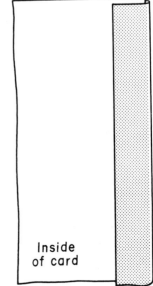

Inside
of card

175 *(above)*   The two ends of covered card, showing the 10 mm (⅜ in.) overlap of cover fabric at the beginning, and the same width projection of card at the end

176 *(below)*   Fold the 10 mm (⅜ in.) overlap of cover fabric to the inside of the card, and stick it in place using the adhesive sparingly

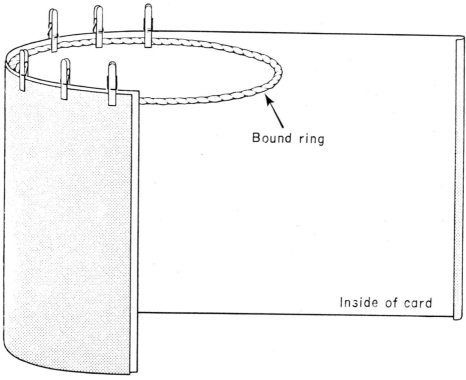

Bound ring

Inside of card

177   Fix the cover fabric to the first ring, allowing it to project approximately 3 mm (⅛ in.) beyond the ring. Hold it in position with spring clothes pegs

Fix the cover fabric to the second ring in the same way. When both rings are pegged in position, the cover is stitched to the rings. For the stitching, disregard the colour of the cover fabric, and use a thread which matches the binding on the rings. A thimble will be helpful when stitching through the cover. On fabric covered card, begin stitching each ring at the end where the fabric is inset. This also applies to bought covered card if the fabric is inset at one end. In any case the stitching must begin at the same end of the cover on each ring. The stitching is worked round the cover to within 50 mm (2 in.) of the second end, to leave space for making the join, and is finished after the join is made. A betweens, size seven, needle is recommended as it is strong but not too thick to weaken the card. Begin stitching in line with the top edge of the ring. Fasten on with a knot and apply a little adhesive to the knot to make it secure. See *figures 178a and b*.

Space the stitches approximately 10 mm (⅜ in.) apart. Accuracy is essential as a hole made in the wrong place will weaken the cover. The stitches formed are slanting on the right side and upright over the binding.

When the first ring has been stitched to within 50 mm (2 in.) of the end, leave the thread and stitch the second ring in the same way. Overlap the two edges of the cover and stick them carefully together to make the join. When the join is secure, finish the last 50 mm (2 in.) of stitching on each edge.

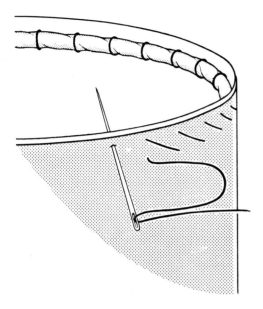

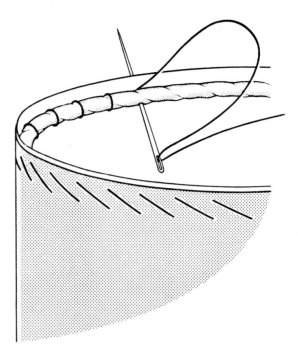

178a   From the right side pass the needle through the binding on the ring

178b   Take the thread over the ring and pass the needle back to the right side, passing it through the binding on the lower edge of the ring

Trimming

The join in the trimming can be made in two ways. *Method A* is suitable for buckram shades as this join is fairly flat. It is also suitable for stretched and pleated shades. *Method B* is suitable for fabric covered card as this makes a more bulky join on the shade.

Method A Cut two lengths of trimming, one equal to the circumference of the top of the shade, and one equal to the circumference of the bottom of the shade with 25 mm (1 in.) turning allowance, see *figure 179*.

179 At the right-hand end of the trimming, fold over a 12 mm ($\frac{1}{2}$ in.) turning to the wrong side. Trim off the corners of the turning to prevent bulk

Apply a little adhesive to the top left hand side of the join on the shade. Place the prepared end of the trimming so that the fold line is in line with the join, and the edge of the trimming projects a fraction above the shade. Keep the trimming taut and stick it in place to within 254 mm (10 in.) of the starting point. Take care not to use too much adhesive. Set the trimming in position for the last 254 mm (10 in.) without sticking it, to check whether the pattern matches at the join. It may be necessary to adjust the tautness of the setting to bring the pattern into line over the join, see *figures 180a and b*.

Apply the trimming to the second edge of the shade in the same way.

180a *(below)* Finish sticking the trimming in place to within 25 mm (1 in.) of the join. Fold the surplus trimming to the wrong side and trim it to leave a 12 mm ($\frac{1}{2}$ in.) turning. Snip off the corners of the turning to reduce bulk

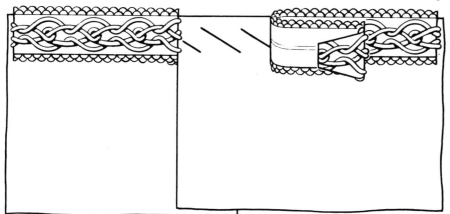

180b *(below)* Stick the last section of trimming in place

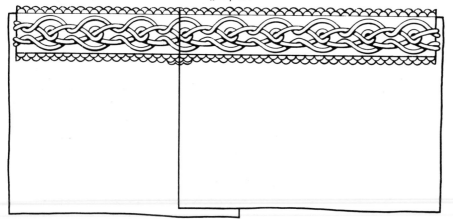

Method B Cut two lengths of trimming as for *Method A*, but with 32 mm (1¼ in.) turning allowance. Snip off the corners at the left-hand end of the trimming.

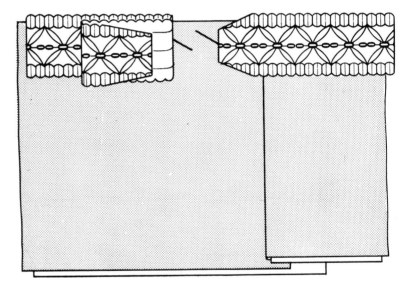

181 Place the prepared end of the trimming so that it overlaps the join by 12 mm (½ in.), and projects a fraction above the shade. Apply the trimming as for *Method A*, but allow a 20 mm (¾ in.) turning on the second end

Stick down the second end to bring its fold in line with the join on the cover. As the turnings face in the same direction, the larger turning allowance will displace the two edges. Treat the second side of the shade in the same way.

NB If using a fringe, do not apply it with any tautness, as this will cause the fringe to pull inwards and so prevent it from hanging straight.

Hand-made Trimming

Cut two strips of iron-on interfacing to the width of trimming required, equal in length respectively to the top and the bottom circumference of the shade. Cut two strips of fabric equal in length to the interfacing strips, with a 32 mm ($1\frac{1}{4}$ in.) turning on each. Cut them equal in width to twice the interfacing width. For a shade which tapers, cut the fabric on the cross, otherwise cut it with whichever straight grain gives the more attractive finish.

With the wrong side uppermost, place one fabric strip on the ironing board. Place a strip of interfacing, adhesive side uppermost, in the centre of the fabric, beginning 12 mm ($\frac{1}{2}$ in.) in from one end and stopping 20 mm ($\frac{3}{4}$ in.) in from the other end.

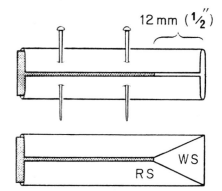

182b At the end where the interfacing is inset by 12 mm ($\frac{1}{2}$ in.), trim the turning, only, to a fishtail shape

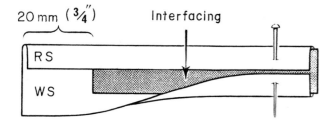

182a Fold the two raw edges to meet over the interfacing, and pin in place. Iron the strip, removing the pins as you go, to fix the two turnings to the interfacing

Begin with the trimmed end, and apply the strip to the shade following the directions given for *Method B*. When the second end is reached, trim the turnings of the prepared strip as in *figure 182b*, and complete the join as for *Method B*.

Prepare and apply the second length of trimming in the same way.

An embroidered cover

It is necessary to plan the embroidery to fit the required size of shade and, when doing this, avoid an arrangement of design which will bring a large motif over the join. A small linking motif, however, can usually be worked after the join has been made, and this helps to give continuity to the design. Use plain lampshade card, and prepare the shade as previously directed. Press or stretch the embroidery as required. With the wrong side outside, place the embroidered fabric round the shade and pin the two edges together, pulling the fabric fairly tightly, but not so tightly that it cannot be removed. Check that the seam line is straight with the grain of the fabric on both sides of the seam. The opposite fabric grain should also link round the shade, particularly if counted thread embroidery has been used and a linking motif is to be embroidered.

Remove the fabric from the shade, and mark the two fitting lines of the seam with tacking as the pins are removed. Make the seam using either fine back-stitch or machining. It is easier to keep the two grains aligned if fine back-stitch is used. See *figures 183a and b*.

If preferred, the turnings can be trimmed to 6 mm ($\frac{1}{4}$ in.) and neatened together with close overcasting.

Press the join and finish the embroidery if necessary. With the right side outside, pull the embroidered cover over the prepared shade, and stick the raw edges onto the card. Apply the trimming as previously described.

It is possible to make an embroidered cover removable for laundering purposes. In this case, shrink the fabric before beginning the embroidery. The fabric must be cut wider than the depth of the shade to allow for neatening the top and bottom edges. The width of turning to allow for this will vary according to the chosen finish.

Prepare the cover as previously described, and either fold a single turning to the wrong side, or make a hem. The finished depth of the cover should be 6 mm ($\frac{1}{4}$ in.) more than the depth of the shade. Hold the turning or hem in place with an embroidery stitch which is in keeping with the embroidery used on the cover. If a single turning has been used, trim away the surplus fabric fairly close to the embroidery stitch holding it in place. Pull the cover over the prepared shade.

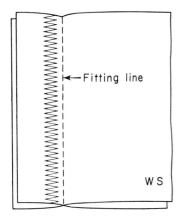

183a Using closely spaced zigzag, neaten the turnings together, placing the stitching fairly close to the fitting line

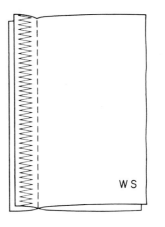

183b Trim away the surplus fabric close to the zigzag

195

When the diameter of the top ring is smaller than that of the bottom one, even with a difference as little as 25 mm (1 in.), the previous method cannot be used. There is, usually, very little difference in the measurements of the ring diameters of a sloping drum shade, but a cone shade has rings with a greater divergence of size. See *figure 171* on page 182.

It is necessary to make a pattern for both these styles of shade. A frame can be used but, if the shade is not too large, two rings are satisfactory. When using two rings make sure that one ring, usually the bottom one, has a pendant or gimbal fitting. Prepare the rings or frame as directed on pages 185–187. If a frame is being used, it is not necessary to bind the struts, but the binding of the top and bottom rings of the frame must be done before taking measurements for the pattern.

Requirements for making the pattern

A large sheet of paper is required, preferably sectional cutting out paper. A set square and a long ruler are helpful. Measurements must be taken carefully, over the bound rings, or the resulting pattern will not fit the frame.
Measurements required:
Height of frame, taken through the centre (not along one of the struts) or the height of the shade if two rings are being used
The diameter and circumference of the top ring
The diameter and circumference of the bottom ring

The pattern

Begin at the lower, left-hand corner of the paper and draw a horizontal line 50 mm (2 in.) above the edge of the paper.
Mark point A as in diagram.
Mark point B to make AB equal the diameter of the bottom ring.
Mark point X in the centre of AB.

Erect a long perpendicular line from X.
Mark point Y to make XY equal to the height of the shade.
Draw a horizontal line through Y, making it parallel with AB.
CD equals the diameter of the top ring with CY equal to YD.
Join AC and BD, and continue these lines until they meet the perpendicular line from X. If the pattern is accurate, the two lines meet at the same point, mark this point Z.
With Z as the centre, draw two arcs of circles: the first with radius ZC: the second with radius ZA. (To draw the circles, use a large pair of compasses, or follow the method given for making a circular pattern on page 148.)
Cut two lengths of string, one equal to the circumference of the bottom ring, and one equal to the circumference of the top ring.
From point A, lay the longer piece of string along the arc, and mark point E. From point C, lay the shorter piece of string along the arc, and mark point F. (A tape measure, held on edge to follow the curve easily, may be used if preferred.)
Join EF and continue the line. This should pass through Z if the pattern is accurate.
Mark G and H, 15 mm ($\frac{5}{8}$ in.) away from E and F, to provide an overlap for joining the shade.
Place a ruler between A and G, and mark the centre.
From this central point, place the ruler to Z and rule a grain line.
Cut out the pattern, cutting along the curve AG, the line GH, the curve HC and the line CA.

It is wise to check the accuracy of the pattern by pegging it onto the two rings, or onto the frame, before cutting out the cover. Minor adjustments can be made, but if there are major discrepancies, it is wise to check the measurements and redraw the pattern.
Place the pattern on the buckram or covered lampshade card, lining up the grain. Mark round the shape and cut out.
If plain lampshade card is being used, place the pattern on the card, mark round it, and

cut out. The fabric can be cut with the grain line of the pattern running with either the warp or weft, according to the desired finished effect. Stick the fabric to the card, overlapping it at one straight edge and insetting it at the other, as for a straight-sided drum shade on page 189.

Make up the shade following the method given for a straight-sided drum shade.

184   The pattern

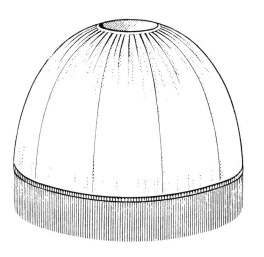

185 Tiffany shade

This style of shade is fairly easy to make and gives a less severe line than the firm shades. It consists of a tube of fabric which is threaded with elastic at either end, and then pulled over a crinoline shaped frame. This is a popular type of cover as it is easily removed for washing. The cover fabric must be light-weight, with good draping qualities. Examples of suitable fabrics are thin cotton such as voile, lace and some of the open-weave acrylics. The acrylics, however, are more difficult to handle as they present problems in seaming. Unless the fabric is pre-shrunk, shrink it before use.

Prepare the frame as directed on pages 185–187. It is wise to bind the top and bottom rings to prevent the struts from damaging the cover fabric. It is unnecessary, however, to bind the struts.

A rectangle of fabric is required equal in length to the circumference of the bound bottom ring plus 25 mm (1 in.) turning, and in width to the measurement of a strut plus 75 mm (3 in.). The warp grain is best placed in line with the width of the fabric. For frames with diameters up to 382 mm (15 in.), the rectangle can be cut from 122 cm (48 in.) width fabric. If the fabric is 91·4 cm (36 in.) wide, and the diameter of the frame exceeds 280 mm (11

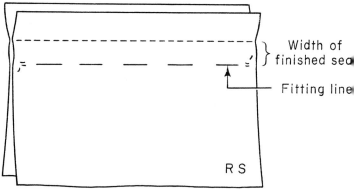

186a Tack the two edges together along the fitting line, that is 12 mm ($\frac{1}{2}$ in.) in from the edge. Machine as far from the fitting line as the width of the finished seam

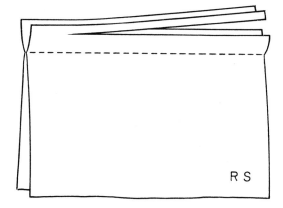

186b Trim the turnings so that they are narrower than the finished width of seam

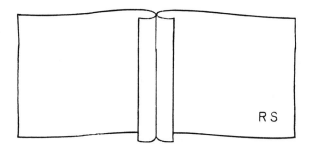

186c Press open the trimmed turnings with thumb and finger or an iron. The raw edges are now just clear of the fitting line

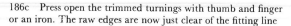

in.), it will be necessary to cut two rectangles to obtain the required length. Cut the two rectangles so that each is equal in length to half the measurement of the circumference plus 25 mm (1 in.).

The fabric must be joined together to form a tube. As this style of shade is usually unlined, a French seam is the best choice and gives a neat, strong finish. The finished width of seam should be as narrow as the fabric will allow, 3 mm ($\frac{1}{8}$ in.) to 6 mm ($\frac{1}{4}$ in.) being suitable widths.

Fold the fabric in half widthways with the wrong sides facing. If two pieces of fabric are being used, place them together with the wrong sides facing so that they can be joined down each side. See *figures 186a, b and c*.

Turn the tube to the wrong side and fold back the seam, creasing sharply along the first line of stitching. This brings the fitting lines over each other and they are then tacked together.

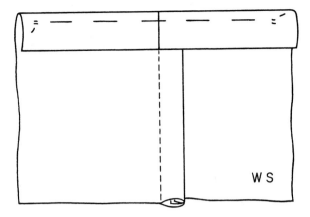

188   Fold the raw edge to the wrong side for 10 mm ($\frac{3}{8}$ in.) and press or tack in place

Fold the edge over again for 10 mm ($\frac{3}{8}$ in.) and tack in place.

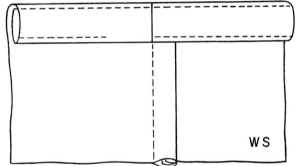

189   Beginning at the seam, machine all round the top edge close to the fold. Machine along the edge of the hem, leaving a 12 mm ($\frac{1}{2}$ in.) gap near the seam for inserting the elastic later

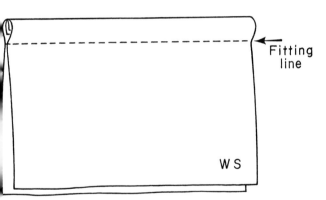

187   Machine along the fitting line

Press along the length of the seam and then press it flat. No fraying edges of fabric should be visible along the seam line on the right side.

Make a casing at the top and bottom edges of the tube in the following way:

From the finished top edge of the cover, measure down the tube for the length of a strut plus 12 mm ($\frac{1}{2}$ in.). At this level tack a fitting line round the tube. Measure round the fitting line and cut a length of fringe equal to this measurement plus 20 mm ($\frac{3}{4}$ in.) for turnings.

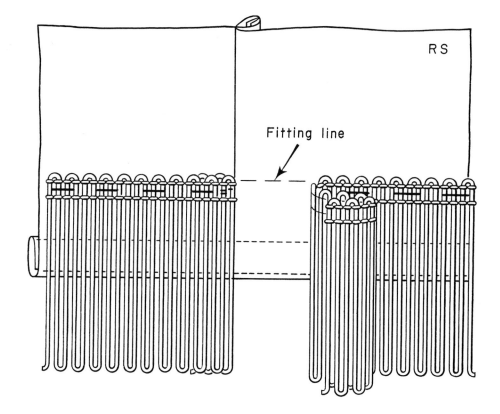

RS

Fitting line

At one end of the fringe fold the raw edge to the wrong side for 10 mm $\frac{3}{8}$ in.). See *figure 190*.

Finish tacking the fringe in place and slip-stitch the two folded edges together. Turn the tube wrong side out and, working from the inside of the tube, machine the fringe in place. If the heading of the fringing has an uneven surface, it may be easier to use a hand setting.

If preferred, the fringe can be set 6 mm ($\frac{1}{4}$ in.) below the fitting line, so that it hangs from just inside the bottom ring instead of in line with it.

Thread the two casings with string and slip the cover over the frame. Draw up the strings to gauge the size of the cover at the top and bottom. Knot the string at the top to bring the cover 12 mm ($\frac{1}{2}$ in.) inside the frame ring all round. At the bottom, knot the string to make

190   Place the prepared edge of the fringe in line with the seam, then pin and tack it along the fitting line to within 25 mm (1 in.) of the starting point. Fold back the surplus fringe so that the two folded edges will meet

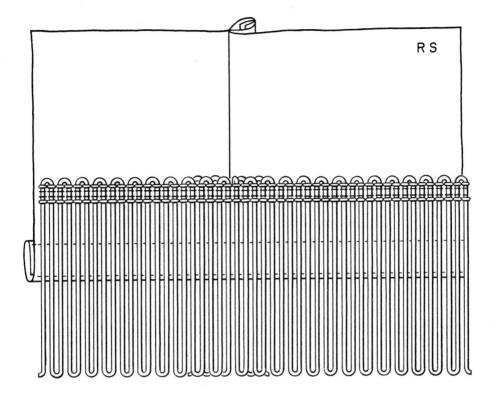

the cover set firmly over the frame with the fringe in the chosen position. The edge of the cover will come within the frame ring. Mark either side of the two knots with a pencil, pull out the string from the casings and remove the cover from the frame.

Measure each length of string between the pencil marks. Cut two pieces of elastic to equal the string lengths, adding 6 mm ($\frac{1}{4}$ in.) for a turning onto each length of elastic. Thread the elastic through the casings, and overlap the ends 25 mm (1 in.) to tighten the fitting adequately. Oversew round the overlapped sections of elastic and slip them inside the casings.

Draw the cover over the frame, easing it into position, so that the fringe heading is level all round.

191 The fringe machined in place. In this case two lines of machining have been worked to hold the fringe heading flat and strengthen the fringe

Stretched shade

Empire frames, which are made with either straight or bowed sides, are used for this type of shade. *Figure 172*, shows a bowed empire shade. As the method of making this shade imposes a certain amount of strain, the frame must be made from wire of a suitable gauge. If the wire bends easily, the frame becomes distorted as it is handled, and a badly fitting cover results. The fabric used for making this type of shade must be flexible so that it can be stretched over the frame. Refer to page 184 for suggested fabrics. A lining gives a more professional finish to the shade, but is not essential. An unlined shade is, perhaps, advisable for a first attempt to give experience in manipulation.

Pins are used to hold the fabric together on the frame as it is stretched into position. Good quality pins should be used which will not mark the fabric and which are strong enough to hold it firmly in place. A beginner will find glass-headed pins easier to handle, but an experienced worker will be able to handle finer pins.

a An unlined shade

Prepare the frame as directed on pages 185–187, binding the top and bottom rings and the two opposite struts near the pendant or gimbal fitting.

Before buying the cover fabric, it is worthwhile using an odd piece of fabric to assess the size required. A certain amount of wastage is inevitable. See *figure 192*.

Trim the square of fabric straight with the grain on all four sides, then fold it cornerwise as shown in *figure 192*. Pin the raw edges together along the two open sides. If the fabric is slippery, it is helpful to tack along these edges.

Place the frame on its side with the bottom ring towards the worker and a bound strut to the left and to the right. Lay the prepared fabric over the frame with the crosswise fold towards the worker, making sure that adequate turning is allowed at the five positions indicated in *figure 192*. Pin the fabric to the frame at the two centre points and at the four corners. These pins may need to be adjusted later. See *figure 193*.

192 A square of fabric is required which, when folded crosswise, is sufficiently large to cover half the frame, with an adequate turning allowance all round. There should be at least 38 mm (1½ in) allowance at A, B, C, D and E

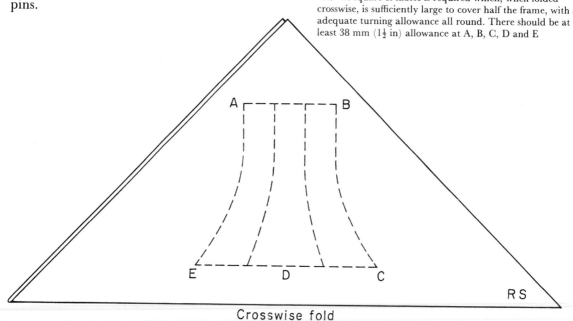

Crosswise fold

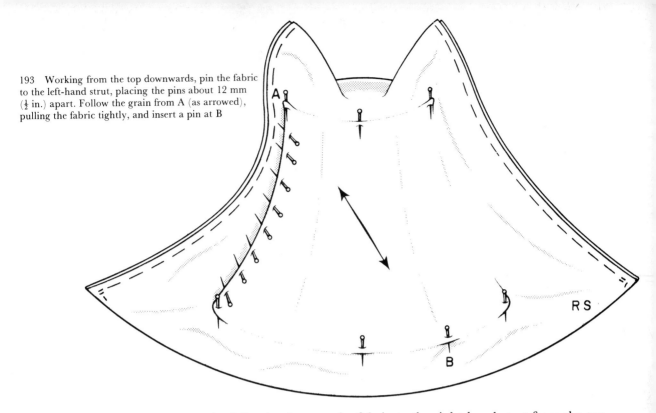

193 Working from the top downwards, pin the fabric to the left-hand strut, placing the pins about 12 mm (½ in.) apart. Follow the grain from A (as arrowed), pulling the fabric tightly, and insert a pin at B

Beginning at B, working to the left, pin the fabric to the bottom ring. As each pin is inserted, tighten the fabric by pulling it tautly from the direction of the left-hand strut. Pin

the fabric to the right-hand strut from the top, this time pulling the fabric tautly from the direction of the bottom ring. See *figure 194*.

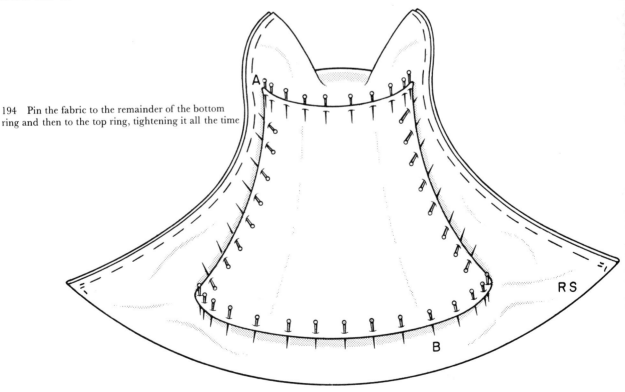

194 Pin the fabric to the remainder of the bottom ring and then to the top ring, tightening it all the time

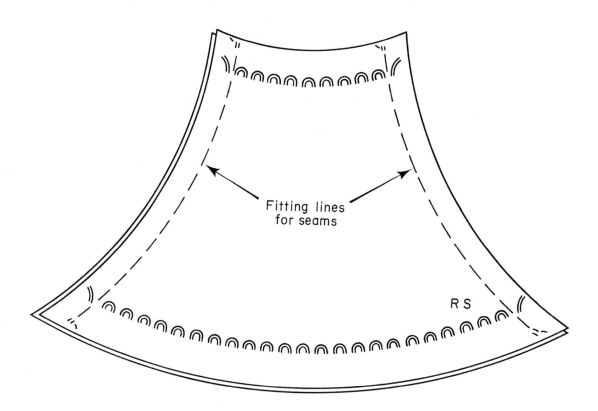

Fitting lines
for seams

R S

195 Tack the fabric together down the sides, extending it 25
mm (1 in.) beyond the marked line in each direction. Mark the
position of the top and bottom rings with thread marking.
Trim away the surplus fabric 32 mm (1¼ in.) outside the four
fitting lines

Pull the fabric at right angles to any wrinkles
which may appear, and as they are removed,
adjust the pins to make the fabric absolutely
taut.

The cover must be removed carefully from
the frame and the fitting lines marked. Remove
it first from the left-hand strut, replacing the
pins in the double fabric, in line with the inner
edge of the strut. This marks the fitting line for
the seam. Placing the fitting line in this position
compensates for the thickness of the binding,
as this is removed from the strut before the
cover is replaced. Repeat this procedure down
the right-hand strut.

Remove the cover from the bottom ring,
and then from the top ring, marking these
fitting lines in line with the outer edges of the
bound rings. Study the pinned lines and, if
necessary, adjust the pins slightly to make four
smooth fitting lines. See *figure 195*.

Separate the two layers of fabric at the top
and bottom edges and snip the thread marks.

Narrow french seams are used to join the
cover fabric down the two sides. (See pages
198 and 199.) Use a fine machine needle and,
to give an elastic seam, choose a flexible thread

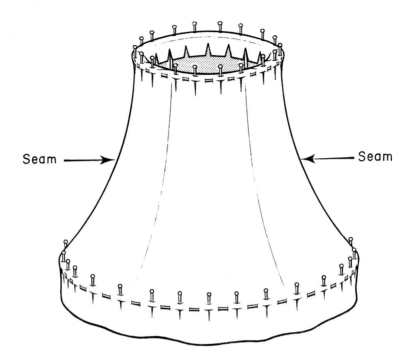

Seam ⟶   ⟵ Seam

196　The fitting lines will be found useful to guide the setting of the fabric and the pinning. The seams should set snugly against the struts

such as pure silk or *Drima*, and set a short stitch length. This will help to prevent the machine stitches from breaking when the cover is stretched over the frame. When making the seams, pay special attention to the accurate use of the fitting lines. If this is not done, the cover will be ill-fitting and the poor seam lines will be conspicuous when the shade is in use. Press the seams very carefully to prevent either stretching or distorting the cover, and finally press them flat, pressing a seam onto each half of the cover.

Remove the binding from the two struts and snip the top turning allowance of the cover to within 15 mm ($\frac{5}{8}$ in.) of the fitting line. Pull the cover over the frame, easing it down gently and setting the seams over the two struts originally bound.

Pin the cover to the frame at the top of each strut, keeping the fitting line in its correct position. Check that the seams are not twisted before pinning them to the bottom ring. Then pin the cover to the base of the remaining struts. Working from each seam alternately, pin the cover to the top and bottom rings, tightening the fabric as each pin is inserted.

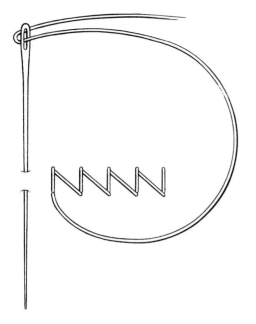

197a Forming the sloping stitch

Study the stretched fabric critically, and if there are any wrinkles, adjust the pins where necessary.

Stitch the fabric to the top and bottom rings, forming alternately sloping and straight stitches as shown in *figures 197a and b*. The fabric must be kept taut as the pins are removed and the stitching progresses. The stitching should be placed on top of the top ring and on the underside of the bottom ring, so that the binding does not show when the shade is finished. The frame should be held in its upright position while the stitching is worked so that the fabric can be stretched as it is stitched. See *figure 198*.

Trim away the spare fabric to within 6 mm ($\frac{1}{4}$ in.) of the fold line at the top, and apply the trimming as for method A on page 192. Finish the bottom edge in the same way.

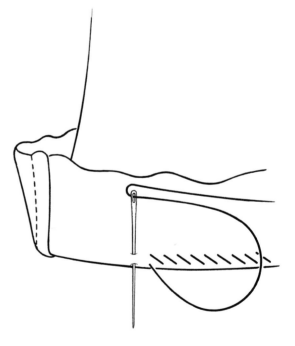

198 Fold back the surplus fabric at the top and bottom of the frame and stitch it as shown. When working this line of stitching on the bottom ring the shade can be turned upside down if preferred

197b Forming the straight stitch

b Lined shade

Refer to page 185 for suggested lining fabrics. Prepare the frame as directed on pahes 185–187, binding the top and bottom rings, and the two opposite struts nearest to the fitting.

First the cover, and then the lining fabric is cut, prepared, stretched and marked in the same way as the cover fabric of an unlined shade.

Seam the cover fabric and stitch it to the frame as for an unlined shade. The first row of stitching, however, can be placed on the outside edges of the two rings as the lining completely covers these two edges.

The lining needs to be approximately 12 mm ($\frac{1}{2}$ in.) narrower than the cover fabric. To reduce the size of the lining, tack two new fitting lines 3 mm ($\frac{1}{8}$ in.) inside the ones originally tacked, and use these new ones for the seam positions. Trim away the surplus fabric round the lining as directed for the cover. Prepare and press the seams, pressing them in the opposite directions to those on the cover. Leave the lining wrong side out.

It is necessary to snip the top turning allowance so that it will fit round the pendant or gimbal fitting. Measure the distance between the strut where the cover seam is set, and the fitting. At this distance away from, and to the left of each seam, snip the top turning allowance to within 3 mm ($\frac{1}{8}$ in.) of the fitting line. If a *Duplex* fitting is used, three snips, taken close to the fitting line will be required to accommodate the three wires of the fitting. The position for these snips can be found by measuring from the struts where the cover seams are set. Continue to snip the turning at 6 mm ($\frac{1}{4}$ in.) to 12 mm ($\frac{1}{2}$ in.) intervals depending on the size of the frame, but bring these snips to within 12 mm ($\frac{1}{2}$ in.) of the fitting line.

Snip the bottom turning to within 12 mm ($\frac{1}{2}$ in.) of the fitting line and at 25 mm (1 in.) intervals.

Place the lining inside the frame with the top fitting line level with the top ring, and pin the seams to the two side struts. Check that the seams are facing in the opposite direction to those of the cover, and that the deeper snips come by the fitting. Pin the lining at the top of the remaining struts. A wrinkle will appear at the fitting wire on each side of the frame. These will disappear when the deeper snips are continued to the fitting line. It is unwise, however, to snip further at this stage.

Turn the frame upside down and, making sure that the lining seams are not twisted, pin them to the base of the struts. Then pin the lining to the base of the remaining struts, tightening it slightly. Turn the shade back to its upright position. If the deeper snips are in the correct places, continue them to the fitting line so that the wrinkles disappear. It will be necessary to remove the pins in the fitting wire areas to make these snips. In most cases the snips may need to extend slightly beyond the fitting line to get a good fit. If the original snip is found to be in the wrong place, make a new snip in the correct position.

Working from each seam alternately, pin at 12 mm ($\frac{1}{4}$ in.) intervals round the top of the frame, setting the fitting line on top of the ring. Invert the frame and, using the fitting line as a guide, pin round the bottom ring in the same way, tightening the fabric as the pins are inserted. If there is any fullness, tighten from the top and bottom of the cover alternately until it is removed. Remove wrinkles as suggested for the cover on page 204. Stitch the lining in place along the outside of the frame, following *figures 197a and b.*

The snips which set round the fitting wires are neatened in the following way:

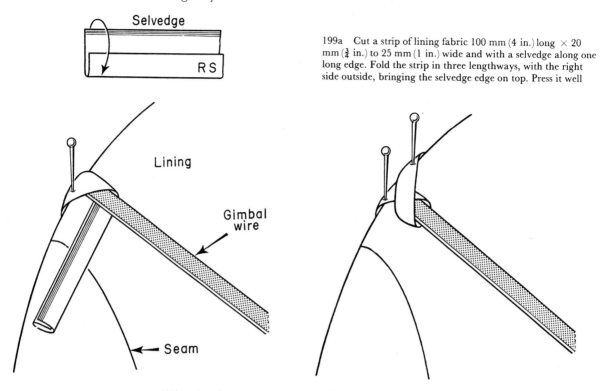

199a   Cut a strip of lining fabric 100 mm (4 in.) long × 20 mm ($\frac{3}{4}$ in.) to 25 mm (1 in.) wide and with a selvedge along one long edge. Fold the strip in three lengthways, with the right side outside, bringing the selvedge edge on top. Press it well

199b and c   Place the strip under the fitting wire and pin one end to the outside of the frame as in figure 199b. Pin the second end as shown in figure 199c

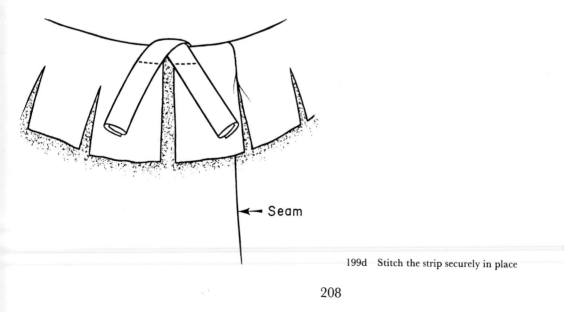

199d   Stitch the strip securely in place

Trim the two layers of fabric to within 6 mm ($\frac{1}{4}$ in.) of the folds including the fitting neatening strips, and apply the trimming as for *Method A* on page 192. Work on one ring at a time to prevent the fabric fraying before it is covered by the trimming.

This style of shade is one of the most difficult to make. It requires manipulative skill and patience; a professional finish is achieved only with fully accurate workmanship.

A drum frame is required. A sloping sided one can be used, but is more difficult to handle than one with straight sides, so it is wiser to begin with the straight drum shape to gain experience. Full directions will be given for a pleated cover on a straight drum frame.

Silk chiffon is the most suitable cover fabric for any pleated shade and, as it is transparent, a lining is essential. The lining fabrics suggested on page 185 are suitable. If crêpe-backed satin is chosen, use the dull side as the right side so that the sheen on the satin enhances the pleats.

Materials Required

The amount of cover fabric required depends on the size of the frame and whether spaced or touching pleats are chosen. A pleat should always be placed over a strut to mask it, and joins are less conspicuous if arranged to come over a strut. A certain amount of wastage is inevitable because of the necessary arrangement of pleats and joins. Larger frames cause more wastage than smaller ones.

Cover fabric

Spaced pleats: approximately 3 × the circumference of the bound ring by the length of a strut plus 50 mm (2 in.).
Touching pleats: approximately 4 × the circumference of the bound ring by the length of a strut plus 50 mm (2 in.).

Lining

The amount required is calculated by taking the circumference of the bound ring plus 100 mm (4 in.) by the height of the frame plus 50 mm (2 in.).
The position of the warp grain The warp grain always runs in line with either the strut measurement or the frame height measurement.

Making the shade

Prepare the frame as directed on pages 185–187, binding the top and bottom rings and the two opposite struts nearest to the pendant or gimbal fitting.

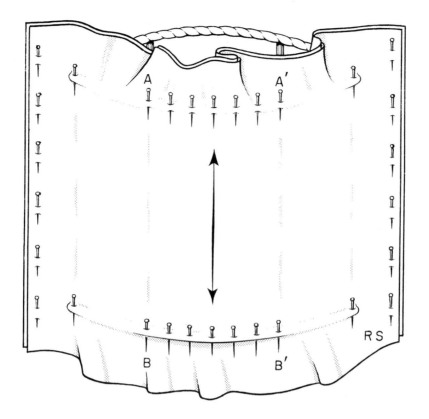

200   Place the prepared lining fabric over the top of the frame
and pin it to the bound rings at the centre points. Pin the
fabric to the four corners. (These pins may need adjusting
later.) Working outwards from the centre in each direction,
pin the fabric to the top ring as far as the first strut in each
case ie A and A1. Keep the weft grain in line with the ring.
Pin the fabric to the bottom ring for the same distance, B and
B1, tightening it against the top ring

Preparing the lining

Make sure that the fabric is straight with the
warp and weft grains along the four edges. Cut
the fabric in half, cutting parallel with the
selvedge edges.

With the wrong sides facing, place two
sections together and pin down the side edges.
If the fabric slips, tack these edges together. A
beginner may find it helpful to tack the top and
bottom edges together as well.

Place the frame on its side with the bottom
ring towards the worker and with a bound
strut to the right and left. See *figure 200*.

Pin the fabric to the top ring as far as the side
struts, then, by tightening it against the top

210

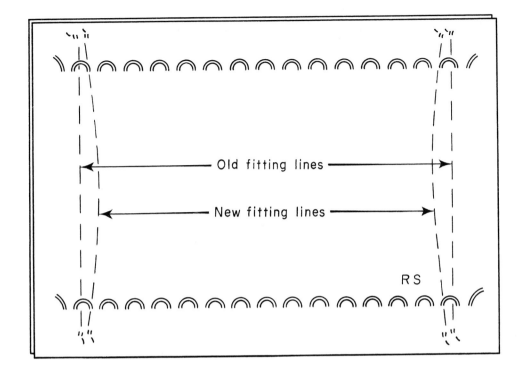

Old fitting lines

New fitting lines

R S

ring, pin it to the bottom ring for the same distance. Pin the fabric to the side struts without tightening it. Remove the lining from the frame and mark the fitting lines as for the stretched cover on page 204. See *figure 201*.

Remove the unwanted tacking lines and, if necessary, trim away the surplus fabric 25 mm (1 in.) outside the four fitting lines. Cut the thread marks.

Prepare and make the french seams as directed on pages 198–199, making them as narrow as the fabric will allow. Press the seams, setting one on to each half of the lining. The lining is now ready to insert at a later stage.

Remove the binding from the two side struts.

201 The lining must now be made a little smaller as it sets inside the frame. Mark two new seam fitting lines 3 mm ($\frac{1}{8}$ in) inside the already existing ones at the ring positions. Bow the new lines slightly in the centre to ensure a good fit

The cover

a With spaced pleats Cut the required number of strips of chiffon, cutting straight with the fabric grains and trim off the selvedge edges. The fabric is not seamed.

Decide on the width of pleat and space desired, remembering that a pleat should come over each strut. Directions will be given for 6 mm ($\frac{1}{4}$ in.) pleats and 3 mm ($\frac{1}{8}$ in.) spacing, which is a popular sizing.

On one strip of fabric, fold under one warp edge to the wrong side for the width of a pleat, in this case 6 mm ($\frac{1}{4}$ in.), making sure that the fold line is straight with the warp grain. Lay the frame on its side with the top ring to the left. Place the prepared edge over a side strut, with the fabric towards the worker, and pin to the top ring with a 25 mm (1 in.) turning outstanding. Reverse the position of the frame, bringing the bottom ring to the left and pin the fold to the bottom ring, tightening it against the top ring. See *figure 202*.

Fold back the fabric at A and B. See *figure 202* and make a 6 mm ($\frac{1}{4}$ in.) pleat, again checking that the fold lines are straight with the warp grain. See *figure 203*.

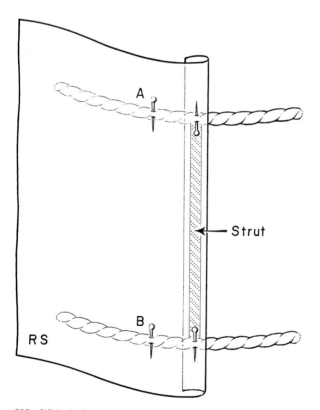

202 With the frame upright, pin the fabric to the two rings at A and B, 15 mm ($\frac{5}{8}$ in.) away from the folded edge. This distance equals twice times the finished pleat width plus a space

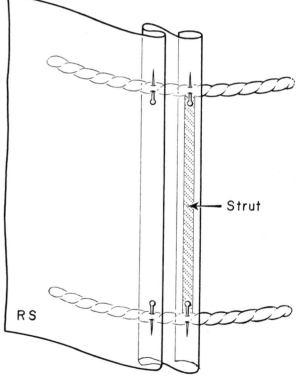

203 Pin the pleat to the top and bottom rings as before and remove the pins from inside the pleat. There should be 3 mm ($\frac{1}{8}$ in.) space between the first folded section and the pleat

Continue pleating in this way until the first piece of chiffon is almost used up, arranging for the join to come over a strut. This will probably be the opposite side strut on a small shade, and the second strut from the starting point on a larger shade. The pleating should end with 15 mm ($\frac{5}{8}$ in.) of unpleated fabric from the fold line of the last pleat. If necessary, trim away any surplus fabric.

It is wise to stitch this section of the pleating onto the two rings before beginning to use the second strip of chiffon. Use the stitch illus-trated in *figure 197a and b* and stitch the fabric to the top and bottom rings, keep it taut and begin stitching at the first pleat, thus leaving the folded section free. This allows for inserting the last raw edge. See *figure 204*.

Continue pleating and stitching in this way until the starting point is reached. Trim the fabric so that it overlaps the first folded section by 6 mm ($\frac{1}{4}$ in.). This brings the two raw edges in line. Arrange the final raw edge to set under-neath the first fold and pin it in place. Stitch the last section onto the rings.

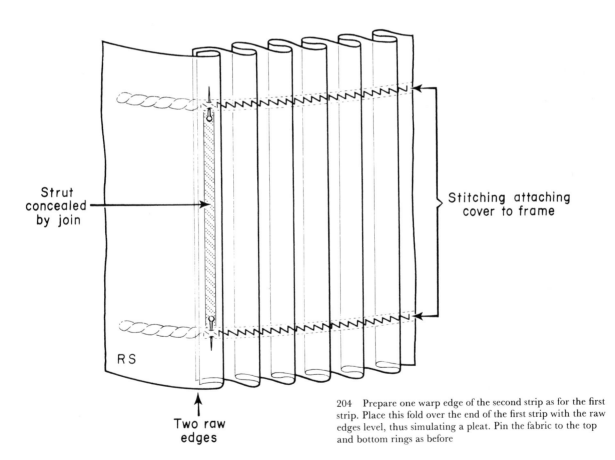

Strut concealed by join

Stitching attaching cover to frame

RS

Two raw edges

204 Prepare one warp edge of the second strip as for the first strip. Place this fold over the end of the first strip with the raw edges level, thus simulating a pleat. Pin the fabric to the top and bottom rings as before

Following the directions for a lined stretched shade, stitch the fabric back along the two rings, insert the lining, neaten the pendant or gimbal fitting and apply the trimming.

b   With touching pleats   This method is almost the same as for the previous shade, but the pins at A and B in figure 202 are set 12 mm ($\frac{1}{2}$ in.) from the first fold line instead of 15 mm ($\frac{5}{8}$ in.). This brings the front fold line of each pleat in line with the under fold of its neighbour.

c   For a drum with sloping sides   See *figure 170*.
   In this style of shade, the pleats are arranged so that they are closer together on the top ring than they are on the bottom ring. This will mean that the pleats are wider at the top than they are at the bottom. It is important that the outer fold line of each pleat is straight with the fabric grain, and that it is set at right angles to the bottom ring.
   When measuring the height of the frame for calculating the lining meterage (yardage), remember to take this measurement through the centre of the frame.

CLEANING LAMPSHADES

Non-washable shades can be kept free from dust by light brushing or vacuuming. Most stretched and pleated shades can be washed. However, the colour of some cover fabrics may run and if there is any doubt, they are best dry-cleaned. Before attempting to wash a shade, test a spare piece of the fabric and trimming for colour fastness if possible.
   Use a solution of warm water and soap flakes or *Stergene* and dip the shade up and down until clean. Rinse it thoroughly in warm water, using the same movement. Remove excess water by blotting the shade with a soft white towel and then hang it on a line to drip-dry.

12 Bed covers

Bed covers are a very important part of bedroom décor, and it is necessary to choose them with discrimination. They must harmonise with the general colour scheme of the bedroom, and the fabric chosen must be suitable for the style of cover and the type of furniture in the room. The bed provides a large, flat area, therefore it requires special consideration as it makes a conspicuous contribution to the appearance of the room.

When buying a ready-made bed cover, or fabric for a bed cover, certain points should be borne in mind. Make sure that your choice will suit the needs of the room as well as your personal taste, and that you have chosen fabric which will withstand regular usage. A bed cover is handled and folded daily, so that a crease resistant fabric is desirable. However, it is not subjected to much friction in use, so a light-weight fabric could be chosen if suitable for the room.

The washability of the fabric is another important point to consider. It is economical and convenient to be able to wash bed covers at home, so choose a fabric which is colour fast in water, and easy to iron. If, however, the bulk of the cover is too great to wash, it is better to choose a dry-cleanable fabric.

Some bed covers are finished with a gathered frill. In this case the fabric should have drip-dry and mini-care finishes, as well as good drapability. A bed cover with a box-pleated edging should be made from fabric which presses easily and holds a sharply creased edge.

If fabric with a printed pattern is used for a bed cover, check that the pattern is set in line with the fabric grain. The main rectangular shapes of the cover must be aligned with both the grain and the pattern.

Sometimes the same fabric is used for curtains and bed cover. When buying this, remember that the effect of light may be different on the vertical folds of the curtains and on the smooth, horizontal area of the bed. Study the fabric in the shop with this in mind.

The size of the room must be considered carefully. Large designs, shiny fabrics and strong colours may look attractive in large rooms, but they can be overwhelming in a small room, and even appear to magnify the size of the bed.

A bed cover uses a considerable length of fabric and is, therefore, a costly item to make. There may be an unused strip of fabric left over if the width of the bed and the width of the fabric chosen do not relate exactly. It is wise to think carefully about the fabric and cost involved, before deciding to make a throw-over bedspread. The candlewick covers fashionable nowadays are available in a wide range of colours and designs. They are seamless as they are made from fabric woven in special widths to fit either single or double beds. The price range is moderately inexpensive, and they may well be a more economic proposition than a throw-over bedspread made at home.

MEASURING A BED

It is important to measure over all the bed-clothes, so that the bed cover will be large enough to cover them completely. Therefore make the bed with its full complement of sheets, blankets and pillows. Add the eider-down to these if it is to be covered by the bed-spread during the day. Measure the bed as shown overleaf in *figure 205*.

MAKING A THROW-OVER BEDSPREAD

If you do decide to make a throw-over bed-spread in order to use a particular fabric, calculate the required amount carefully, after

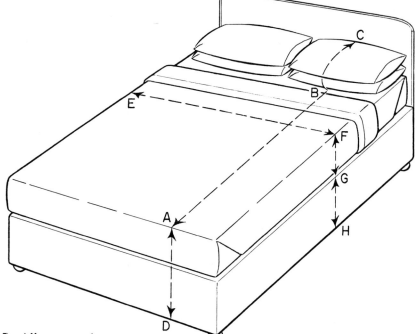

measuring the bed (*figure 205*). Allow a tuck-in of 150 mm (6 in.) under the pillows, and an overlap of 100 mm (4 in.) at the top, and a seam allowance of 20 mm ($\frac{3}{4}$ in.). Allow a hem turning of 32 mm ($1\frac{1}{4}$ in.) to 38 mm ($1\frac{1}{2}$ in.) according to the nature of the fabric.

Arrange for a width of fabric to come in the centre, with an even width strip joined on either side. When using patterned fabric, place a design motif centrally in the wide panel and match the pattern over the seams. This must be allowed for when calculating the meterage (yardage) to buy.

Join the strips with a machine fell seam, see page 74. Plain fabric can have the seams trimmed with braid to give an attractive finish to the bedspread. In this case, make a plain seam on the right side of the fabric and trim the turning to just less than half the width of the braid, eg for a 25 mm (1 in.) braid, trim the turnings to 10 mm ($\frac{3}{8}$ in.), and press the turnings open flat. Pin and tack the braid over the seam to cover the turnings, easing it very slightly to prevent puckering the finished seam. Machine it in place down each side.

Make 25 mm (1 in.) wide hems, with mitred corners, round the four edges of the bedspread.

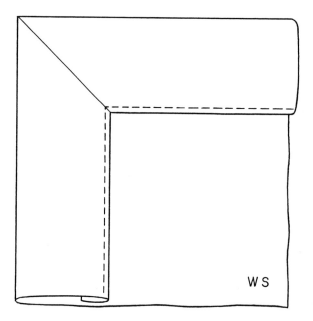

206   A mitred corner with machined hems

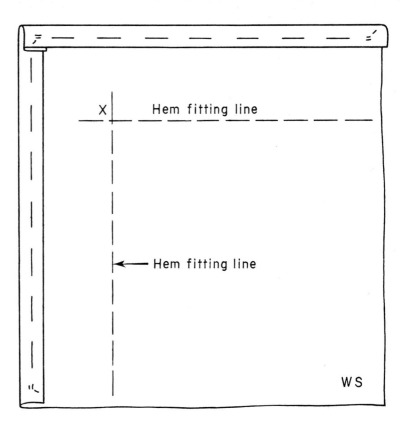

X   Hem fitting line

◀── Hem fitting line

W S

207a   Folding straight with the fabric grain, turn the 6 mm ($\frac{1}{4}$ in.) first turning to the wrong side, and tack for about 100 mm (4 in.) either side of the corner. Tack the fitting line of the hem, straight with the grain, 25 mm (1 in.) inside the folded edge, accurately shaping the corner at X. Press the corner

To mitre the corner follow *figure 207a (above) and 207b and c (overleaf)*.

    If the fabric tends to fray badly, use a 12 mm ($\frac{1}{2}$ in.) first turning.

    To finish the hem, fold and pin the first turning along each side between the mitres, tacking if necessary, then set and tack the hems. For an inconspicuous appearance, slip-hem the hems, but they may be machined if a quick finish is desired. See *figure 206 opposite*.

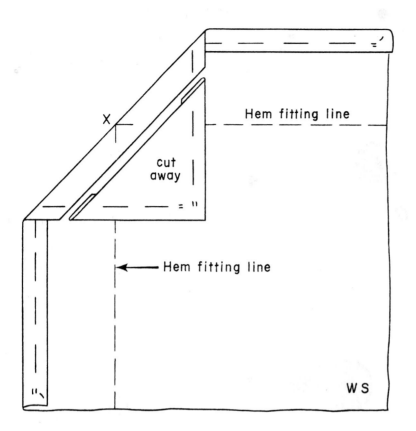

Hem fitting line

X

cut
away

Hem fitting line

W S

207b *(above)*   Mark points 50 mm (2 in) from the outer corner. Fold over from these points, bringing point X in the centre of the fold. Press this fold and, leaving 6 mm ($\frac{1}{4}$ in) turning, cut away the corner

207c *(left)*   Fold the corner in half, wrong side out, pin and tack from X along the mitre fitting line, keeping the hem turning edges exactly level. Back-stitch along the mitre line

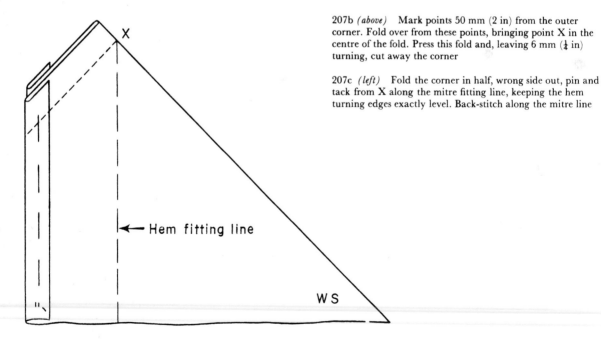

X

Hem fitting line

W S

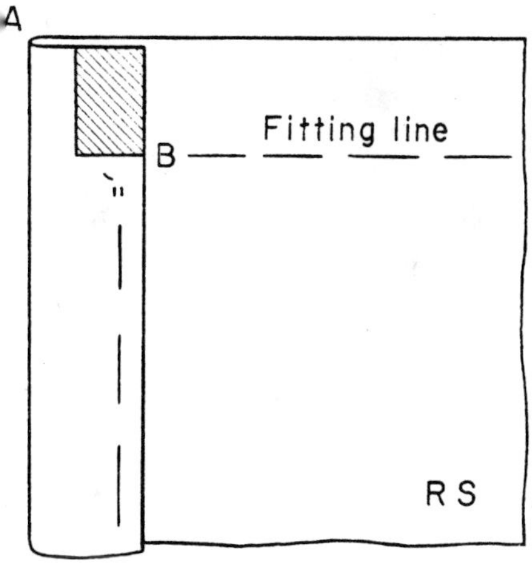

208 *(left)* To prepare the corner, turn and tack the 12 mm ($\frac{1}{2}$ in.) turning on one side of the corner. Trim away the shaded portion, fold A to B and press or tack the triangle thus formed

As an alternative to a plain hem, the edge of the throw-over can be finished with braid or fringing. In this case a 12 mm ($\frac{1}{2}$ in.) turning is adequate. Prepare the edge by tacking the turnings to the right side, making neat, square corners. See *figure 208.*

To finish the corner, fold and tack the 12 mm ($\frac{1}{2}$ in.) turning on the other side of the corner.

When all four corners and edges are prepared, press the turnings to give a sharp outer edge to the throw-over. Set the braid level with the outer fold and covering the raw edge of the turning. Pin and tack the braid, easing it slightly to prevent puckering. Make a mitred fold at each corner. *Figure 209a and b* show how to prepare 25 mm (1 in.) wide braid for a left-hand corner.

For a right-hand corner, reverse the placing.

When setting fringing, the width of the throw-over turning is controlled by the width of the fringe edging, as this is set to cover the turning on the same principle as the braid setting. The corners, however, are more satisfactory if rounded. Mark points 50 mm (2 in.) either side of the corner, and chalk a smooth curve between these points. Make a paper pattern as a guide if preferred. Fold the turning carefully round the curve, tack with small stitches and press flat. When setting the fringe edging round the curve, ease it as much as possible. This will give a better finish at the corners.

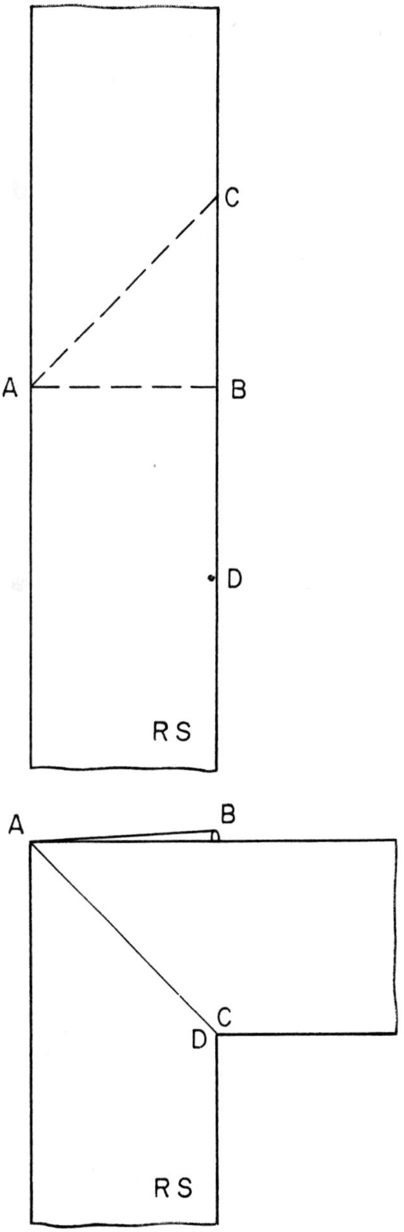

209a and b A comes level with corners of throw-over. Fold across the braid, wrong side outside, and crease the line AB. Open out the braid and mark 25 mm (1 in.) either side of B (C and D). Crease AC on the right side and bring C down to D

Fabric

This type of bed cover is suitable only for light-weight fabrics, as the flounce will not hang attractively if the fabric is either stiff or heavy. Light-weight quilted nylon can be used with minimum fullness.

Measuring the bed

See figure 205, page 216.
Length Measure from the foot of the bed as far as the pillow position AB, and continue measuring right over the pillows to C. Add 100 mm (4 in.) for an overlap at the top.
Width Measure the width of the bed EF, placing the tape-measure carefully to ensure covering the bed-clothes adequately. This gives the measurement for judging the width of the central panel of the bed cover.
Depth Measure the depth of the bed from F to within 12 mm ($\frac{1}{2}$ in.) of the floor, (ie F through G to H). This gives the width for cutting the flounce.

The central panel

The width of the central panel must equal the width of the bed. Very often the width of the fabric proves to be convenient, but sometimes this is not the case. If the fabric is too wide, it must be cut down to fit. Plain fabric can have a single strip cut off along one selvedge, but patterned fabric may need a strip cut off along each selvedge, to keep the pattern design centrally balanced.

If the fabric is too narrow, an additional strip must be joined along each side of the main piece. Even if these strips are quite narrow, there must be one each side to give a balanced appearance to the finished panel. On patterned fabric attempt to match the pattern across the seams.

The flounce

The flounce will not hang attractively if it is either skimped or too tightly gathered, so allow 1·5 (1$\frac{1}{2}$) times the finished length for minimum fullness, or up to twice the finished length for maximum fullness. Maximum fullness should be used only with very light-weight fabrics, otherwise the flounce becomes bunchy and difficult to attach to the central panel.

The pillow gusset

In order to allow the central panel to rise smoothly over the pillows, and the frill to set straight along from the foot to the top of the bed, a gusset has to be inserted to accommodate the depth of the pillows. This gusset differs in shape according to the width of the bed. See *figures 210 and 211*, which show the gusset patterns for use with the depth of two pillows.

Figure 210 shows the gusset pattern for wide single and double beds, where the pillows lie

210

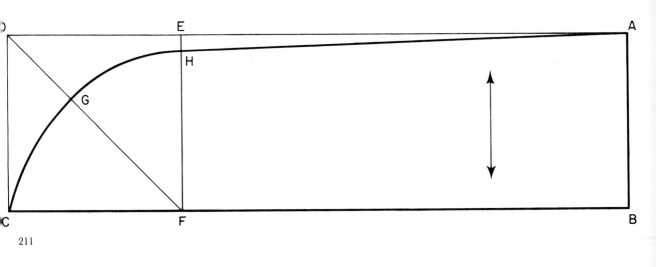

within the edges of the bed. Directions are given below for making the pattern.

Draw a perpendicular line 108 mm ($4\frac{1}{4}$ in.) long, and mark points A and B.

Draw a horizontal line from B, at right angles to AB, and 406 mm (16 in.) long.

Mark point C and join AC.

Mark in the grain line parallel with AB.

Figure 211 shows the gusset pattern for narrow single and double beds, where the pillows reach the outer edge of the bed. Directions are given below for making the pattern.

Draw a rectangle 457 mm (18 in.) × 128 mm (5 in.) and label it ABCD as in the diagram.

Mark E 128 mm (5 in.) from D, and F 128 mm (5 in.) from C.

Join EF and DF.

On the line DF, mark point G 65 mm ($2\frac{1}{2}$ in.) from D.

Mark H 12 mm ($\frac{1}{2}$ in.) below E and join AH. Draw a curve from H, through G to C. (The thicker line in the diagram shows the pattern shape.)

Mark in the grain line parallel with AB.

Direction of warp grain

Central panel: from head to foot
flounce: from top to bottom
pillow gusset: from top to bottom

Turning allowances

Allow a 50 mm (2 in.) turning at the bottom of the flounce, and a 20 mm ($\frac{3}{4}$ in.) turning on all other edges. If the fabric frays badly, wider allowances will be necessary.

Cutting plan

The cutting plan varies according to the size of the bed and the width of the fabric, so it is not possible to suggest a plan which would suit all bed covers. It is useful to plan out the cutting of the individual bed cover on squared paper, using a suitable scale, so that the most economical meterage (yardage) can be discovered.

Cutting out

Mark out the sections required for the central panel and the flounce. Pin on the pillow gusset patterns. Check the correct use of the fabric grain and that adequate fabric is available for the required turning allowances before beginning to cut. Mark all necessary fitting lines.

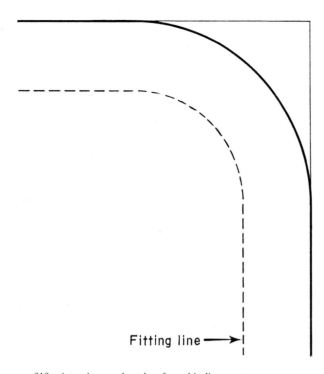

Fitting line ⟶

212   A tracing can be taken from this diagram to use as a pattern for cutting the corners. The original square corner of fabric is shown, with a rounded corner to follow for the cutting line, and an inner rounded corner which marks the fitting line, allowing the 20 mm (¾ in.) turning for setting the flounce

213   Pin the sloping edge of the gusset with its fitting line along the fitting line of the panel. Point A should be 120 mm (4¾ in.) from the edge of the panel, to provide the 100 mm (4 in.) overlap plus 20 mm (¾ in.) turning. Tack and machine between A and C

Making the cover

The central panel   If additional strips have to be joined down each side of the main piece, use either a machine fell seam or a double machine stitched seam, see page 74. In either case, make the seams as narrow as the fabric will allow.

The two corners at the foot end are rounded, so that the flounce sets and hangs smoothly.

Cut the rounded corners at the foot end of the central panel. See *figure 212*.

Setting the gussets to the central panel

a   The triangular gusset. See *figure 213*.

b   The rounded gusset.

Pin the curved edge of the gusset to the central panel, setting it from the same point A, as shown in *figure 213*. If carefully manipulated, the curved end can be set flat and unstretched to the panel. When tacked, the turning of the gusset should be fluted, but the fitting line should be smooth. Machine in position to correspond to AC in *figure 213*.

The flounce   Cut and join the flounce lengths to give the required amount of flouncing for setting to three sides of the bed cover. Use a French seam, see page 198, for joining the flounce lengths of very light-weight fabrics, otherwise use a double machine stitched seam, see page 74.

The gathering   Stitch the gathers with number 40 cotton to match the fabric in colour. The gathering stitches should be left in the fabric permanently to control the turning firmly

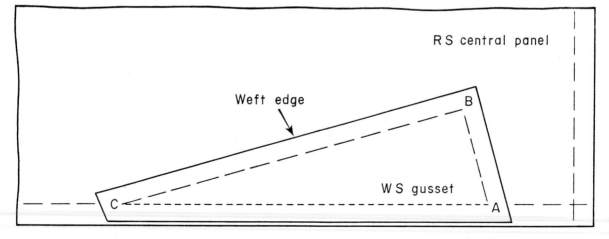

when finishing the seam. Begin and finish the gathering 32 mm (1¼ in.) from the raw edges at either end of the flounce. This leaves free the 20 mm (¾ in.) turning allowance, plus the finished hem width of 12 mm (½ in.)

a Gathering with machine attachments Either a ruffler or a gathering foot can be used if they provide the right amount of fullness. This must be tried out on a strip of the fabric, measuring it both before and after stitching. Stitch on the right side of the fabric.

If a ruffler is used, stitch along the fitting line. A second row of stitching is not required.

If a gathering foot is used, machine first along the turning 6 mm (¼ in.) outside the fitting line, and then machine a second line of gathering along the fitting line. This order of stitching is necessary as the second row increases the fullness.

b Gathering with a lengthened machine stitch This necessitates some preparation of the gusseted central panel and the top edge of the flounce. On the fitting lines, tailor tack points 32 mm (1¼ in.) in from the side raw edges on the two gussets and also at each end of the flounces. This provides a flat area of fabric when making the side edge hems later on.

Measure the fitting line of the gusseted central panel between the two marked points. Divide this measurement into 7, 8 or 9 equal sized sections, according to the size of the panel. Tailor tack these sections.

Measure the top edge of the flounce between the two marked points. Divide this measurement into the same number of equal sized sections as the gusseted panel.

To work the gathering, set the stitch length control of the machine to give the longest stitch. On old sewing machines it will also be necessary to loosen the upper tension. Place the fabric wrong side uppermost. In each of the marked sections, stitch a line *along* the fitting line, and a second line 6 mm (¼ in.) *outside* the fitting line. Leave about 100 m (4 in.) of thread at each end of each line of stitching.

With the wrong side of the flounce uppermost, fasten off the cottons at the right-hand end of each gathered section. This places a fastened off end and an open end side by side at each junction in the gathering, and is easier for manipulation. To fasten off the ends, pull the right side threads through to the wrong side. Tie each pair of threads together three times, then tie the two pairs of threads together three times.

Pull up the gathering threads from the right side of the flounce. This gives, finally, a taut

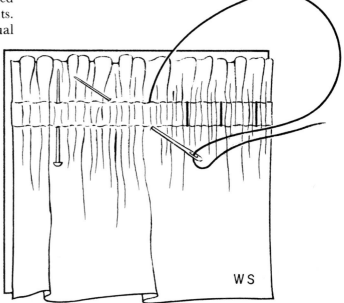

WS

214 Upright tacking

223

thread on the right side, controls the fullness when setting the gathers and gives a flatter finish. Hold the two threads together when pulling, and ease the fabric along gently to avoid breaking the threads. Gather the flounce section, making the gathered sections fit the sections marked on the central panel. Do not knot and cut off the pulled gathering cottons, in case some later adjustment is necessary. Pull the right side threads through to the wrong side and wind the surplus lengths of cotton round a pin.

Adjust the gathers evenly in each section. This requires care and accuracy for an attractive result.

Setting the flounce   To set the flounce, pin the tack-marks to their opposite numbers on the central panel, working between the gusset points in the first place. Pin between the tack marks, setting the pins about 50 mm (2 in.) apart and at right angles to the raw edge, the point going in through the fitting lines and out through the upper line of gathering. The gathers will be firmly held, but adjustable between the pins, for a final check of even setting. Ease the flounce at the rounded corners to give a smooth line.

Tack the flounce to the central panel using upright tacking, (*figure 214,* page 223). Ease and adjust the gathers evenly, using the fingers and/or a pin. Keep the gathers at right angles to the fitting line.

With the flounce uppermost, machine the seam, working from the following directions:
1   Using a pin, pierce through the machine stitch at the fitting point C of the gusset in figure 213. Note its position on the flounce side and lower the machine needle directly into this point.
2   Machine along the seam, setting the stitching just inside the fitting line gathering cotton to prevent it showing on the right side.
3   Machine slowly, easing the gathers to keep them at right angles to the machine stitching.
4   At point C of each gusset, unpick three or four upright tacking stitches, so that the central panel turning can be folded back out of the

215 (*opposite above*)   Snip the hem turning of the overlap section, snipping in line with the outer fold of the hem previously tacked. This frees the 6 mm ($\frac{1}{4}$ in.) turning for the side hem of the overlap. Machine, trim and zigzag along the sloping side of the gusset as previously described, beginning level with the outer edge of the tacked hem

way. Pin and tack the flounce to the gusset from point C to head end, using the technique already described.
5   Reset the seam into the machine with flounce uppermost, and stitch the remaining two sections of the seam, along the fitting line.

Neatening the seams and making the side hems   The seam neatening has to be done in three stages, in order to deal with the shaping at the point of the gusset and to combine it with making the hems at the edges of the flap, gusset and flounce. Work in the following order:
1   Press the turnings of the gusset and flounce seam, taking care to prevent the iron overlapping the fitting line and crushing the flounce.
2   Machine together the flounce and gusset turnings 10 mm ($\frac{3}{8}$ in.) outside the fitting line, as far as the raw edge of the gusset turning beyond point C. Trim away the surplus turning to 3 mm ($\frac{1}{8}$ in.) outside the machining, leaving a 12 mm ($\frac{1}{2}$ in.) turning in all. Zigzag or overcast over the raw edge.

Snip diagonally across the end of the seam turning to reduce bulk in the hem as it crosses the seam.
3   Fold, pin and tack a hem along the side edge of the gusset and flounce, using a 6 mm ($\frac{1}{4}$ in.) first turning and a 12 mm ($\frac{1}{2}$ in.) second turning. *See figure 215.*

When tacking, stitch the hem to the unfinished seam turning of the gusset, but do not stitch through to the central panel. Leave the hem tacked for the time being.
4 and 5   Follow the instructions in the captions to *figure 215 and 216.*

The top hem on the central panel   At the top of the central panel there is a 20 mm ($\frac{3}{4}$ in.) hem turning with trimmed corners. Turn a 12 mm ($\frac{1}{2}$ in.) wide hem along this edge, using a 6 mm ($\frac{1}{4}$ in.) first turning. Machine the hem and oversew the hem ends.

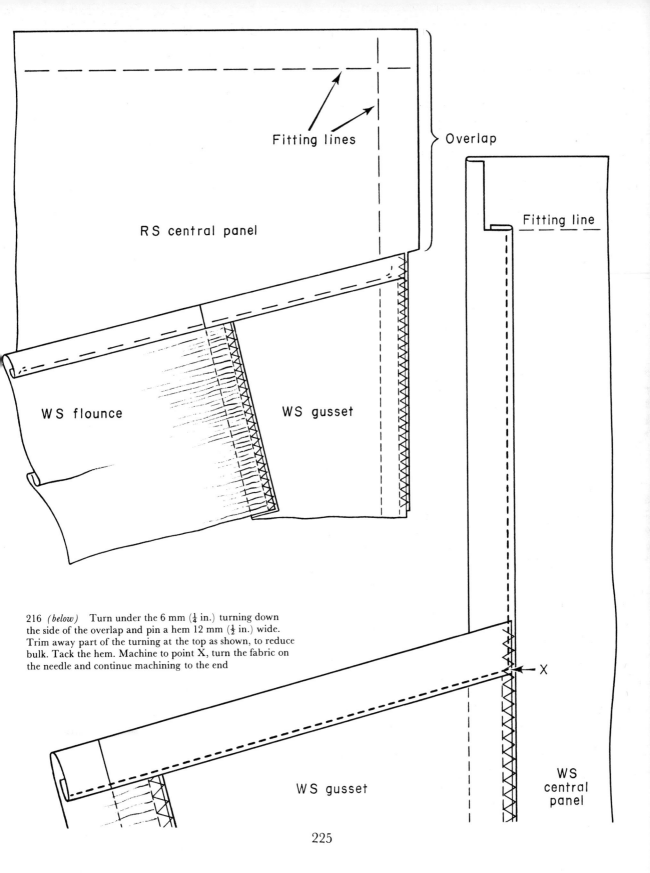

Fitting lines

Overlap

Fitting line

RS central panel

WS flounce

WS gusset

216 *(below)* Turn under the 6 mm ($\frac{1}{4}$ in.) turning down the side of the overlap and pin a hem 12 mm ($\frac{1}{2}$ in.) wide. Trim away part of the turning at the top as shown, to reduce bulk. Tack the hem. Machine to point X, turn the fabric on the needle and continue machining to the end

X

WS gusset

WS central panel

225

Piping a bed cover with a pillow gusset and a gathered flounce

For information about piping, refer to the section beginning on page 156.

a Piping a cover with a triangular gusset:

Seam the sloping edge of the gusset to the central panel as for the previous cover. Pipe the gusseted central panel before setting the flounce.

b Piping a cover with a rounded gusset:

Pipe the central panel excluding the head end. Pipe the straight, lower edge of the gusset. Set the curved edge of the gusset to the central panel, and finally set the flounce.

MAKING A BED COVER WITH A PILLOW GUSSET AND A GATHERED FLOUNCE FOR A BED WITH A FOOT-BOARD

In most ways this bed-cover resembles the previous one and there is no difference at all in the planning and making of the gusseted head end of the cover. In this case, however, the flounce is made in two sections, one for each side of the bed, and a tuck-in allowance for the foot is added to the length of the central panel. A solid foot-board needs a 100 mm (4 in.) tuck-in but, if the foot-board is barred, bring the tuck-in just below the open-work.

Measure the central panel length as before, but add the necessary tuck-in allowance plus 20 mm ($\frac{3}{4}$ in.) hem turning. Bearing this measurement in mind, tailor-tack a point to guide the position for setting the end of the flounce at the foot end of the bed.

Cut the flounce for each side of the bed, making it the length of the bed plus required fullness, plus two hem allowances each of 20 mm ($\frac{3}{4}$ in.)

Prepare the flounce, and on the upper edge fitting line mark points 32 mm ($1\frac{1}{4}$ in.) in from each end. The gathering will come between these points.

Gather and set the flounce following the principles outlined for the previous cover.

The preparation of the hems, and the neat-ening of the seams at the foot end, are dealt with in a similar way to those at the head end.

FITTED COVERS FOR DIVAN BEDS

Divans are popular nowadays for study bed-rooms and bed-sitting rooms, as they provide a couch in the day-time and quickly convert into a bed at night-time. The day-time use necessitates a cover which is firm and durable, therefore the stronger furnishing fabrics, such as furnishing tweeds and repp, are usually chosen.

The pillows bear out the day-time couch appearance if detachable covers are made for them. These can match the divan cover fabric, or provide attractive colour contrast to suit the room décor. They can be made pillow shaped, or the pillow can be rolled to fit a bolster-shaped cover. The covers can be made from directions given in the cushion section, beginning on page 145. The following styles are for use with day-time cushions:

1 A tailored piped cover. This cover has a plain skirting joined to the central panel with a piped seam. It is finished with piping at the lower edge.

2 Boxed covers. These have a boxing, usually piped, with a valance attached. The valance can be either plain with an inverted pleat at each corner, or box-pleated all round.

Measurements required

The measurements must be taken with the bed-clothes in place, but without pillows on the divan.

a For the central panel:
Length of divan
Width of divan
Allow 20 mm ($\frac{3}{4}$ in.) turnings on all edges

b For the plain skirting:
(length of divan × 2) plus (width of divan × 2).
depth from top of mattress to within 20 mm ($\frac{3}{4}$ in.) of floor

Allow 20 mm ($\frac{3}{4}$ in.) turnings on all edges.

c For boxing:
(length of divan × 2) plus (width of divan × 2)
depth of mattress
Allow 20 mm ($\frac{3}{4}$ in.) turnings on all edges.

d For valance:
   i With straight sides and an inverted pleat at each corner:
(length of divan + 254 mm (10 in.) for pleat allowance) × 2.
(width of divan + 254 mm (10 in.) for pleat allowance) × 2.
depth from base of mattress to within 12 mm ($\frac{1}{2}$ in.) of the floor. Allow 20 mm ($\frac{3}{4}$ in.) turnings along the top edge and for the seams joining the valance strips into the total length required. Add 38 mm ($1\frac{1}{2}$ in.) turnings along the hem edge.
   ii With pleats all round:
(length of divan × 2) plus (width of divan × 2) plus the required amount for pleating, see page 231.
Turning allowances as for the previous valance

If day-time covers in matching fabric are to be made for the pillows, the extra meterage (yardage) required for these should be added to the cover calculations.

Direction of the warp grain

Central panel   from head to foot
Plain skirting ⎤ down the depth or along the
Boxing   ⎬ length to give the best use of
Valance   ⎦   the fabric

Meterage (yardage) calculation

The central panel requires the full width of fabric.
The skirting panels are best cut with the warp along the length, as the depth will not exceed half the width of furnishing fabric. The seams can be arranged at the four corners without wastage of fabric which gives a smarter, more box-like effect to the cover.

Making the cover

Cut and trim the central panel as directed on page 220, and mark the fitting lines.
Cut the two side panels of the skirting, and the head and foot panels, and mark the fitting lines.
Prepare the piping for the four sides of the central panel (see page 160), using a medium thickness cord, and set it as directed for a rectangular shape on page 161.
Join the four panels of the skirting with plain seams. See page 77.
Lay the piped central panel on the divan and pin about 610 mm (24 in.) of the skirting in position. Match the fitting lines accurately, and set the pinned seam along the upper edge of the mattress. Check the hem fitting line of the skirting and adjust it if necessary to bring it 20 mm ($\frac{3}{4}$ in.) above the floor. Unpin the skirting. Cut the crossway strips 70 mm ($2\frac{3}{4}$ in.) wide for the piping on the hem edge of the skirting.

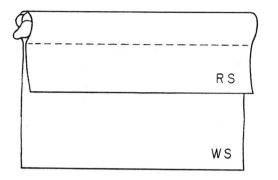

217a   Enclose the piping cord inside the crossway strip with a
12 mm ($\frac{1}{2}$ in.) upper turning

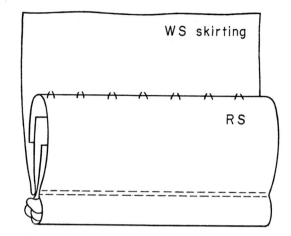

218   Fold over the raw edge of the outer turning of the piping
for 12 mm ($\frac{1}{2}$ in), and set it behind the skirting turning. Tack
close to the fold, slip-hem the edge and remove the tacking

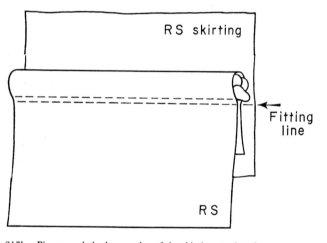

217b   Pipe round the lower edge of the skirting, setting the
piping onto the right side, along the fitting line. Refer to pages
161 and 162 for making the final join of the piping, before
machining in place as shown

Fold the turnings of the skirting and piping back to the wrong side and press them in position.

The depth of the piping will bring the skirting to within 12 mm ($\frac{1}{2}$ in.) of the floor.

Join the skirting to the piped central panel, following the principles outlined for a square scatter cushion on page 164.

228

A PIPED BOXED COVER WITH CORNER INVERTED PLEATS

Meterage (yardage) calculations

The central panel requires practically the full width of the fabric. The boxing and valance are best cut with the warpway along the length, so that the boxing seams come at the corners. The valance seams will be hidden by the inverted pleats. This use of the warp gives the more economical meterage (yardage).

The cutting plan (in two sections)

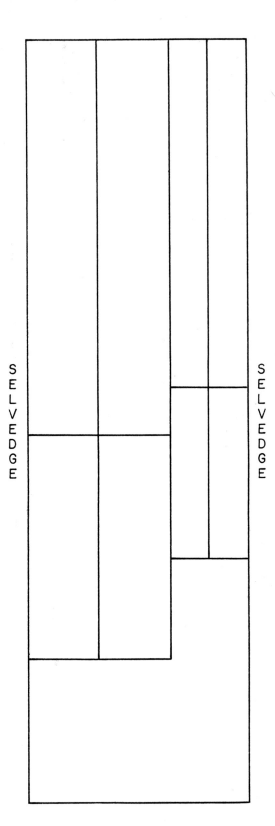

219a *(above)*   The central panel

219b *(right)*   The valance and boxing strips with space reserved for crossway strips for piping. In all cases the turning and pleating allowances have been included

229

Making the cover

Cut the central panel as directed on page 220. Prepare and pipe the central panel and the boxing as directed for a boxed cushion on page 172, but apply the piping to the lower edge of the boxing before setting the upper, unpiped edge to the central panel.

The valance

Join up the valance strips into one circular section and press the seams open flat. Fit the top section, complete with boxing, onto the divan. Pin about 610 mm (24 in.) of the upper edge of the valance to the boxing, matching the fitting lines. Check the hem fitting line of the valance and adjust if necessary. Unpin the valance, fold, tack and stitch the hem. Machining gives a quick finish to the hem, but close slip-hemming, being invisible on the right side, gives a better standard of finish, particularly on plain fabric. Braid should not be applied as it gives too thick an edge for satisfactory pleating. A line of satin stitching, worked by machine could be used if suitable for the fabric. It could match the piping in colour if this is in contrast to the main colour.

Press the hem when finished.

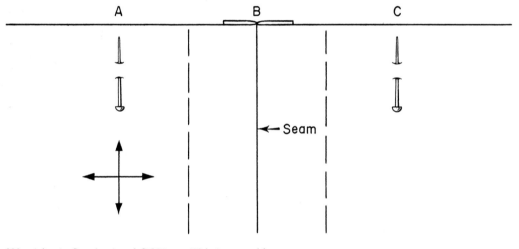

220a *(above)*   Set pins A and C 254 mm (10 in.) apart with the seam **B** in the centre. The dotted lines indicate where the inner folds of the pleat will come. The arrowed lines indicate the positions of the fabric grain

220b *(below)*   The inverted pleat folded into position. The folds are set straight with a fabric grain

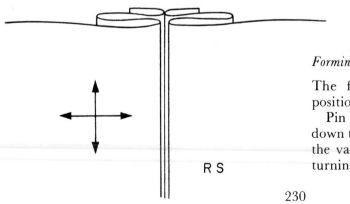

Forming the inverted pleats

The four pleats are formed at the seam positions, (*figures 220a and b*).

Pin and tack across the top of the pleat and down the centre folds. Press the pleat lightly on the valance, but firmly along the upper edge turning.

230

The upper edge of the valance is set to the lower edge of the boxing. Begin the setting at one corner with the valance uppermost. Place the right sides together with the fitting lines over each other. If the boxing is piped, this brings the piping between the valance and the boxing. Pin the two parts together as far as the next corner, taking care to set the corner accurately. Tack firmly along this section, using a strong needle and tacking thread. Continue pinning together and tacking each section of the valance and boxing along the fitting line.

With the boxing side uppermost, machine the seam all round the cover, using a piping foot on the machine. Use a long machine stitch, number 40 thread, and a strong machine needle. Machine with care along this very thick seam.

To flatten and neaten the seam on the wrong side, machine the turnings together 12 mm ($\frac{1}{2}$ in.) outside the fitting line. Trim the turning to within 3 mm ($\frac{1}{8}$ in.) of this machining, and zigzag, or overcast, over the raw edges.

Press the flat top section of the cover. Remove the tacking stitches from one pleat at a time and press them firmly, using a pressing cloth if necessary.

A PIPED BOXED COVER WITH A BOX-PLEATED VALANCE

The central panel is cut as for the previous cover. The valance is better cut with the warp grain downwards. The boxing can be cut with either the weft or the warp running along its length, eg a striped fabric would be quite pleasing cut weftway, a patterned fabric, however, must be cut warpway to match the valance grain and give continuity to the pattern. A plain fabric can be cut weftway to avoid seams other than those at the corners, providing this direction of the grain does not give a marked change of colour in contrast to the valance.

The valance

The box-pleats can be arranged to meet edge to edge all round the valance, which uses the maximum amount of fabric. A more economical way of planning the valance is to space the box pleats with an equal width space between each pleat. If a more interesting arrangement is desired, and the fabric is suitable, the box-pleats can be grouped. There must be an even number of pleats in each group to facilitate the corner setting.

It is impossible to give an accurate guide for the length of fabric required for the valance, as the pleating depends on fabric limitations, divan plus bedding measurements and the choice of pleat arrangement. The pleating must be worked out carefully so that the box pleats fit into the length and width of the divan, making an identical arrangement at each corner. For edge to edge pleating, arrange for two pleats to meet at each corner; for spaced single pleats, arrange the corners with two pleats meeting; for grouped pleating, bring the centre of a group to each corner.

The fabric must be considered carefully as any pattern or interest in the weave will be affected by the folding of the pleats, and may have to control the width of the pleating in order to give the best possible finished effect.

Forming the box pleats

See figures 221a and b overleaf

To estimate the length of fabric required for a box-pleated valance, it is helpful to cut a strip of paper equal in length to the width of the fabric by 100 mm (4 in.), and rule it with guide lines for pleating. Fold the paper to try out various arrangements of pleating, and discover the loss in length in each case. Remember to allow 20 mm ($\frac{3}{4}$ in.) seam turnings for joining the valance strips. The seams must be placed as indicated in *figure 221a*, so that they can be pressed flat and do not interfere with the folding of the pleats.

It is usually impossible to find a width of pleating which will fit exactly into both the length and the width measurements of the divan. To overcome this problem, choose the desired pleat width and arrange a corner. Then plan the pleats for first one short and then one long side of the divan, making modifications in either the pleat width or spacing, to bring the next two corners in line with the pleating plan of the first one. Invariably it will be found necessary to make the pleats fractionally nar-rower or wider on the long side than on the short side. Further strips of paper can be cut and pinned together for this preliminary test-ing. Remember to cut them to correspond to the fabric width and also to arrange for each join to come under a pleat. When the best arrangement has been found, the amount of fabric required for the valance can be calcula-ted.

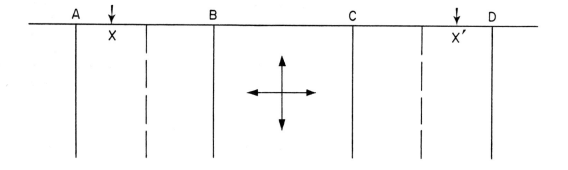

221a   BC is the finished width of box-pleat. To form the pleat, fold B over A and C over D. The arrowed lines indicate the positions of the fabric grains. The fold lines of the pleats retain a more sharply pressed edge if they are folded in line with the warp grain. X and X1 mark suitable positions for placing a seam when joining the valance strips

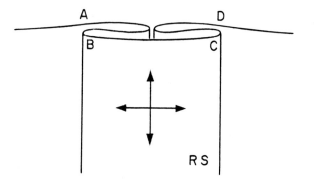

221b   The folded box-pleat on the right side. It will be seen that each pleat uses up twice its finished width of fabric

Calculating the meterage (yardage)

Once the pleating has been planned, and the amount of fabric required discovered, it will be necessary to plan a lay for the cover in order to estimate the amount of fabric required in all.

Making the cover

Cut the central panel and the boxing strips and pipe and join them together as for the previous style.

Cut the required number of valance strips and join two together with a plain seam pressed open flat. In the seamed area fold and pin the first pleat, bringing the seam line into its required position, at point X or X1 in *figure 221a* This pleat will set at a corner on one side of the divan, so fold another pleat, or pleats, to make the full corner arrangement. Mark the centre of this arrangement. Continue pleating on either side until the two widths of fabric are almost used up. Assess the position of the next seam on the left-hand end of the pleated strip, trimming away any surplus fabric if necessary. Machine and press the second seam. Continue pleating over the second seam until there is adequate pleating to fit across the foot of the divan. This may necessitate a third seam for edge to edge pleating. Test this section of the prepared pleating against an appropriate side of the boxing. If accurate, tack the pleats in place along the two outer folded edges of each pleat, and across the top of the arranged length. If not accurate, make suitable adjustments.

Continue pleating in this way, section by section, until the valance is complete. Pin about 610 mm (24 in.) of the valance fabric in position to check the lower hem fitting line. Correct this if necessary, then tack the hem using a 6 mm ($\frac{1}{4}$ in.) first turning and a 12 mm ($\frac{1}{2}$ in.) second turning. This is a very long hem to slip-hem by hand, so it can be machined. If one is available, the machine slip-hemming foot gives a very good result on most fabrics.

The box-pleated valance is now set to the prepared boxing as outlined on page 176.

Basis: 1 in. = 25·4 mm (exactly)

A Imperial measurement

B Metric measurement

(actual conversion to

three decimal places)

C Metric measurement

(adapted to more

practical measurement

for use in text)

A	B	C	A	B	C
$\frac{1}{8}$	3·175	3	$2\frac{1}{8}$	53·975	55
$\frac{1}{4}$	6·350	6	$2\frac{1}{4}$	57·150	58
$\frac{3}{8}$	9·525	10	$2\frac{3}{8}$	60·325	60
$\frac{1}{2}$	12·700	12	$2\frac{1}{2}$	63·500	65
$\frac{5}{8}$	15·875	15	$2\frac{5}{8}$	66·675	66
$\frac{3}{4}$	19·050	20	$2\frac{3}{4}$	69·850	70
$\frac{7}{8}$	22·225	22	$2\frac{7}{8}$	73·025	72
1	*25·400*	*25*	3	76·200	75
$1\frac{1}{8}$	28·575	30	$3\frac{1}{8}$	79·375	80
$1\frac{1}{4}$	31·750	32	$3\frac{1}{4}$	82·550	82
$1\frac{3}{8}$	34·925	35	$3\frac{3}{8}$	85·725	85
$1\frac{1}{2}$	38·100	38	$3\frac{1}{2}$	88·900	90
$1\frac{5}{8}$	41·275	40	$3\frac{5}{8}$	92·075	92
$1\frac{3}{4}$	44·450	45	$3\frac{3}{4}$	95·250	95
$1\frac{7}{8}$	47·625	48	$3\frac{7}{8}$	98·425	98
2	50·800	50	4	101·600	100

A	B	C	A	B	C	A	B	C
$4\frac{1}{8}$	104·775	105	$6\frac{1}{8}$	155·575	155	$8\frac{1}{8}$	206·375	206
$4\frac{1}{4}$	107·950	108	$6\frac{1}{4}$	158·750	160	$8\frac{1}{4}$	209·550	210
$4\frac{3}{8}$	111·125	112	$6\frac{3}{8}$	161·925	162	$8\frac{3}{8}$	212·725	212
$4\frac{1}{2}$	114·300	115	$6\frac{1}{2}$	165·100	165	$8\frac{1}{2}$	215·900	215
$4\frac{5}{8}$	117·475	118	$6\frac{5}{8}$	168·275	168	$8\frac{5}{8}$	219·075	220
$4\frac{3}{4}$	120·650	120	$6\frac{3}{4}$	171·450	170	$8\frac{3}{4}$	222·250	222
$4\frac{7}{8}$	123·825	125	$6\frac{7}{8}$	174·625	175	$8\frac{7}{8}$	225·425	225
5	127·000	128	7	177·800	180	9	228·600	230
$5\frac{1}{8}$	130·175	130	$7\frac{1}{8}$	180·975	182	$9\frac{1}{8}$	231·775	232
$5\frac{1}{4}$	133·350	135	$7\frac{1}{4}$	184·150	185	$9\frac{1}{4}$	234·950	235
$5\frac{3}{8}$	136·525	138	$7\frac{3}{8}$	187·325	188	$9\frac{3}{8}$	238·125	240
$5\frac{1}{2}$	139·700	140	$7\frac{1}{2}$	190·500	190	$9\frac{1}{2}$	241·300	242
$5\frac{5}{8}$	142·875	142	$7\frac{5}{8}$	193·675	195	$9\frac{5}{8}$	244·475	245
$5\frac{3}{4}$	146·050	145	$7\frac{3}{4}$	196·850	198	$9\frac{3}{4}$	247·650	248
$5\frac{7}{8}$	149·225	148	$7\frac{7}{8}$	200·025	200	$9\frac{7}{8}$	250·825	250
6	152·400	150	8	203·200	205	10	254·000	254

236